A. N. Whitehead and Social Theory

A. N. Whitehead and Social Theory

Tracing a Culture of Thought

Michael Halewood

ANTHEM PRESS
LONDON · NEW YORK · DELHI

Anthem Press
An imprint of Wimbledon Publishing Company
www.anthempress.com

This edition first published in UK and USA 2013
by ANTHEM PRESS
75-76 Blackfriars Road, London SE1 8HA, UK
or PO Box 9779, London SW19 7ZG, UK
and
244 Madison Ave. #116, New York, NY 10016, USA

First published in hardback by Anthem Press in 2011

British Library Cataloguing-in-Publication Data
A catalogue record for this book is available from the British Library.

Library of Congress Cataloging-in-Publication Data
The Library of Congress has cataloged the hardcover edition as follows:
Halewood, Michael.
A.N. Whitehead and social theory : tracing a culture of thought /
Michael Halewood.
p. cm.
Includes bibliographical references (p.) and index.
ISBN 978-0-85728-796-0 (hardback : alk. paper)
1. Social sciences–Philosophy. 2. Sociology–Philosophy.
3. Whitehead, Alfred North, 1861–1947. I. Title.
H61.15.H34 2011
300.1–dc23
2011028421

ISBN-13: 978 1 78308 069 4 (Pbk)
ISBN-10: 1 78308 069 8 (Pbk)

This title is also available as an ebook.

CONTENTS

ACKNOWLEDGEMENTS

Many and varied are the people who have helped and supported me during the process of producing this book; I owe them much and I am grateful. My initial interest in the work of Whitehead was nurtured by, amongst others, Andrew Barry (who first introduced me to him), Mariam Fraser, Celia Lury, Mike Michael and Alberto Toscano. Others who have helped maintain and develop this engagement are Didier Debaise, Roland Faber, Andy Goffey and Steven Shaviro. However, over the last ten years or so, it has been Isabelle Stengers and her work that have most supported, challenged and deepened my understanding of Whitehead.

Rob Stones provided advice and support for the publication of this book and Janka Romero at Anthem Press has been a mine of information. Astrid Lorange's zesty enthusiasm for the project was much appreciated.

More generally, there are many who have had input. I would like to thank my parents, Conor Carville, Joe Daniel, Deirdre Lambe, Mark Lawson, Lynne Pettinger, Darren Thiel, Christian Vaughan-Spruce, Vanessa White, Alex Wilkie and Anna Maria Grigoraş.

In April 2010, I used material from a draft version of this book to give three lectures at the University of Turku and the University of Tampere, both in Finland. I am grateful to the staff and students of these institutions for their comments, questions, suggestions and hospitality, especially Seppo Poutanen.

None of the chapters contained in this book is a simple reprint of previously published material. However, some sections do address themes and use material which has been published elsewhere. A section of Chapter One was published in 'A.N. Whitehead, Information and Social Theory', *Theory, Culture and Society*, 22.6 (2005): 73–94. Elements of Chapter Two are from M. Halewood and M. Michael, 'Being a Sociologist and Becoming a Whiteheadian: Toward a Concrescent Methodology', *Theory, Culture and Society*, 25.4 (2008): 31–56. Chapter Four includes material published as 'Fact, Values, Individuals, and Others: Towards a Metaphysics of Value' in R. Faber, B. Henning and C. Combs (eds), *Beyond Metaphysics* (New York: Rodopi Press, 2010), 227–47. Chapter Five includes material from 'Sociology, Societies, and Sociality' in

M. Dibben (ed.), *Applied Process Thought Volume II* (Frankfurt/Lancaster: Ontos Verlag, 2009), 293–317. A section of Chapter Six was published as 'Butler and Whitehead on the (Social) Body' in R. Faber and A. Stephenson (eds), *Secrets of Becoming. Negotiating Whitehead, Deleuze and Butler* (Fordham University Press: New York, 2011), 107–26. I am grateful for being able to reproduce these here.

LIST OF ABBREVIATIONS

The following abbreviations have been used for the works of Whitehead which are cited throughout this text. They have been ordered in terms of approximate frequency of use.

PR	–	*Process and Reality*
AI	–	*Adventures of Ideas*
MT	–	*Modes of Thought*
SYM	–	*Symbolism. Its Meaning and Effect*
SMW	–	*Science and the Modern World*
CN	–	*Concept of Nature*
SP	–	*Science and Philosophy*
RM	–	*Religion in the Making*
PRPS	–	*The Principle of Relativity with applications to Physical Science*
AE	–	*The Aims of Education and Other Essays*

Chapter One

A CULTURE OF THOUGHT – THE BIFURCATION OF NATURE

Alfred North Whitehead (1861–1947) was the most sociological of philosophers. This in two ways: first, he viewed all enduring things as 'societies'; second, he believed that one major role of theory is to challenge the deepest preconceptions and assumptions which permeate our attempts to understand and explain the world. What such claims mean and what their consequences might be will be considered throughout this book. Its overall aim is to outline Whitehead's philosophy; the challenges that it makes and the opportunities that it offers social theory with regard to a specific set of problems and concerns, namely those of realism and causation, value, subjectivity, the body, sexual difference and capitalism. Yet it must be stressed that Whitehead was a philosopher not a sociologist and his ideas are not to be envisaged as simply and directly applicable to social theory. He will not miraculously solve or explain away a set of conceptual problems relating to contemporary society or analyses thereof. Having said this, Whitehead's work has some fundamental implications for the status and procedures of social theory and social theorists which could lead to a reconceptualization of some of its founding claims and methods of analysis. Whitehead's philosophy constitutes a bold cosmological vision which diagnoses the fault lines of modernity and its conceptual apparatus by identifying what might be termed its "culture of thought". It also offers a prognosis which might enable the production of novel, differently textured modes of thought. This introductory chapter will, having given a brief biographical sketch of Whitehead, outline the specific assumptions and conceptual problems which Whitehead sees as suffusing the contemporary world and theory. As will be seen, the major constituent of modern thought identified is the acceptance of what he calls "The Bifurcation of Nature". The discussion of the problems inherent in this worldview make up the key conceptual fulcrum around which this book turns, namely the notion of "a culture of thought". This will, in turn, indicate the problematics which will be taken up and elaborated in the following chapters.

Whitehead was born in 1861 in Ramsgate, Kent, in the south of England. He went up to Trinity College, Cambridge, in 1880 where he remained as an undergraduate, fellow and senior lecturer until 1910. His field of interest at this time was pure and applied mathematics and he specialized in symbolic logic. During this period he collaborated with Bertrand Russell, and they wrote the ground-breaking *Principia Mathematica* between the years 1903–10. In 1910 Whitehead left Cambridge and moved to London where he eventually took up a professorship at Imperial College, University of London. This period witnessed a shift in Whitehead's interest toward mathematical physics and more especially the work of Einstein on relativity. As will be seen throughout this book, the consequences of the notion of relativity for science, philosophy, history and the understanding of society and societies were an important and ongoing concern of Whitehead. This is evident in both his direct discussion of Einstein's theories in his 1922 publication *The Principle of Relativity with applications to Physical Science* (PRPS) and in the later elaboration of his own version of the principle of relativity as fundamental to his philosophical approach which he termed "philosophy of organism" in his major 1929 work *Process and Reality* (PR).

Whitehead's move to London led not only to an extension of his ideas to mathematical physics but also to the practicalities and purpose of universities and education in general. He took up high-ranking administrative positions in the Senate of the University of London and worked to open up the colleges and curriculum to both women and local communities (SP, 18–19). This interest in the role of education carried on throughout Whitehead's life and culminated in the publication of his 1929 collection of essays *The Aims of Education* (AE). In 1924, at the age of 63, Whitehead was invited to another Cambridge, that of Massachusetts, USA, where he was asked to take up a professorship in philosophy at Harvard University. Here he worked until 1937 and it is during this period that he produced most of the works that will be discussed in this book, namely *Science and the Modern World* (SMW, 1925), *Religion in the Making* (RM, 1926), *Symbolism. Its Meaning and Effect* (SYM, 1927), *Process and Reality* (PR, 1929), *Adventures of Ideas* (AI, 1933) and *Modes of Thought* (MT, 1938). It is sometimes reported that after giving his first lecture at Harvard, Whitehead commented that this was the first philosophy lecture that he had ever attended (e.g. Stengers 2008a, 100). This is not to suggest that Whitehead lacked philosophical knowledge. He had been reading and discussing philosophy since his early years at Cambridge (SP, 13–14) but the lack of any professionalized legacy and constraint, which might well be conferred by a lifetime in a philosophy department, is evident in the close but almost heretical renderings of major philosophical texts which run throughout his later works. Steven Shaviro in his recent and important work,

Without Criteria (2009), describes Whitehead's method of reading the "great philosophers" as one which 'mines…unexpected creative sparks, excerpting those moments where, for instance, Plato affirms Becoming against the static world of ideas, or Descartes refutes mind-body dualism' (Shaviro 2009, x). This creative, rather than deconstructive, approach is one which Isabelle Stengers (2002, 2008a) assigns both to Whitehead and to her own work and which she refers to, in the subtitle of her enormously important work on Whitehead, *Penser Avec Whitehead* (Stengers 2002), as 'a free and savage creation of concepts'.[1] It is this inventive yet scholarly take on the history of thought, and the specific role of concepts and abstractions, that Whitehead developed toward the end of his life which this book will attempt to elucidate in terms of their import for social theory. In doing so, it will provide the first sustained account of such interrelations, building on the positive but partial references and usages of Whitehead's work and terms that have been developed by certain key contemporary theorists such as Donna Haraway who has stated that 'Alfred North Whitehead was a great influence on me' (Haraway 2000, 21),[2] Bruno Latour (for example, Latour 1999a, 141; Latour 1999b, 315) and, more recently, Judith Butler.[3]

Whitehead was not only a mathematician, mathematical physicist and a philosopher, he was also a historian of the philosophy of science. Throughout his work he was interested in tracing the manner in which modern science developed and accepted new concepts and how these bled into apparently common-sense understandings of the world, especially from the seventeenth century to the present day. He also outlines how such concepts were derived from or related to the realm of philosophy and, on occasions, led to antagonisms between science, philosophy and more generalized questions about the status of knowledge and reality. His analysis is not always purely abstract or philosophical, though it often is, but also surveys the everyday, commonplace assumptions about reality and experience which run throughout contemporary thought and society. It is an important theoretical task to identify and interrogate such assumptions and this is one which will be undertaken in this book.

Metaphysics and Sociology

Before moving on to the initial analysis of Whitehead's relevance to social theory, it is worth spending a little time considering some questions which might already be troubling those who feel it important to distinguish between the methods and purpose of sociology, social theory and philosophy.

The danger of adopting a philosophical stance with regard to analyses of the social is that it would seem, by definition, to remove all the "social" elements. Insofar as philosophy aims for a "pure" and dislocated consideration of thought, it disregards the details of the play of power and ideology which permeate the social world, including ideas and thoughts about such a world. It neglects to see that the very act of philosophy is socially situated and needs to be explained with regards to its specific historical and cultural location, not vice versa. The case is even starker with regard to metaphysics. This branch of philosophy which traditionally dealt with supposedly fundamental questions and first principles, but which required no reference to experience or to what might now be called "empirical evidence" to supports its arguments, has fallen into disrepute. Its link to medieval theology and the propensity of its arguments to indulge in apparently irrelevant debates, such as that of the number of angels which can fit on the head of a pin, led to its rejection by the cadre of modern philosophers.

Yet the major work of Whitehead, *Process and Reality* (PR), is one of metaphysics and comprises the major resource for the analyses developed in this book. Although it is hoped that the reasons and justification for a treatment of the work of Whitehead will unfold as the chapters proceed, the following passages will make some elementary moves to situate the vital importance of Whitehead's concepts for those of sociology and social theory.

One of the most striking aspects of Whitehead's work is that he is concerned not just with what we think but *how* we think. However, he does not use the usual social descriptions to outline how we think; that is, he does not invoke any prior notions of community, culture, economic relations or human nature. Such notions themselves need to be explained, not assumed. Instead, he focuses on the inextricable link between the concepts that we have inherited and how they were developed, as well as how they are currently deployed. And, as just mentioned, such investigations cannot take anything for granted, not the social, the political, the cultural or even the human. It is this lack of any fixed starting point and the willingness to deal with our concepts and their consequences in the most abstract of terms that makes Whitehead's work metaphysical. What makes it "sociological" in the usual sense of the word, is Whitehead's readiness to challenge our deepest conceptual assumptions. This is a new kind of metaphysics, one which is not a search for first principles as such, but a thorough investigation of the workings of the conceptual scheme that we have inherited.

Traces remain of what might seem like traditional metaphysics, especially in *Process and Reality*. The second chapter of this work is titled "The Categoreal Scheme" amidst which are found "The Category of the Ultimate", "Categories of Existence", "Categories of Explanation" and nine "Categoreal Obligations" (PR, 18–30). Furthermore, Whitehead introduces many technical terms such as "actual entities", "eternal objects", "prehensions" and so on. Despite these appearances, this does not mean that this text should be envisaged as just another work on metaphysics and hence outdated and irrelevant. Instead, two important, interlinked points must be insisted upon both here and throughout the following chapters:

i. The technical terms that Whitehead uses are not to be learned and applied to the world.
ii. His metaphysics is not a description of reality-as-it-is, in the sense of a discovery of the previously unfathomed secrets of the universe (it is not the true picture of all existence in its fundamental state).

To think in such ways, to assume that there is a key which can unlock the depths of reality, is, according to Whitehead, to have already fallen into the traps set by the concepts that we have inherited and to passively accept what has been termed in this book modernity's "culture of thought". These pitfalls and limitations are precisely what Whitehead's metaphysics is designed to illustrate and help us avoid. Shaviro puts it as follows: 'Whitehead's metaphysics is a ramshackle construction, continually open to revision, and not an assertion of absolute truths' (Shaviro 2009, xiii). Whilst the term "ramshackle" may be a little strong, the important point remains: Whitehead's metaphysics is not interested in providing final answers or solutions but in providing novel ways of thinking.

These novel modes of thought might be aided by some of the themes which run throughout Whitehead's work, such as "becoming", "relativity" and "construction". Later chapters will investigate the status of these and the contribution that they can make to social theory, but again it should be noted that these are not overarching answers or simple solutions; they are not simply to be learned and applied to the social realm. (For example, it is not simply a matter of saying that the social body is always becoming. More work will have to be done to satisfy the opportunities and requirements that Whitehead offers us. Later chapters will attempt to do this work.)

To summarize: the point is to interrogate our concepts, to recognize the limits that they place on us and to seek ways of re-energizing the problems which have led us to think in this way, in order to produce novel concepts and insights. With this in mind, it is time to turn to the details of Whitehead's work.

A Culture of Thought – The Bifurcation of Nature

'In each period there is a general form of the forms of thought; and, like the air we breathe, such a form is so translucent, and so pervading, and so seemingly necessary, that only by extreme effort can we become aware of it'

(AI, 14). This is the first demand that Whitehead makes of his reader. To stop, to pause and to be prepared to reconsider and investigate that which enables thought and also that which hinders it. The "form of the forms of thought" is the first indication of what, in the title of this book, has been referred to as "a culture of thought". This is not something which provides the ground for our thinking, it is not a base upon which arises a set of ideas. As is indicated by the use of the word "form", this is a notion which refers to the manner of thinking, the way it is carried out and carried on. It is a 'tone of thought' (PR, 5). The prevalent tone, or tones, of thought are what constitute a culture of thought. Such thought and thinking, according to Whitehead, must involve the construction of abstractions. 'You cannot think without abstractions; accordingly, it is of the utmost importance to be vigilant in critically revising your *modes* of abstraction. It is here that philosophy finds its niche as essential to the healthy progress of society' (SMW, 73, with emphasis in original; see also Stengers 2008a for a discussion of Whitehead's notion of abstraction). The task of theoretical investigations is, therefore, to locate and revise the manner in which abstractions are made. But, it must be stressed that there is no such thing as purely abstract thinking or wholly abstract knowledge. The supposition that thought is, in and of itself, purely abstract and can lead to pure knowledge is indicative of an assumption and presumption which characterizes the specific and constraining mode of thought which lingers throughout modernity. 'The notion of a sphere of human knowledge characterized by unalloyed truth is the pet delusion of dogmatists, whether they be theologians, scientists, or humanistic scholars' (MT, 94). For Whitehead, thinking is an abstractive activity which itself is always a located activity. Each abstraction occurs in a specific field or with regard to a specific problem; this is what provides it with both its purpose and its effectivity. Some abstractions are concerned with quarks, some with analyses of the poetry of Wallace Stevens, and some with the link between social class and education. To claim that such abstractions are self-sufficient is to forget that they arise from a more fundamental interconnection of things as they are. Abstraction and the activity of thinking are genuine processes which arise within reality but are neither a reflection nor a representation of reality as: 'every abstraction neglects the influx of the factors omitted into the factors retained' (MT, 196).

The above discussion of the status of abstraction is not intended to provide a full, or fully convincing, account of the importance of this term for Whitehead. It is offered as a first foray into some of his most abiding concerns, an indication of the depth of his critique. An elaboration of his alternative understanding of abstractions will be discussed throughout this book. To point ahead, the notions of the body, sexual difference, subjectivity and capitalism will all be immersed in problems and questions of abstraction, which have their place both in the world and in thinking about the world. For the moment, and as a next step in outlining Whitehead's thought, the dominant abstraction which Whitehead locates as the ongoing and most influential within modernity is that of "the bifurcation of nature".

It was suggested previously that Whitehead's philosophical publishing career commenced with his move to Harvard in 1924. This is not quite the case. In 1920 he published a text which serves as a juncture between his scientific and philosophical concerns, namely *Concept of Nature* (CN). This text asks: what kind of ultimate entities must there be which can be inferred from the character of our sense-experience? 'I submit to you that among the necessary prolegomena for philosophy and for natural science is a thorough understanding of the types of entities, and types of relations among those entities, which are disclosed to us in our perceptions of nature' (CN, 48). It therefore raises the spectre of ultimate questions about reality but does so without recourse to providing an explicit and developed metaphysics (Whitehead will provide this nine years later in his major metaphysical work *Process and Reality* (PR)). *Concept of Nature* (CN) situates Whitehead's concerns squarely within the changing early twentieth-century scientific accounts of the character of existence, most especially with regard to relativity and quantum theory, and the relation of these to human experience and perception. For the purpose of the argument being made here, the most crucial aspect of this text is Whitehead's clear delineation of that fundamental aspect of thought which arose with and still stalks modernity – the bifurcation of nature. As Stengers (2002) argues, the attempt to delineate and critique both the premises and consequences of the bifurcation of nature, as well the setting out of a theoretical framework which refuses to accede to its grip on thought, is a task which animates all Whitehead's later philosophical endeavours. As such, the bifurcation of nature is a theme to which Whitehead returns again and again, subtly restating and resituating its influence and operations. This bifurcation is not a "thing" which can be located and dissected. It is a "form of the forms of thought" and, as such, will only appear in the deployment of thoughts and concepts. The bifurcation of nature is not a structure which hides behind or determines thought; it is indicative of the located operations of thought in modernity. In a sense there is a similarity with Foucault's attempts in *The Archaeology of Knowledge* (1972) and *The Order of Things* (1974) to characterize the changing modes and contents of thought and knowledge and their implication in wider societal processes. However, Whitehead allows for more messiness than Foucault might in both the development and influence of such forms of the forms of thought. This makes providing a definition of this notion problematic but it is in *Concept of Nature* that Whitehead comes closest.

> What I am essentially protesting against is the bifurcation of nature into two systems of reality, which in so far as they are real, are real in different senses. One reality would be the entities such as electrons which are the study of speculative physics. This would be the reality which is there for knowledge; although on this theory it is never known. For what is known is the other sort of reality, which is the byplay of the mind. Thus there would be two natures, one is the conjecture and the other is the dream.
>
> Another way of phrasing this theory which I am arguing against is to bifurcate nature into two divisions, namely into the nature apprehended in awareness and the nature which is the cause of awareness. The nature which is in fact apprehended in awareness holds within it the greenness of the trees, the song of the birds, the warmth of the sun, the hardness of the chairs, and the feel of the velvet. The nature which is the cause of awareness is the conjectured system of molecules and electrons which so affects the mind as to produce the awareness of apparent nature. The meeting point of these two natures is the mind, the causal nature being influent and the apparent nature being effluent. (CN, 30–1)

Here Whitehead pinpoints the ostensibly unbridgeable gap between reality as conceived by science and reality as experienced by humans. This is one of the intransigent conditions of modernity; that the real reality is reserved for the unseen, yet fundamental, operations of those entities (molecules, electrons, etc.) which comprise a facticity utterly devoid of intrinsic meaning and utterly divorced from the meaningful realm of human existence. This reduces nature to an inert, implacable basis which is deprived of any purpose or inherent quality. Furthermore, the realm of experience (of warmth, redness, softness) and the description of such experience (in poems, art, hermeneutics etc.) is posited as solely a human affair and creation. This divorce can lead either to the celebration of this latter realm as the indicator of the specificity of the human as that sole element of existence which is, almost miraculously, endowed with language, value, and consciousness. Or, it can entail a reduction of such language, value and consciousness, as well as any descriptions of these, to interesting but unreal aspects of a dislocated human culture. Worse, it might lead some to suggest that the words, beliefs and thoughts of humans are merely inconsequential or irrelevant meanderings of a peculiar offshoot of existence, especially when compared with the grandeur of "Nature", (selfish) genes or God.

As will be seen throughout this book, this division of reality has sedimented into strict and calcified divisions of labour between distinct areas of thought. The "professionalization" of academic thought with the establishment of strictly demarcated schools, faculties and departments within the modern university from the nineteenth century onwards has reinforced the assumption that different subjects deal with different subject matters (SMW, 244–5). For example, and as will be discussed at length in Chapters Five and Six, contemporary analyses are often predicated on the resolute distinction between the "natural", biological body which falls under the purview of science and the "social", cultural body which is addressed by social theory. Here, the very facticity of the body is at stake. Do scientists have the sole right to discuss and manipulate the material body? Are attempts to incorporate the biological body into social analyses bound to lapse into a form of essentialism, thereby forgoing the important and political critiques which have demonstrated the constructedness of gender and sexuality? This leads to the crucial question of the efficacy of social and cultural analyses and of the reality of the sociocultural realm itself. If the constructedness of the body is solely a result of what humans think, say and act in relation to the body then does this not suggest that the material body itself does not matter at all, it is a mere blank canvas, an inert substratum upon which human illusions are placed, imagined or written? Whitehead gently ridicules this dividing of the academic spoils, which insists that the meanings, values and politics of the world reside solely in a human realm which is indifferent to, and distinct from, a prior, material realm, when he comments, ironically, that 'The poets are entirely mistaken. They should address their lyrics to themselves, and should turn them into odes of self-congratulation on the excellence of the human mind. Nature is a dull affair, soundless, scentless, colourless; merely the hurrying of material, endlessly, meaninglessly' (SMW, 68–9).

This bifurcation of nature, as Stengers puts it, 'literally plagues modern thought' (Stengers 2008a, 98). However, it must be stated that, at this point, Whitehead has not fully made his case. The present discussion is merely a first signal as to the importance he assigns to this notion; it is not envisaged as a once and for all proof that it is a prerequisite of being modern that one accepts a clear split between a real ("natural") reality which lies behind or beyond the human, social realm. There is no one mode of thought which subtends our thinking. There are only those occasions, sites, fields and debates which may or may not, to a greater or lesser extent, presuppose or rely upon, in a more or less diffuse way, some degree of complicity with a supposed division between a real reality and human experience. The investigation of the specific sites of these conceptual and practical debates will be taken up in the later sections of this book. The strength of Whitehead's argument should not be assessed simply in terms of his initial account of the bifurcation of nature. Rather, the influence and extent of this aspect of thought will be developed and considered in relation to the individual problems and cases under scrutiny, such as subjectivity, the status of the body, sexual difference, and the character of capitalism.

Another warning should be established here. The subtitle of this book refers to 'a Culture of Thought'. This might suggest that there is only *one* culture of thought which either stalks modernity or Whitehead's thought. This is not the case. There is a slight but deliberate ambiguity to the choice of the phrase "culture of thought"; it is intended to indicate the importance of recognizing the inextricable link between what we think and how we think. That is to say, that there is a texture and tone to thought but this does not render thought unreal, ineffective or relativistic. A culture of thought is necessary to thinking but it does not fully determine thinking and it does not occupy a separate and more fundamental realm to the operations of thought; it manifests itself in multiform abstractions, debates, journal articles, data-sets, conferences, seminars, lectures, course outlines, newspapers, conversations in coffee bars, restaurants and pubs. It would be equally valid, therefore, to refer to "cultures of thought" but this option has not been taken up here as this might suggest a form of relativism or disjunction between realms of thought or a hierarchy of abstractions and concepts. However, it should be noted that there is no supposition of an external, systematic, framework of thought which comprises one, originary, culture of thought which is distinct from its manifestations in vital and contested contemporary debates.

As stated above, Whitehead's description of the bifurcation of nature has not, as yet, been "proven". It is not clear that such a concept can be the subject of a proof, for as Whitehead says, there is a point at which philosophy must move beyond such confined limits: 'philosophy, in any proper sense of the term, cannot be proved. For proof is based upon abstraction... The attempt of any philosophic discourse should be to produce self-evidence' (MT, 67). Nevertheless, there is still a requirement to make a case, to provide "self-evidence". Hence, the following sections of this chapter will address different elements of Whitehead's scrutiny of the genesis of the bifurcation of nature through a discussion of three pivotal philosophical and scientific concepts which still linger within modern thought, even if they are not rendered explicit therein. These are: Aristotle's notion of "primary substance"; the subject-predicate axis of thought; the seventeenth-century notion of "secondary qualities" and its enduring influence on contemporary conceptions of nature as inert, passive and dead.[4]

Philosophy, Science and Contemporary Thought

Whitehead maintains that certain elements of Aristotelian logic with its reliance upon a conception of a "primary substance" still have a pervasive effect on what is considered to constitute a valid argument and way of reasoning. It should be noted that, although Whitehead does not always make this clear in *Process and Reality* (PR), his argument is against Aristotle's version of logic rather than against all of his metaphysics. His concern is the results that have accrued for philosophy, science and modern thought from the tacit adoption of Aristotle's description of "primary substance". This concept holds that there is a ground or static base which comprises utter reality and which exists separately from the perceptions, thoughts and conceptions of (human) subjects. 'The unquestioned acceptance of the Aristotelian logic has led to an ingrained tendency to postulate a substratum for whatever is disclosed in sense awareness, namely, to look below what we are aware of for the substance in the sense of the "concrete thing"' (CN, 18). 'In this way, the exclusive reliance on sense-perception promotes a false metaphysics' (AI, 281). That is, the philosophical and scientific emphasis upon perception as the royal road to knowledge or understanding replicates the misconception that *underneath* experience is a basis which placidly subtends that experience 'so that the course of nature is conceived as being merely the fortunes of matter in its adventure through space' (CN, 20). The leads to the conception that it is the attributes of matter rather than matter itself which are present to, and the basis for, human perception, knowledge and consciousness.

Much of *Process and Reality* (PR) alludes to various problems associated with such a position. For the moment, there are three points arising from the Aristotelian viewpoint, all of which are interrelated. First, the division of the universe into two distinct realms, with substance on one side and the qualities of substance on the other, produces a gulf between absolute reality and the characteristics of such a reality. This, in turn, produces the mutually exclusive fields of materialism and idealism (depending upon which side of the gulf is given priority). Moreover, the facticity of substance is distinct from the qualities that are predicated of particular instances of such a substance. These qualities thereby inhabit a separate and abstract realm; their real existence inheres beyond their particular instantiations. Second, it is impossible to account for, or allow for, the interconnection of individual items of materiality. That is to say, when primary substance exhibits itself, it does so as a complete and individual fact. There is, of course, a distinction made by those who maintain that substance itself comprises one complete entity – monism – and those who regard substance itself as comprising various, complete, individuated items – atomism. But the basic problem remains the same. 'Each substantial thing is thus conceived as complete in itself, without reference to any other substantial thing' (AI, 169). Descriptions of facticity thus amount to no more than a limited description of a supposedly individual point at an individual time. Each item becomes a solitary thing, an object, unrelated to any other. It is therefore impossible for information to pass between such objects. This position both denies, and is unable to account for, any notions of dynamism, fluency or process. Third, the splitting of existence into a primary substance which is distinct from those (human) subjects who experience or perceive such a substance also creates a gap between that which knows and that which is to be known. Whitehead identifies this as characterizing the main, mistaken concerns of modern epistemology. 'All modern epistemologies, all modern cosmologies, wrestle with this problem. There is, for their doctrine, a mysterious reality in the background, intrinsically unknowable by any direct intercourse' (AI, 170).

But the real error derives from the synthesis of this metaphysical conception of matter with Aristotle's logic, and especially with the linking of epistemology to linguistic forms in a way which still inhibits science, philosophy, the humanities and social theory today. Whitehead is clear that although a connection has been made between the form of modernity's language and the form of its thought, it is not a necessary one and it needs to be clarified in order to be challenged. Whitehead refers to this specific division as the "subject-predicate axis" and identifies it as an integral element of the bifurcation of nature, one which infects and limits our modern culture of thought. According to Whitehead, the modern outlook arises from the slow influence of Aristotle's Logic, during a period of two thousand years, which asserts that logical and rational thought is based upon and is expressed in its surest form through the simplest form of sentences.

> For example, the sentence "This water is hot" attributes the character of high temperatures to the particular mass of water in the particular bathtub. The quality of "being hot" is an abstraction. Many different things can be hot, and we can think being hot without thinking of any particular thing in a bathtub which is hot. But in the real physical world, the quality of "being hot" can only appear as a characteristic of concrete things which *are* hot. (AI, 169. Emphasis in original.)

Whitehead argues that Aristotle's notion of primary substance(s) as comprising the realm of utter facticity, separate from the experience or perceptions of such facticity, splits the universe into two fundamental (and fundamentally different) realms. There is the realm of substance, things, objects, etc. which comprises the physical (natural) world. In contradistinction to this is the realm of subjects, which perceive, know or cognize this other realm (or fail in all of these). This is what Whitehead refers to as the splitting of the world into "known and knower". On one side there is that which knows or perceives, on the other is that which is known or perceived. 'The subject is the knower, the object is the known. Thus, with this interpretation, the object-subject relation is the knower-known relation' (AI 225). Subjects are human, objects are nonhuman. In this way, Whitehead demonstrates how Aristotelian logic insists that existence replicates the linguistic patterns of simple sentences or, vice versa, that simple sentences replicate the fundamental structure of reality.

This linguistic-reality dyad creates a disjunction between such a primary substance and the qualities or characteristics that are attributed to it. For, qualities or attributes are predicated of a primary substance which itself remains fixed or constant and indifferent to such accidental changes. "X is red", "X are inferior", "X causes criminality". In each of these sentences "X" takes the place of primary substance. Each "X" could be substituted by a different "substance" (a tomato, men, a gene, for example). In such a system, the task of science is to provide the correct attributions to substance, and the task of epistemology is to account for how knowledge of the "correctness" or "incorrectness" of such attributions is possible. However, both systems reinforce the distinction between something that really *is* (primary substance) and its qualities or characteristics (heat, weight, criminality, for example). A gulf is thus created between the world-as-it-is and information about the world-as-it-is. This has led to epistemological and logical convolutions since at least the time of Kant. It is in these terms that Whitehead states that the influence of Aristotle is not only widespread but pernicious. 'The evil produced by Aristotelian "primary substance" is exactly this habit of metaphysical emphasis upon the "subject-predicate" form of propositions' (PR, 30). The deployment of the word "evil" in this context points to the depth of error which Whitehead believes still permeates much science, philosophy and contemporary thought.

Another aspect of the bifurcation of nature arises from seventeenth-century scientific doctrines on matter which developed certain, specific approaches that complicated, yet reinforced, the fundamental split between inert nature and the human subject or mind. 'Systematic doctrines of light and sound as being something proceeding from the emitting bodies were definitely established, and in particular the connexion of light with colour was laid bare by Newton' (CN, 26–7). This outlook maintains that matter comprises the primary reality which is "out there" and which is to be known by the mind. At the same time, it also confounds the manner in which the relation between the known and the knower is to be understood. Now, the relation is not to be envisaged as that of the mind merely perceiving the attributes of an otherwise inert matter. Rather, the relation between knower and known is to be conceived as one in which matter, in some way, transmits attributes of itself to the mind, via sense perception, whilst itself remaining the same. Also, there is the second difficulty of accounting for the fact that that which is perceived (by the mind) is different from that which is transmitted: 'we do not even perceive what enters the eye' (CN, 27). So, light particles or waves enter the eye and are focused on the retina but what is perceived is not "light particles" but a specific colour (for example, green) but "green" itself does not seem to enter the eye. On such a theory "greenness" can only be explained by resorting to what Whitehead calls a "psychic addition". 'The theory of psychic additions would treat the greenness as a psychic addition furnished by the perceiving mind, and would leave to nature merely the molecules and the radiant energy which influence the mind towards that perception' (CN, 29–30). This establishes the modern, irredeemable breach between the real world and human experience thereof. A profound gap is established whereby the real reality is ascribed to the world and a lesser or illusory form of reality is ascribed to the mental states which accompany human experience of the world. 'The colour and the sound were no longer in nature. They are the mental reactions of the percipient... Thus nature is left with bits of matter, qualified by mass, spatial relations, and the change of such relations' (MT, 180). Greenness is not of the natural world, it is of the world of the human mind, to be studied by psychologists, social psychologists and poets, whereas the molecules which give rise to such greenness are studied by scientists and are conceived of as utterly un-green. 'For some, nature is the mere appearance and mind is the sole reality. For others, physical nature is the sole reality and mind is an epi-phenomenon' (MT, 205). Later chapters will outline how Whitehead develops a philosophical position which evades such distinctions and gaps and which is able to account for experience as an integral element of existence. At this point, however, it is the critical aspect of Whitehead's approach which is being developed.

One abiding aspect of Whitehead's challenge to philosophy, science and social theory is his demarcation of the complex yet inconsistent retention of specific outdated concepts within their theoretical armoury. For example, with regard to the previous discussions of the notions of primary substance and secondary qualities, these would be mere speculations on the history of ideas if they did not still have an important but reductive effect on current conceptualizations of science. In turn, these would be merely of interest to historians of science and philosophers of science if they did not also mould the forms of thought which linger in the background and influence the thoughts, activities and approaches of scientists, social theorists and, indeed, all those who partake of modernity. So, as Whitehead points out, contemporary theoretical science itself, to a large part, would no longer wish to adhere to a concept of existence based on an enduring, primary substance. 'The atom is only explicable as a society with activities involving rhythms with their definite periods. Again the concept shifted its application: protons and electrons were conceived as materialistic electric charges whose activities could be construed as locomotive adventures' (PR, 78). Whitehead argues that science is not a homogeneous entity, and that its approaches and concepts do not form a consistent class; contradictory concepts can be maintained at the same time. For example, the insistence upon the positing of genes in terms of an outdated, inert atomicity, as self-identical objects with prior causal power, is not only well entrenched but dangerous. So, one of the tasks of theory, according to Whitehead, is to point out some of the confusions surrounding current scientific conceptions and to attempt to develop a conceptual apparatus that will avoid such errors and provide a more sustained, perhaps even a "truer", account of the complexity of the interrelations of matter, science and subjectivity.

An early indication of the relevance of Whitehead to informing such contemporary debates is to be found in Haraway who has, since her earliest texts (Haraway 1976), been an advocate of his work. Interestingly, her longest discussion of Whitehead to date is to be found in her analysis of dominant scientific conceptualization of genes as dislocated objects, which she calls 'gene fetishism' (Haraway 1997, 142 and 141–8 passim). "Gene fetishism" is the mistaken belief that genes are objects in the traditional philosophical and scientific sense. For Haraway, such a belief is blind to the interrelatedness of all items of matter. As such, "gene fetishism" is a defence mechanism 'against the knowledge of the actual complexity and embeddedness of all objects, including genes. The fetishist ends up believing in the code of codes, the book of life, and even the search for the grail' (Haraway 1997, 146). Haraway makes extensive use of the work of Whitehead in the course of her account: 'The third strand in my helical spiral of gene fetishism is spun out of what Whitehead called the "fallacy of misplaced concreteness"' (1997, 146). Whitehead defines this fallacy as 'the accidental error of mistaking the abstract for the concrete' (SMW, 64). Haraway uses this term of Whitehead's to explain how gene fetishism attempts to grant an unwarranted level of concrete, objective existence to genes. Gene fetishists fail to realize that their concept of the gene amounts to no more than an abstraction that posits genes as distinct and discrete objects when *in fact* they are always embroiled in a more complex set of interrelations. This is not to suggest that either Haraway's or Whitehead's arguments imply that there are no actual objects, that nothing is concrete. 'The mere phrase that "'physical science is an abstraction", is a confession of philosophic failure. It is the business of rational thought to describe the more concrete fact from which that abstraction is derivable' (AI, 186). Whitehead is not intent on explaining away science or dismissing its importance. On the contrary, he wants to provide fuller, more coherent, more incisive accounts. As will be seen, in order to provide valid descriptions of that which is genuinely concrete, one must be able to account for the processual character of reality. This will always involve descriptions of interrelation, as Haraway also suggests.

Nevertheless, Whitehead does not grant science any immediate priority in accessing the "truth of the world". It is too deeply immersed in concepts that are now outdated for that; it still tacitly relies upon the dichotomy apparent in the bifurcation of nature and the seeming impasse created by the subject-predicate axis. Yet, this is not to dismiss science wholesale for Whitehead maintains that it is within modern science itself that such conceptualizations of matter have been challenged, through its overturning of much of Newton's approach. 'The story commences with the wave-theory of light and ends with the wave-theory of matter' (AI, 200). The resultant contemporary (scientific) conception of objects, space and matter is as follows:

> In the modern concept the group of agitations which we term matter is fused into its environment. There is no possibility of a detached, self-contained local existence. The environment enters into the nature of each thing. Some elements in the nature of a complete set of agitations may remain stable as those agitations are propelled through a changing environment. But such stability is only the case in a general, average way. This average fact is the reason why we find the same chair, the same rock, and the same planet enduring for days, or for centuries, or for millions of years. (MT, 188–9)

Whitehead is clear, as is Haraway in her discussion of gene fetishism, that the implications of such a dissolution of matter have not been fully accepted by science. Its culture of thought harbours the notion of self-contained and self-identical objects externally related to each other, which Newton described all those years ago. Science still invokes concepts of matter which are incompatible with its own contemporary conceptual framework; this is one of its great but perhaps unrecognized paradoxes: 'in the present-day re-construction of physics fragments of the Newtonian concepts are stubbornly retained. The result is to reduce modern physics to a sort of mystic chant over an unintelligible Universe' (MT, 185). Science and its culture of thought are implicated within the culture of thought of modernity but they are not determined by it, caused by it, or a mere epi-phenomenon of it. Social theory cannot explain science away as merely a social construct as some early combatants in the so-called "Science Wars" maintained. Science is an aspect of modernity but one which often mistakes its own status, as do its detractors and defenders. The utter imbrication of science with other theoretical, practical, social, legal, artistic and everyday endeavours is an element of modernity which is often misrecognized (see Latour 1993a). Science is not separate from society but nor is it fully reducible to it: 'the autonomy of the natural sciences has its origin in a concept of the world of Nature, now discarded' (MT, 197). Importantly, Whitehead maintains the right of theory (including social and cultural theory) to judge, and establish hypotheses or descriptions which, even if not True, then are at least as true or "truer" than those of science. Whitehead's ultimate appraisal of science is that: 'Science only deals with half the evidence provided by human experience. It divides the seamless coat – or, to change the metaphor into a happier form, it examines the coat, which is superficial, and neglects the body which is fundamental' (MT, 211). This provides a theoretical and practical position for social theory to engage with such questions in a manner where its statements cannot be so easily dismissed as merely speculations on the social or cultural significance of a physicality or materiality that is ontologically prior to such analyses and over which science somehow has greater authority. The importance of the concept of experience will be taken up in Chapter Two and the centrality of the body to both existence and theory will be addressed in Chapters Three, Six and Seven.

Ultimately, Whitehead's rejection of the bifurcation of nature and the "evil" that it produces rests on his assertion that it comprises a 'radical inconsistency at the basis of thought [which] accounts for much that is half-hearted and wavering in our civilisation. It would be going too far to say that it distracts thought. It enfeebles it, by reason of the inconsistency lurking in the background' (SMW 94). This "radical inconsistency" is emblematic of the culture of thought of modernity. The aim of Whitehead's philosophy is to be more coherent and more consistent (PR, 3–4); he is a hopeful philosopher and his contribution to social theory is a positive one, as will become clear as each topic is addressed in turn. The later sections of this book will outline both the influence of the inconsistency inherent in specific topics within social theory and will also deploy a Whiteheadian analysis to suggest ways of reorienting and reapproaching these problems. This will not involve simply deconstructing, dismissing or forgetting the concepts and the debates which polarize scientific and social accounts of reality, nature, society, the body, sexual difference, and so on. Instead, it will take such debates as a challenge to produce new modes of thought. 'A clash of doctrines is not a disaster – it is an opportunity' (SMW, 230).

The procedure and topics of this book, therefore, reside both within and without the traditional concerns of philosophy and of social theory. Although the subsequent discussions are not set out in the usual manner or format of a text on the philosophy of social science, this is not to say that it is not envisaged as a contribution to this field. Overall, it is intended to comprise a provocation to the usual approach to the philosophy of social science and as an opportunity to reframe and reconsider its fundamental purpose and approach. Despite its lack of separate chapters on the questions of structure and agency, the individual and society, objectivity and value-freedom, this does not entail that the topics and concepts developed here are not crucial to these debates. Building on the work of Whitehead, it will hopefully become more and more clear that to start within such debates is to tacitly accept the parameters that they have established and thereby to limit the creation of novel concepts and fresh perspectives. Instead, it will be argued that many of the conceptual assumptions which permeate and animate these debates can be traced back to an implicit acceptance of some elements of the bifurcation of nature. Social theory is a creature and reflection of modernity; it, too, is a product of the segmentation and professionalization of thought which developed and hardened in the nineteenth century. In order to move beyond such a segmentation, this book will take the opportunity of utilizing the work of Whitehead to establish a new relation between philosophy and social theory.

The depth of Whitehead's challenge to contemporary thought will thus become clear as the consequences of Whitehead's diagnosis unfold. As stated earlier, it is not easy simply to prove (or disprove) a conceptual scheme or way of thinking. As Whitehead says: 'If we consider philosophical controversies, we shall find that disputants tend to require coherence from their adversaries, and to grant dispensations to themselves. It has been remarked that a system of philosophy is never refuted; it is only abandoned' (PR, 6). Theoretical problems are not always solved by digging deeper, by endlessly refining or tweaking concepts. At some point it must be realized that a set of concepts has lost its purchase and its charm. Resolute attempts to rescue such concepts lead to the increasingly desperate position where 'Failure to include some obvious elements of experience in the scope of the system is met by boldly denying the facts' (PR, 6). There is then the consequent danger of theory becoming a mere superficial game, which is quite rightly derided as being irrelevant to the real world by those involved in more "practical" or "empirical" research. Whitehead, therefore, sets out some specific demands for theory, namely that it be coherent and that it adequately explains and incorporates those elements of experience which are so clear to all those who are not lost in their own theoretical labyrinths. Before proceeding to substantiate these claims, I will end this chapter with a very brief summary of the deficiencies which Whitehead identifies in traditional approaches to theory as well as indicating the positive moves that he will make to avoid these. These are not intended as full accounts but rather as indications of the flavour and reach of Whitehead's arguments which will be explored in more detail in the chapters that follow. These deficiencies might, rather boldly, be summarized in the two following phrases: Critical thought is not Critical enough; Realism is not Realistic enough.

Whitehead describes Descartes as one of the chief instigators of the modern form of critical thought. He does not pillory him for this, he simply points out that his mode of critique is one which does not go far enough; Descartes neglects to interrogate those assumptions which enable him to make his critique, those elements which he takes for granted whilst he establishes his procedure of radically doubting everything. And what enables this very process of doubt is what Whitehead terms the 'social environment' (PR, 203 and passim). This is another prima facie indication of the "sociological" character of Whitehead's philosophy. But, this is a very specific conception of the social and is very different from the one which is normally deployed in sociology and social theory (this will be discussed further in Chapter Four). The social environment, as Whitehead envisages it, is comprised of all those things, concepts, words, practices within which and from which the contemporary world, events and people are located, act and change. To return to Whitehead on Descartes, as Stengers puts it: 'Nothing is more strange to Whitehead that Descartes strategy of "radical doubt" which sets out to make a clean slate of all those inferences which could be seen as fictional or untrue, but forgets everything which is presupposed by such a procedure, for example the fact that his decision and his inquiry presuppose, at the very least, the words to formulate the legitimate reasons for rejecting, one after another, all those things in which faith can no longer be placed' (Stengers 2002, 293). Whitehead's philosophy is a generous one in that it wants to be able to include more, to explain more, namely all the elements of experience and reality. He chastises Descartes and much critical thought for immediately, and without due justification, ruling out of bounds, or ignoring, certain elements of experience and certain elements which enable thought.

The same criticism – that his philosophy makes assumptions that it does not make explicit – is levelled by Whitehead at Hume; a thinker who is often seen as the empiricist counterpart to Descartes' rationalism. The problem with Hume, according to Whitehead, is that he seems happy to extend his scepticism to the point where he questions the existence of cause as really existing in the world, as it is not something that we can ever genuinely see or have an impression of, but he does not apply the same principle to his discussion of "habit", the term that he uses to explain how the notion of cause manages to arise in the (human) mind. 'It is difficult to understand why Hume exempts "habit" from the same criticism as that applied to the notion of "cause." We have no "impression" of "habit," just as we have no "impression" of "cause"' (PR, 140). Again, the challenge that Whitehead makes is that such critical thought is not critical enough, it only surveys one aspect of the problem and slips in unwarranted explanations to shore up its assumptions. Habit is not something of which we have an impression. Therefore, in Whitehead's view, it should be subject to the same strictures that Hume places on the notion of cause. This is not to suggest that Whitehead believes that cause or habit do not exist. Chapter Three and Chapter Five will outline the important role that a reformed account of cause has in Whitehead's philosophy and the related importance of the role of the body in accounting for causation. The point Whitehead makes is that it is not a valid procedure to explain one term or concept with another presumed yet hidden one. There must be a democracy of critique which does not privilege any item of existence or experience. Shaviro, commenting on Whitehead's reading of Hume, states that 'There is no reason why mental events should be treated any differently than any other sort of events; they are all part of the same stream of experience' (Shaviro 2009, 31). Quite what Whitehead envisages by experience will be discussed further in Chapter Two. For the moment, what is important here is the second major element of Whitehead's challenge namely, that 'Realism is not Realistic enough'.

The impetus of any realistic philosophical approach would clearly seem to be to account for that which is real. However many realist philosophers have taken the demand for realism as assuming that what needs to be explained is the really real which is, obviously, distinct from the unreal, fictitious and imaginary. This apparently sensible step is, however, one which has betrayed its own procedures. It assumes, prior to any investigation, that there is a distinction between that which is real and that which is imaginary. It has delimited and limited the scope of its inquiry in an unwarranted fashion. As Stengers puts it: 'Critical thought accepts so many things without criticizing them' (Stengers 2002, 74). Empiricists have not been empirical enough; they have accepted certain aspects of experience as providing clear and distinct information about the world and denigrated other aspects as fictive or imaginary but they have done so before all the evidence is in. Whitehead is clear that such a procedure is unjustified; the task for theory is to be able to provide the most general account which enables all items of the world and of experience to be incorporated (including that which is normally referred to as fictive or imaginary). There are to be no gaps. The need for such an account is what drove Whitehead from his specific investigations of the philosophy and history of science, "civilization", religion and symbolism (CN, SMW, RM, SYM, respectively) to undertake his magnum opus, *Process and Reality* (PR), at the age of 66, after a full and internationally successful academic life. Whitehead did not write this book in order to make a name for himself in the philosophical world but in order to respond to the questions that he had set himself throughout his career. As the title of his major work suggests, reality, for Whitehead, must be considered to be a process rather than some kind of substratum (or "primary substance") which it is the task of (human) knowers to know (a prevalent and abiding assumption which, as will now be clear, replicates the mode of thought which has infected philosophy from the time of Aristotle).

To return to the question of the status and procedure of realism, Whitehead starts with no presuppositions, with no assumptions, as to what reality consists in and in what reality consists. As Harman, albeit in a different context, puts it: 'At the outset, the philosopher has no idea what is real and what is unreal' (Harman 2009, 74). As Whitehead, even more dramatically, puts it: 'Philosophy may not neglect the multifariousness of the world – the fairies dance, and Christ is nailed to the cross' (PR 338). This is not to suggest that Whitehead believes either in fairies or Christ. It is, rather, a statement which demonstrates his utter refusal to make any prior judgement as to what constitutes reality or what needs to be accounted for by theory. Whitehead was no romantic, he was a practising scientist and clearly stated that 'I assume as an axiom that science is not a fairy tale' (CN, 40). Yet this does not grant science the sole authority to describe or account for the real. This would not only invoke a version of the bifurcation of nature, it would also exclude, through an unwarranted fiat, social theory and the humanities from partaking in, or contributing to, analyses of the real.

The pressing need to recast the assumptions and conceptual machinations which inform the bifurcation of nature and the associated divisions between science, philosophy and social theory is one major task of this book. Social theory needs to make a bold re-engagement with the problems and concepts of reality, the natural, the body, etc. in order to provide more robust, fuller accounts, indeed to engage with *more* of the world. This is, in short, the importance of Whitehead.

Chapter Two

INTRODUCING WHITEHEAD'S PHILOSOPHY – THE LURE OF WHITEHEAD

The previous chapter outlined Whitehead's diagnosis of the culture of thought of modernity and the fault lines that sow inconsistency at its heart. This chapter will outline Whitehead's positive philosophical contribution and, concomitantly, the opportunities that he offers contemporary thought and social theory in general. Whitehead's work is not self-explanatory and it comprises philosophical, metaphysical, scientific, historical and sociological elements. It will not be possible to examine all these in detail or to do full justice to the intricacies of his work. Instead, this chapter is offered as an invitation to consider the most fundamental aspects of Whitehead's thought. Borrowing a term from Whitehead, this chapter aims to propose the "lure" (PR, 184 and passim) that his concepts offer. The discussions which follow will introduce Whitehead's key philosophical stance with regard to a range of topics but do not constitute an 'introduction' to Whitehead's philosophy.[1] This chapter and this book are not simply an exegesis of his work which can then be applied to a certain set of problems. As Stengers (2002, 2008a) has stressed, it is not as if Whitehead provides a ready-made set of conceptual answers. Rather, he invites us to stop, to consider what and how we are thinking and then to construct novel responses to the problems we inhabit and which inhabit us and our world. This attention to the fabric of our concepts and problems, to that which enables us to think and also limits our thoughts, requires that we attend to those most abiding, assumed and presupposed aspects of our culture of thought which we usually take for granted or ignore. As Stengers puts it, rather than accepting the concepts which we inherit, we must aim for 'a maximization of friction; recovering what has been obscured by specialized selection' (Stengers 2008, 95). The task ahead is to delve more deeply into that which is normally passed over, to investigate the tensions and frictions which enable our concepts to operate so as to discover both that which has been included in their construction and what has been missed out.

To commence, as might seem to be done at points in the previous chapter, by suggesting that Whitehead's philosophical stance "comes out of nowhere", as if it were possible to start abstract thinking afresh and untainted by the legacy and assumptions of modernity, would be erroneous. Whitehead is well aware of the constrictions to thought that are present as a result of this history of concepts, most especially the bifurcation of nature. What Whitehead refuses to do is assume that any one element, such as a distinctive form of economic-social relations, the intertwining of an ever more complex differentiation of the division of labour with new forms of sociality, or shifting historical forms of social action, is sufficient in itself to account either for modernity or its culture of thought. All these may well play important roles, but they cannot initially be taken as the foundations, guide, or reasons for contemporary society without preliminary investigations into the character of such concepts and reality. Hence, his attempt to produce a novel, twentieth-century metaphysics is firmly placed as an attempt to "maximize the friction" latent within the legacy of our culture of thought, in order to develop an approach which, rather than deconstructing or resolving this bifurcation as postmodernists and certain contemporary philosophers of social science aim to do, is able to bypass its most insidious effects. In this way, Whitehead's philosophy is utterly situated, even if might not appear to be so at first sight.

Perhaps the clearest clue as to the main elements of Whitehead's philosophy is to be found in the title of his major work, *Process and Reality* (PR). What he is attempting to explain is how reality, and the 'stubborn fact' (PR, xiv and passim) that presents itself in the universe, can be consistently theorized within a theory of the universe as dynamic. Whitehead states that: 'the history of philosophy...tends to ignore the fluency, and to analyse the world in terms of static categories' (PR, 209). As has been seen, he views this tendency as an inimitable part of the history of Western philosophy and modern science resulting in the traditional and dominant position which has falsely viewed the universe as rendered into discrete Newtonian objects. Yet, Whitehead also argues against those who simply focus upon the flows and mobility of the world and solely address becoming, as well as those, such as Spinoza (1992), who (apparently) prioritizes infinite substance as the "real" condition of the universe out of which its modifications appear. In such accounts, that which is stressed is the almost universal nature of becoming, at the expense of the ability to account for immediate items of matter; postmodern emphases on irreality and flows and flights are not the answer. Whitehead asserts that it is easy to describe the world simply in terms of motion, flux, infinity or becoming. What is more difficult is to develop an account of the facticity of the world within the fluency of existence without recourse to some kind of philosophical or scientific materialism.

The task which Whitehead has therefore set himself is to account for the objects of the world without replicating the outdated and inconsistent concepts which dog science and philosophy (and, by implication, social theory). Even more daunting, Whitehead has insisted that such an account must rid itself of the suppositions which infect modernity's culture of thought and yet must still be able to incorporate everything that manifests itself in the world and in experience. Furthermore, Whitehead wants to take on board and portray the fluency of the world, as does relativity theory with its refusal of static conceptions of time and space. What is, perhaps, most remarkable about Whitehead's view of this endeavour is that he sees it as entirely consonant with common sense. 'Philosophy is the welding of imagination and common sense into a restraint upon specialists, and also into an enlargement of their imaginations' (PR, 17). He locates the problems and concepts which suffuse even the most abstract philosophy within everyday experience; he explains his point by quoting from a hymn:

> Abide with me; Fast falls the eventide. Here the first line expresses the permanences, "abide," "me" and the "Being" addressed; and the second line sets these permanences amid the inescapable flux. (PR, 209)

This sense of change and permanency, fixity and flow, being and becoming are, for Whitehead, elements which permeate the lives of everyone who experiences the passing of day into night and who feel themselves to be some kind of enduring entity within this passing. The development of a theory which is able to include both of these elements of experience is, however, not so simple.

Subjects and Experience

Whitehead's critique of contemporary conceptions of objects might suggest that he will emphasize the role and status of subjects within his work. In one sense this is exactly the case, but a strong word of warning must be made at this point. When Whitehead uses the term "subject" he does so in a very specific sense and to immediately assume that he means *human* subject would be to miss his point. If Whitehead were simply to assert the primacy of the human mind, self or subjectivity he would simply be fixating on one element of the bifurcation of nature namely, that of the primacy of human experience characterized in terms of consciousness, the mind or rationality. But he wants to avoid having to accept the validity of this very distinction when setting up his philosophy. Whitehead is insistent and consistent in his declarations that consciousness and the more general operations of the human mind cannot be taken for granted. They are not that which subtends experience or human existence but are factors within existence which themselves need to be explained. To start with consciousness or the mind, as Descartes does, is to slip in that which is meant to be explained as itself explanatory of the proposed explanation. 'Experience has been explained in a thoroughly topsy-turvy fashion, the wrong end first' (PR 162). Whitehead is not denying the importance of consciousness for humans. He is simply stating that the manner of its existence and operations cannot be taken for granted; it is not something that we experience continuously: 'The simplicity of clear consciousness is no measure of the complexity of complete experience... our experience suggests that consciousness is the crown of experience, only occasionally attained, not its necessary base' (PR, 267). Again, this is not to state that Whitehead believes that consciousness has no role but that its status should not be too readily assumed, and certainly not posited as foundational. A misrecognition of the extent of Whitehead's critique of consciousness by early "American" sociological interpreters of Whitehead, including Mead, Parsons and Schutz led, perhaps, to the initial enthusiasm but later disavowal of the relevance of Whitehead to social theory; an unfortunate legacy which this book is attempting to redress (see Halewood 2008 for a fuller discussion of the initial reception of Whitehead by early twentieth-century sociology).

Any reading of Whitehead as a proponent of the primacy of consciousness is all the more surprising given that he stresses that philosophers have often been too quick to latch on to the alleged clarity that conscious experience appears to offer and to treat it as the core of experience when it is really only one element within a whole host of experiences. The same applies to other elements of humanity which have also been posited as the core of its being; elements such as rationality and agency.

> It is said that "men [sic] are rational." This is palpably false: they are only intermittently rational – merely liable to rationality. Again the phrase "Socrates is mortal" is only another way of saying that "perhaps he will die." The intellect of Socrates is intermittent: he occasionally sleeps and he can be drugged or stunned. (PR, 79)

Theory has tended to treat reason, consciousness and agency as nouns, as objects, as if they exist substantially within the world and possession of them enables us to arise and be defined as humans. John Dewey, a contemporary of Whitehead on the American philosophical stage, puts it thus: '"Thought," reason, intelligence, whatever word we choose to use, is existentially an adjective (or better an adverb), not a noun. It is a disposition of activity' (Dewey 1958 [1925], 158). The crucial point here is that it is the activity, the *processes*, of thinking or reasoning which are primary. Even more importantly, such processes do not happen in abstract but always occur within a certain situation and in a certain way; they have a quality to them which is best described adverbially. The manner and quality of such experiences as integral to all experience (and hence to all existence) is a major element of Whitehead's thought which will be discussed throughout this book. For the moment, and to summarize, Whitehead, in an often quoted passage, describes his position thus: 'Descartes in his own philosophy conceives the thinker as creating the occasional thought. The philosophy of organism inverts the order, and conceives the thought as a constituent operation in the creation of the occasional thinker' (PR, 151). In *Modes of Thought* he puts it as follows: 'Clear, conscious discrimination is an accident of human existence. It makes us human. But it does not make us exist. It is of the essence of our humanity. But it is an accident of our existence' (MT, 158).

Whitehead has now dismissed both objects and consciousness as fundamental to reality or an understanding of it. However, it might have been noted that he has not dismissed the importance of experience. And here we are at the key step within Whitehead's philosophical journey. As opposed to Descartes, who assumes all experience to be conscious experience, or Hume, who starts with perceptual (tacitly human) experience, Whitehead is more modest and yet more daring. He views such experiences as bearing witness to a wider, more expansive field of experience than is usually noticed or admitted within theory. He does not judge any of these experiences, does not rank or categorize them as more or less relevant before he embarks on his cosmological adventure. He does not, as some realists are wont to do, exclude any form or content of experience out of hand (the imagined, the fanciful, the phantasmagorical, for example). Instead, he takes the radical step of focusing on experience as primary to all existence. This is not to make a phenomenologist of Whitehead (as that term is usually conceived); experience, for Whitehead, neither relies upon nor solely refers to consciousness or the lived conditions of humanity.[2] To limit such experiences to humans at the outset is an unjustified, limiting step as well as an invalid theoretical assumption. So, Whitehead's solution to the problem of viewing the world as comprised of objects *and* subjects, with the associated lapse into the bifurcation of nature, is to focus on the experience of subjects as the primary basis of reality. His metaphysics is one which liberates experience from the chains of their reliance upon either subjects or objects (be they human or "natural"). Experience will serve as Whitehead's ontological cornerstone. He sums up his approach in the following maxim: 'apart from the experiences of subjects there is nothing, nothing, nothing, bare nothingness' (PR, 167).

The remaining sections of the present chapter will flesh out some of the other important, positive elements of Whitehead's philosophy which are required for later analyses. In doing so, it will outline some of the key elements of Whitehead's philosophy in order to open up and indicate the lure that he offers contemporary thought. The list is not exhaustive and these are not intended as definitions; they are a sketch of the conceptual framework which Whitehead constructs. Five main notions will be discussed: "Actual Entities", "Prehensions", "Power", "Relativity" and "Creativity".

Actual Entities

Whitehead is clear that he wants to move beyond the Newtonian view of objects as self-identical, self-contained entities as this leads to a conception where the 'universe is shivered into a multitude of disconnected substantial things... But substantial thing cannot call unto substantial thing' (AI, 170). On such a view it is impossible to account for the relations between objects (or between objects and subjects) as each object is envisaged as entirely self-sufficient and dislocated from all other objects (or subjects). This does not mean that Whitehead denies the existence of actual things. Rather, he wants to characterize the existence of actual things in terms which can allow for a genuine interrelation between them. Furthermore, he describes both the constitution of such actual things, and the possibility of their interrelation, through his insistence that it is experience which is key. He achieves this through the adoption of the term "actual entity" as expressing the primary mode of existence:

> It is fundamental to the metaphysical doctrine of the philosophy of organism, that the notion of an actual entity as the unchanging subject of change is completely abandoned. An actual entity is at once the subject experiencing and the superject of its experiences. It is subject-superject and neither half of this description can for a moment be lost sight of. (PR, 29)

The coming together of diverse experiences into a novel unity is the process of becoming a subject (which Whitehead refers to as its 'concrescence' (PR, 41–2)). There is no subjectivity prior to this combining. There is no ongoing mind or identity which lurks behind or sustains a continuing individuality. Instead, on each occasion of a novel combination of diverse elements, there is the development of a new superject. No longer is subjectivity that which is limited to humans; no longer is it an enduring facet of a person or a guarantor of a continuing self-identity. The term "superject" with its connotations of a throwing beyond the present should alert us to this lack of a substantial base to subjectivity: that which experiences is some kind of a subject but the process of this experiencing entails a going beyond (hence the term "superject").

The very word "superject" elicits the dynamic character of existence and overcomes simple conceptions of the past, present and future. It is the 'past hurling itself into a new transcendent fact. It is the flying dart...hurled beyond the bounds of the world' (AI, 227). Being is constituted through the launch of the past into the future. This is the being of becoming. Moreover, '*how* an actual entity *becomes* constitutes *what* that actual entity *is*... Its "being" is constituted by its "becoming". This is the "principle of process"' (PR, 23; emphasis in original). Whitehead's conception of existence is always focused on the "*how*" of becoming (in Dewey's sense of the term, existence is adverbial). "How" an actual entity becomes creates what that entity *is*. The importance of this notion of "how an actual entity becomes" will be taken up below (and the consequent rendering of value as implicit in facticity will be taken up in Chapter Three). For the moment, it should be noted that all "things", all items of materiality are subjects (in terms of constituting a superject). But, each such item, each such subject, is a novel creation. As it is the process of becoming which is given priority in Whitehead's ontology, the terms "object" and "subject" lose their usual sense – 'subject and object are relative terms' (AI, 226). That is to say, each actual entity only exists for as long as it is becoming. When it has become it "perishes". This does not mean that it somehow vanishes out of the universe. Instead, it becomes a potential item of data for the creation of new entities. In this sense it is an "object". This reinforces Whitehead's claim that by delineating the reality of the process of experience he is able to describe both the primacy of becoming *and* the facticity of existence.

Prehensions

The process of existence is not, according to Whitehead, some kind of undulating, undifferentiated, flow or flux. He manages to maintain both becoming and differentiation by insisting that each becoming unfolds in a different manner, incorporating different elements to every other becoming. In order to more fully explain the constituency of an actual entity and how its very being enables, indeed requires, its interrelation with and co-constitution by other entities, Whitehead introduces the notion of "prehensions": 'the first analysis of an actual entity, into its most concrete elements, discloses it to be a concrescence of prehensions, which have originated in the process of becoming. All further analysis is an analysis of prehensions' (PR, 23). The word "prehension" is not a neologism, Whitehead did not invent this term. It is a little used word which means "grasping" and which Whitehead adopts as pivotal in accounting for the manner in which things come to be. Prehensions enable Whitehead to account for differentiated becomings within a wider system of process *and* to retain a grasp on the "concrete", on the materiality of reality.

Whitehead's description of actual entities, as has just been summarized, is designed to illustrate the reality of "stubborn fact" within a universe which is characterized by continual process. As such, it is an abstract theory of the conditions of existence. The point of Whitehead's analysis is to provide a systematic conceptual framework which encompasses the facticity and potentiality inherent in all existence and which avoids the snares and traps of the bifurcation of nature. Actual entities do not comprise the material world as encountered (by humans) and there is no benefit in trying to map actual entities onto elements of the world as experienced by humans; for example, by envisaging them as fundamental particles such as electrons or quarks. Their role is not to describe the world "as it is" but to enable novel conceptual constructions which more fully and adequately account for the diversity and process of reality (so, for example, 'a molecule is a historic route of actual occasions'[3] (PR, 80)). Yet, it will be incumbent, eventually, upon Whitehead to relate this high abstraction to the contemporary world and this will be explained and interpreted in the latter sections of this book. The point to be made, at present, is that Whitehead wants to shift the emphasis from the notion of objects and subjects to that of experience; experiences are what make up the eventful character of existence. That is to say, the world is not made up of inert objects but of those events of experience which we undergo.

So far, this chapter has outlined how Whitehead grants subjectivity to all items of materiality insofar as they constitute superjects. This is not immediately a description of human subjectivity (though, ultimately, the same process of the reception of the external world along with the manner of such reception, as constituting the moments of individual existence, will also apply to humans). Before proceeding, it should be pointed out that there is some discrepancy amongst Whitehead scholars as to how far it is possible to use the term actual entities to describe that which is commonly held to be the "enduring objects" of the contemporary world, for example, rocks, plants, planets, dogs, sweets, cheeseboards. Technically, Whitehead refers to such "things" solely as 'societies' (PR, 89–92), though at times he refers to such things in terms of a 'nexus' (e.g. PR, 63). The present discussion is only concerned with outlining the challenge that Whitehead makes to usual conceptions of existence; the status of enduring objects in terms of societies will be more fully discussed in Chapter Four. The purpose and status of the analysis being made here is aptly summarized by Stengers when she states:

> The point is not to wonder about the legitimacy of Whitehead's speculative definition of what truly exists, as if *Process and Reality* unfolded some kind of ultimate perspective. A perspective is certainly produced, but it cannot be separated from an experience of disclosure; and this experience does not concern actual entities as such, but the very possibility of changing the problem, to escape the oppositions our modern definitions induce. (Stengers 2007, 45)

To return to the notion of prehensions: these act as a way of portraying an interrelation between actual entities which does not predicate some form of subtending subject. Instead the subject (superject) is constructed and constructs itself through the combining of specific, yet diverse, prehensions. 'There are an indefinite number of prehensions, overlapping, subdividing, and supplementary to each other' (PR, 235). For Whitehead, that which is prehended is not inert matter, instead, prehensions are the *feeling* of another entity. Again, Whitehead has chosen a surprising term to explain his conceptual construction. The term "feeling" would seem to invoke a whole host of humanly subjectivist notions; emotions, irrationality and so on. In one sense this is exactly what Whitehead is attempting to do. He is trying to shock us out of our scientist, materialist complacency by insisting on the quality of experience which inhabits all experiences. As he himself comments: 'It throws an interesting light on the belief in a well-understood technical phraseology reigning…that an accomplished philosopher censured in print, my use of the word Feeling as being in a sense never before employed in philosophy (AI, 297).

In Whitehead's framework, feelings, prehensions and experiences are certainly not limited to humans. A stone feels the warmth of the sun; a tree feels the strength of the wind. Feelings are not inert data, waiting "out there" to be felt. These feelings make up the concrescence of each entity, in its act of experience: 'Feelings are "vectors"; for they feel what is *there* and transform it into what is *here*' (PR, 87; emphasis in original). It is in this most literal sense that 'life is robbery' (PR, 105). So, Whitehead argues that 'there is a flow of feeling' (PR, 237). Prehensions are the basis for the interrelation of actual entities and can be thought of as constituting some kind of generalized perceptive interrelation (which is not predicated on human perception): 'a simple feeling is the most primitive type of an act of perception, devoid of consciousness' (PR, 236). This is one crucial step that Whitehead makes in attempting to construct a conceptual system which is not predicated on consciousness or humanity but which is able to explain and to incorporate consciousness. He does this, as will be seen in Chapter Three, through a radical reconception of the status of perception. However, it must be remembered that Whitehead's thoughts on such questions are, again, likely to differ greatly from those of other philosophers. Consequently, his notion of perception is not one which includes any notion of representation. For: '"representative perception" can never, within its own metaphysical doctrines, produce the title deeds to guarantee the validity of the representation of fact by idea' (PR, 54). This is because the very separation of that which is represented (the object) from that to which it is represented (the subject) will always rely on some form of materialism or idealism, or will invoke one of a range of trenchant philosophical dualisms. Such a separation is also another instance of the inconsistency dragged into modern thought by a tacit acceptance of the bifurcation of nature. With a nod ahead to one of the important aspects of poststructuralism, Whitehead is deeply suspicious of the concept of representation, for the very possibility of its operation presupposes, and relies upon, the distinction between the object of such representation and the subject to which or within which such representations occur. For Whitehead, subjects do not perceive objects. Rather, subjects (superjects) are formed through prehensions, or through "perceptions" which are really perceptive feelings.[4]

Power

Whitehead's analysis should not be construed as merely abstract metaphysical speculation. He is clear that the very constitution of subjectivity (and objectivity) is embroiled in power: 'the problem of perception and the problem of power are one and the same, at least so far as perception is reduced to mere prehension of actual entities' (PR, 58). For, although Whitehead does not develop a fully fledged theory of power, it is clear that the notion is integral to his understanding of the coming to be and endurance of all existence. Indeed, insofar as power is a necessary aspect of existence, so a proper understanding of the operations of power is necessary for any analysis of existence. Whitehead puts it thus: 'the notion of "power" is...the principle that the reasons for things are always to be found in the composite nature of definite actual entities' (PR, 19). So, the "correct" analysis of actual occasions into their component parts is not simply a deconstruction in the sense of a dissipation or an explaining away. Rather, it is a detailed account of both the conditions which prevail and the novelty that is entailed in any becoming. 'The philosophy of organism holds that, in order to understand "power", we must have a correct notion of how each individual actual entity contributes to the datum *from which* its successors arise and *to which* they must conform' (PR, 56).

One of the great strengths, therefore, of Whitehead's work, and one of the direct contributions it can make to social theory today, is to be found in a dual insistence. On the one hand, there is the need for a rigorous analysis of that which combines to instantiate enduring objects (or subjects) and the manner in which combinations appear, noting that such analysis will always lay bare the operations of power. Yet, at the same time, it should be remembered that such analysis is no mere counting of items but a description of the way, the manner, in which such combinations occur. An integral part of this will be a recognition of the role of novelty, or lack thereof. However, some care should be taken when addressing Whitehead's concept of power. There may be a temptation to read back into his work a straight-forward justification of more contemporary framings of power, such as that of Foucault. Whilst it is clearly possible to see certain similarities, it would be a mistake to simply transfer Whitehead's thoughts on power directly into the social realm. His understanding of power is inherently philosophical and cosmological. And, faithful to his general outlook, power must always be understood as relational. He cites Locke[5] to make his point: 'fire has a power to melt gold...and gold has a power to be melted... Power thus considered is twofold; viz. as able to make, or able to receive, any change... power includes in it some kind of relation' (PR, 57–8). Thus, for Whitehead, power is integral to the process of concrescence, to existence and to our analyses of the world, not as some kind of "add-on", human derivation or construction, but as an integral element of how things really are.

Relativity

Throughout his philosophy of organism, Whitehead seeks to balance the concreteness of actual entities with the dynamic, processual character of existence. As has been seen, one main way in which he accomplishes this is through his theory of prehensions. It is these which enable him to balance the vector character and the materiality of the process of existence. In order to strengthen and clarify this position, Whitehead turns to his notion of relativity which is a crucial and abiding element within his philosophy and which he describes as follows: 'it belongs to the nature of a "being" that it is a potential for every "becoming." This is the "principle of relativity"' (PR, 22). This reiterates the importance of prehensions as they are the mode through which the link between the actuality of one entity and that of another is made (and explained). This also raises the centrality of potentiality for all existence; the necessity of potentiality for the appearance of actuality. In this way, Whitehead challenges the notion of matter and nature as dislocated and dead, and thereby avoids "bifurcating nature".

Whitehead envisages his principle of relativity as an important philosophical contribution which not only accords with and extends elements of contemporary physics, but also challenges accepted doctrines of individualized existence.

> The principle of universal relativity directly traverses Aristotle's dictum, "A substance is not present in a subject." On the contrary, according to this principle an actual entity *is* present in other actual entities... The philosophy of organism is mainly devoted to the task of making clear the notion of "being present in another entity." (PR, 50. Emphasis in original.)

Hence Whitehead introduces the notion of heterogeneity into his philosophical scheme. This is because each item of existence, each superject is the combination of elements, of prehensions that were previously diverse, into a novel unity through the process of concrescence. Such heterogeneity is, once again, no mere metaphor or invocation of a social construction. The coming-to-be of all items of matter involves genuine construction. Nature is a construction. But this is not a simple explaining-away so beloved of some sociologists of science. 'Philosophy destroys its usefulness when it indulges in brilliant feats of explaining away' (PR, 17). This is a call to engage in a new form of investigation which recognizes the utterly constructed and interrelated aspects of all existence and the necessary embroiling of that which is commonly thought of as discrete, namely objects and subjects. But this heterogeneity is not limited to being *within* actual entities. Through the principle of relativity, Whitehead enables heterogeneity between actual entities. 'They differ among themselves' (PR, 18). And one way in which this occurs is through Whitehead's deployment of his principle of relativity with respect to time, space and duration.

The classical theory of time envisages a linear progression in which time proceeds uniformly. In such a conception two things are contemporary if they inhabit the same segment of time and space. Colloquially speaking and jumping to the "human" level, two students could be referred to as contemporaries if they attend the same university at the same "time". That is to say, they inhabited the same place in a mutually coextensive slab of temporality and this spatio-temporal locale was simply a segment of the larger spatio-temporal realm of the universe considered as that ultimate vessel which is occupied by all objects. On such accounts, time is the measure by which such objects are said to coexist, preexist or follow on from each other. Whitehead, in another example of his integration of certain findings of modern science to his argument, rejects this concept:

> Curiously enough, even at this early stage of metaphysical discussion, the influence of the "relativity theory" of modern physics is important. According to the classical "uniquely serial" view of time, two contemporary actual entities define the same actual world. According to the modern view no two actual entities define the same actual world. (PR, 65–6)

So, although the theory of relativity might only be observable in cases such as 'the perihelion of mercury, and the positions of the stars in the neighbourhood of the sun' (CN, 169), this does not mean that there is not a myriad of time-space systems which are normally ignored (in conscious human experience). This adoption of relativity is of vital importance as it allows for the concrete existence of actualities which do not rely on a common locus for their definition. That which links all entities is the manner in which they come to be, but this manner of coming-to-be is not itself a thing and does not comprise some enduring essence of an entity. Each entity is defined anew on each occasion. Heterogeneity is rife. Thus the two university contemporaries are not constantly "contemporary" on the relativistic account. Rather, at some times and points they are and at other times and points they are not. In this way, Whitehead's theory allows for the description of an entity as inhabiting differing spatial and temporal systems concurrently.

Creativity

Whitehead further explains the manner in which actual entities are interrelated, and the link between individuality, process and becoming through one of his most important terms, that of "creativity". Perhaps the most surprising element of Whitehead's deployment of the word "creativity" is that he coined this very term. This bears repeating. Prior to his use of "creativity" in *Religion in the Making* in 1926 (RM, 77) this word was not extant in the English language (see Meyer 2007 for a fuller bibliographical account). "Creativity" is a term of Whitehead's own devising. In 1925, in *Science and the Modern World* (SMW), and a year or so before his first use of "creativity", he instead used the word '*creativeness*' (SMW, 140; emphasis in original). But it is only really in *Process and Reality* (PR), in 1929, that he fully adopts the term "creativity" as best expressing the mode, character and ubiquity of the role of novelty within existence. The almost immediate uptake of this word and its overbearing demeanour in contemporary language and everyday life might mask both the "originality" of Whitehead's intention in coining this word and the specificity of his rendering of the concept. Just as C. S. Peirce invented the word "Pragmaticism" in order to distinguish it from the then current usage of "pragmatism" and referred to his own new term as 'ugly enough to be safe from kidnappers' (Peirce 1958, 186), it might be worth reconsidering the ugliness of the word "creativity". It is a noun developed by adding a rather clunky "ivity" to the stem of the verb "to create". It is akin, perhaps, to insisting nowadays on the need for the term "inventivity" to distinguish it from that of "inventiveness" in order to pinpoint a specific aspect of the inventive process which the latter term does not capture. So, once again, there is a need to pause and consider what Whitehead is asking of us when he proposes to make creativity fundamental to his scheme. Shaviro has emphasized this importance of this step when he states: 'These concepts (creativity, novelty, innovation) (or at least these words) are so familiar today – familiar, perhaps, to the point of nausea – that it is difficult to grasp how radical a rupture they mark in the history of Western thought' (Shaviro 2009, 71). They have become part of our culture of thought and sit unquestioned as background affective elements which inform and limit our actions and ideas, especially as long as their status remains uninterrogated. In assessments of applications for research funding, television talent shows, career development plans, provision of local government services, sexual activity, and so on and so on, it is often assumed, by definition, that creativity is a "good" thing, which always produces benefits; that creation is inherently and unquestionably something to be celebrated. Whilst Whitehead's texts do contain a certain degree of affirmation of creativity, this does not entail a conceptual benediction of all that is created.

> A new actuality may appear in the wrong society, amid which its claims to efficacy act mainly as inhibitions. Then a weary task is set for the creative function, by an epoch of new creations to remove the inhibition. Insistence on birth at the wrong season is the trick of evil. In other words, the novel fact may throw back, inhibit, delay. (PR, 223)

So, it should be noted that whilst Whitehead's concept of creativity is a crucial one for this philosophy, its main role is to develop an account of the process and potentiality of the world which avoids resorting to fixed conceptions of subjects and objects. As such, it might enable methodologies to be developed which recognize heterogeneity, relativity, concreteness, process, becoming *and* mundanity. For, as Whitehead makes clear, such terms imply each other and cannot be taken in isolation:

> To arrive at the philosophic generalization…an apparent redundancy of terms is required. The words correct each other. We require "together", "creativity", "concrescence", "prehension", "feeling", "subjective form", "data", "actuality", "becoming", "process". (AI, 304)

There is, therefore, a need for a lack of quiescence when faced with the concepts of novelty and creativity and a requirement to establish their parameters. This is exactly what Whitehead offers.

"'Creativity" is the universal of universals characterizing ultimate matter of fact' (PR, 21). 'For the fundamental inescapable fact is the creativity in virtue of which there can be no "many things" which are not subordinated in a concrete unity' (PR, 211). Creativity operates as that which explains the process through which diverse prehensions become one thing. It also indicates Whitehead's insistence that such a process is not only accomplished by humans but is an integral aspect of the becoming of all moments of existence. It is in this sense that Whitehead uses the term creativity to describe the activity which characterizes the coming-to-be of any thing which exists. Creativity is an important strand of Whitehead's attempt to describe a universe in process; it operates as the link between the completed actual entities which act as data and the ongoing experiences which constitute novel subjects.

And, as has been seen, this involves some notion of relativity. Creativity helps explains the process, the movement, from the potentiality provided by completed actual entities (which have "finished" their becoming) to the arising of new superjects. Thus, '"the actual world" is always a relative term, and refers to that basis of presupposed actual occasions which is a datum for the novel concrescence' (PR, 211). Or: 'viewed in abstraction objects are passive, but viewed in conjunction they carry the creativity which drives the world' (AI, 230–1).

This might give the impression that creativity occupies the role of a supplementary category which either subtends or rises above actual instances of existence. However, Whitehead avoids this reading by making a distinction between absolute and real potentiality:

> Thus we have always to consider two meanings of potentiality: (a) the "general" potentiality, which is the bundle of possibilities, mutually consistent or alternative…and (b) the "real" potentiality, which is conditioned by the data provided by the actual world. (PR, 65)

"General" potentiality functions as an abstract condition which provides a metaphysical positioning and consistency to Whitehead's argument. "Real" potentiality refers to Whitehead's insistence that creativity is only to be found through and in those occasions of becoming which populate the world. This distinction between "general" and "real" potentiality is an incisive one which has important consequences for the relevance of Whitehead to social theory. If his thought were a mere celebration of the abstract notion of general potentiality as indicative of a universe comprised of infinite becomings, thereby suggesting that only the flux and flow of existence comprise the reality of existence, then his work might offer no more than another rendition of the worst excesses of postmodernist theory. The insistence on the importance of "real" potentiality helps Whitehead to escape such a charge. Real potentiality describes the limited expressions of potentiality which inhere in the world at a given time. As Marx puts it, 'Men [sic] make their own history, but they do not make it just as they please; they do not make it under circumstances chosen by themselves, but under circumstances directly encountered, given and transmitted from the past' (Marx 1977, 300). Real potentiality accounts for both the facticity of the historical and, hence, the contemporary world, but it gives no extra-mural or covering explanation as to why this world rather than another has arisen. Moreover, real potentiality indicates that such a world, and the people within it, is not, and are not, inert or passive objects. But creativity is not, for Whitehead, some kind of free-floating spirit or energy to be tapped into by blessed or gifted individuals. Whitehead insists that creativity is in no way to be limited to human activity or consciousness and that a wider understanding of creativity, based on the relativity of the potential and the actual, must be recognized. 'How the past perishes is how the future becomes' (AI, 305). Again, this points to the importance of the manner of existence as opposed to the mere facticity of existence. There is an utter embroiling of potentiality and facticity as will be discussed in more detail throughout this book.

The current chapter has attempted to outline the most provocative and the most productive aspects of Whitehead's thought. It has striven to indicate the tone of Whitehead's concepts and how they might lure novel responses to specific problems within social theory. It is not envisaged that this discussion will have "proved" Whitehead's philosophy or that the reader will have fully accepted his challenging philosophical position. However, it is hoped that as the chapters proceed, and the analyses become more and more directly related to contemporary questions within social theory, then the efficacy of Whitehead's work and ideas for our culture of thought will become more evident and substantive.

Chapter Three

'A THOROUGH-GOING REALISM' – WHITEHEAD ON CAUSE AND CONFORMATION

The problem of the concept and existence of cause is one which haunts natural science and social science; the productive and destructive elements of this notion are an abiding element of our culture of thought. If nature is truly made up of causes and necessities which supervene our control, desires or intentions then, all too soon, the natural world becomes a clockwork, deterministic realm where the operations and machinations of the laws of nature, of genes, of physical forces, have a logical and existential priority which entails that human action and purpose is reduced to an ineffective, superficial consequence of deeper and darker reasons. One response to the seeming implacable law-ruled reality which such a neutral, natural, causal desert portrays has been developed by those elements of social theory and the humanities which posit an entirely distinct realm of human society, culture and action with its own rules, reasons and causes. The description and delimitation of a distinct realm of human purpose and history was envisaged as removing the problem of positing human action simply as an epiphenomenal outcome of the natural world. But it did not remove the problem of the rigidity of the concept of cause and its operation within this supposedly distinct social realm. That is to say, the very character of the initial philosophical demarcation of cause as that which has necessary consequences retained its metaphysical grip as did the corollary of this position, namely that each cause must always produce its relevant effect or that each event or phenomenon must be traceable to its cause: social class determines educational achievement, for example.

Of course, science and social theory have not been blind to such problematics and much effort and writing has gone into insisting upon the complexity and multifaceted, nonlinear, probabilistic character of correlation (as opposed to strict causation). However, Whitehead would argue that such accounts have not solved the problem of cause, they have merely replaced it. The influence of the initial concept of cause as developed within science and philosophy still lurks in present debates: 'the two attitudes involved are inconsistent. A scientific realism, based on mechanism, is conjoined with an unwavering belief in the world of men [sic] and of the higher animals as being composed of self-determining organisms' (SMW, 94). Hence, those who aim to avoid the deterministic vision of a causal, external nature by constructing the concept of a discrete social or cultural realm which is occupied by specific human actions, reasons, causes and effects have simply split existence into two realms in an unwarranted fashion. This witnesses another version of the bifurcation of nature and serves not to solve the problem of cause but merely to compound it, as it shifts the question to another realm; that of the humanly social. Again, this may be to overstate the case and this chapter will have to do more work to substantiate this critique. The aim here is, therefore, to highlight the importance of the notion of cause for the conceptual remodelling of social theory that Whitehead demands.

To achieve this, the chapter will give a brief review of the philosophical problematic of cause as propounded by Hume. This will include an outline of three main elements: an account of that which Hume was arguing against; the strange status of cause in modern science; a discussion of attempts to reconcile or avoid the problems of positivism and empiricism within contemporary social theory, as expressed through Critical Realism. This will be followed by an account of Whitehead's argument that cause *is* a genuine element of reality but that it has been misrecognized by science, philosophy and social theory alike. This misrecognition has two main aspects: the exclusion of the body from epistemological and empirical accounts of reality and our knowledge thereof; a denial of the importance of "conformation" as a genuine element of existence. The role of value as implicit within such existence, as an element of all phenomena, be they natural, social, psychological or biological, is an integral part of Whitehead's argument, but a full discussion of this will have to be put off until the next chapter.

The Problem of Cause

Most students of social science, sociology and social theory will, at some point in their career, have a lecture which outlines how David Hume (1711–76) established both the importance of empiricism and the problem of causation. Often, this latter problem is then subsumed into the problem of the empirical and scientific status of sociology, or otherwise. For Whitehead, such a conflation, as opposed to an interrogation of the premises and locale of the tenets of empiricism and causation within the wider conceptual framework of modernity, only serves to enable causation's most insidious elements to dwell amongst us and our thoughts, even if we appear to reject them. In order to fully appreciate the direction and force of Hume's argument, it is required to establish exactly what he was arguing against, and why.

When Hume challenged the prevailing philosophical notion of cause, his aim was not simply to assert the primacy of empiricism and thereby set the scientific, experimental paradigm on its merry way. Hume was pointing to the difficulties inherent in the rationalist conception of cause, its emphasis on logical and metaphysical necessity, and the hold that it had over the culture of thought of the time. Strict rationalism had insisted that it was possible to derive *necessary* elements which explained both the character of rationality and the character of existence. The claim was that it was possible to produce logical formulae, such as the principle of noncontradiction (if something is one thing then it is not another, different thing), or metaphysical principles, such as that of cause and effect (any cause must have an effect, every effect must have a cause), which not only held as prime characteristics of thinking and rationality but were the basis of the very nature of reality and of the possibility of knowledge thereof. Such a version of rationalism posits a world constituted of ultimate and necessary principles from which other statements about the world can be derived. Its main thrust is that the world is logically or metaphysically self-explanatory in a manner to which the rational mind has a privileged access.[1]

For Hume, such an approach is unjustified as, he argues, an interrogation of the mind and the experiences of the mind does not reveal such ultimate principles but rather a complex concatenation of impressions and sensations. With regard to the notion of cause and effect, this has specific consequences; the complex world of experience does not, of itself, demonstrate the operation of cause *in* the world (as rationalists maintain):

> Our *memory* presents us only with a *multitude* of instances wherein we always find like bodies, motions, or qualities, in like relations. From the mere *repetition* of any past impression, even to infinity, there will never arise any *new original idea*, such as that of *necessary connection*. (Hume cited in PR, 133–4. Emphasis in original.)

For Hume, cause, which he here terms "necessary connection", is not of the world; it cannot be assumed to be of the world as it can never been "seen" in the world. If we watch a car hit a lamppost we tend to describe the event as one in which we see the car cause the lamppost to bend. But, all our perception really offers us is an impression of the movement of a car followed by the movement of the lamppost. The notion of cause (necessary connection) is not present therein. Cause is not of the world. Furthermore, it is not possible to identify any one event which actually or logically always follows from another event. There is no unique, constant, inevitable flow from any given cause to any given event. The sun will not rise forever (it will burn itself out and implode, eventually); stones do not fall when dropped if the gravitational field is too weak, etc.

> In a word, then, every effect is distinct from its cause. It could not, therefore, be discovered in the cause; and the first invention or conception of it, *à priori* [sic], must be entirely arbitrary. (Hume cited in SMW, 5. Emphasis in original.)

This "arbitrary" factor is supplied by the mind which, through habit, conjoins similar events and assigns the notion of cause to them. But such a conjunction is a result of the operations of the human mind not of the world itself which, Hume argues, is not causal, in the rationalist sense of the term. It has already been seen that Whitehead views Hume's slipping in of the concept of habit as unjustified (see Chapter One). But this is not the important point here. What is of interest, rather, is the insistence that empiricism, and consequently any scientific mode of thought which is premised upon empiricism, cannot subscribe to the rationalist notion of cause as inherent in the world.

However, modern science, especially in its positivist mood, has not always heeded the warnings of Hume and has retained elements of the rationalist concept of cause in its description of the laws of nature (which cannot be broken), for example, in the notion that genes somehow "cause" organisms to act or behave in specific ways.

> For example, when geneticists conceive genes as the determinants of heredity. The analogy of the old concept of matter sometimes leads them to ignore the influence of the particular animal body in which they are functioning. They presuppose that a pellet of matter remains in all respects self-identical whatever be its changes of environment. (MT, 189)

Again, this is not the place to fully investigate such matters.[2] The point here is simply to point up the inconsistency with regard to the concept of cause which sometimes lurks within modern science, or public understandings thereof.

Many contemporary scientists and social scientists would insist that they too reject the rationalist notion of cause and have developed probabilistic accounts which simply identify patterns of interrelation between specific events or phenomena. In doing so, they claim to bring to light the likelihood of one event following another (the rise of statistics) rather than asserting any metaphysical principle as to the existence of cause in nature, society or the mind. Rather than decry or accuse such scientific approaches, the important point to note is that there is a tension inherent in contemporary understandings of the scientific method with regard to the role and status of cause which reflects the retention of outdated philosophical positions with regard to this difficult concept. For example, within social theory, Critical Realism has attempted to develop more sophisticated accounts both of the ontological status of that which is addressed by natural and social science and the complex operation of cause in both the natural and social world. The following brief outline of Critical Realism is not intended as a full account of the varied, nuanced, positions which have been developed by its supporters over recent years,[3] instead it is intended as an outline of some of the basic positions and assumptions of Critical Realism and as an indication of the extent to which these inhabit or replicate positions which are in need of reorientation, given the subsequent analysis of Whitehead on cause and conformation. As such, the twin notions of reality as stratified and the assumption of an irreducible distinction between the natural and social realm will be addressed, especially with regard to the concept of causation. Whitehead's work confronts some of the most cherished assumptions and presumptions of social theory with regard to its subject matters and procedures. But, as will be seen, this is not to explain away reality. It is to suggest that novel modes of thought are required which will move beyond minute discussions of the specific status of natural science, and the interrelation of structure and agency, in order to develop new approaches to analyses of the world, and to provide conceptual tools which can explain more of reality.

The development of Critical Realism from the 1970s onwards has sought to avoid the polarity which social theory had arguably fallen into by envisaging positivism and interpretivism as the only alternatives for the theoretical models of social theory. Of course, this polarity has since also been challenged by feminism, queer theory, poststructuralism and Science and Technology Studies, amongst others. Bhaskar's (1978) initial intervention in this field was concerned with establishing a realist account of science. One of the major premises of his approach is that recent thought has overemphasized the epistemological; indeed it has reduced all questions about the status of existence to ones about the status of our knowledge of such existence. This he terms the 'epistemic fallacy' (Bhaskar 1978, 36) which he defines as the mistaken belief that: 'statements about being can be reduced to or analysed in terms of statements about knowledge' (Bhaskar 1978, 36). Whitehead would concur: 'all difficulties as to first principles are only camouflaged metaphysical difficulties. Thus also the epistemological difficulty is only solvable by an appeal to ontology' (PR, 189). Thus, the attention which Critical Realism pays to ontology, to the notion of a reality which is not simply produced by or reflected in human knowledge, or lack of knowledge, is to be welcomed. The investigation of the character of such a reality is, for Bhaskar, to be developed through "transcendental arguments" which demonstrate how a 'philosophical ontology is developed by reflection upon what must be the case for science to be possible' (Bhaskar 1978, 39). Again, there is a resemblance to the procedure that Whitehead develops in *Concept of Nature* (CN. See Chapter One for a fuller discussion of this) although he does not use the term "transcendental". For Bhaskar, the transcendental element refers to the framing of questions in the following terms 'what must be the case for "x" to be possible?' (Bhaskar 1979, 10). Within a theory of science, this entails the positing of an independent reality (or the conditions of possibility of such a reality) which must exist in order for scientific activity to occur (as it plainly does): 'given that science does occur or could occur, the world *must* be a certain way' (Bhaskar 1978, 29; emphasis in original). Rather than taking the simple empiricist line that all that is presented to sense-perception is all that there is, the transcendental element of Critical Realism insists that that which is presented presupposes and partially discloses that which enables such presentations. For example, the change in density which comes from the placing of salt in water is only possible on the condition that molecules can change their structure in different environments and that the relative density of liquids is variable, and so on. Or, someone reading a newspaper looking at job adverts bears witness to a more fundamental set of conditions which are situated in the wider conditions of a world where, mostly, newspapers are not fiction and contracted employment is a real fact of contemporary existence. Or, a dog awaiting its owner by the door which starts to bark excitedly on hearing familiar footsteps presupposes the conditions of pet-ownership and dog-exercising as enjoyable for canines. Such superficially banal statements are actually first indications of an important step that Critical Realism makes in moving beyond mere facticity toward the processes and potentiality inherent within all existence; a move which Whitehead himself wishes to make. The difference between the two approaches is, briefly, that Critical Realism attempts to explain the relation between such process and potentiality and its empirical, everyday manifestations, by dividing reality up into layers.[4] Furthermore, it tends to take the post-Kantian line of limiting the operation of the transcendental to human thought, rather than enabling the world to transcend itself. This has the further consequence of reinforcing the distinction between the natural world of real existence, which science studies, and the social world of human existence within which such scientific investigations take place. In this respect, Critical Realism reiterates the bifurcation of nature.

For Bhaskar, and Critical Realists more generally, one major strength of their position is that it supplies what they term a "depth realism", that is to say, it is not reducible to immediate experiences of the world but is able to discover the deeper, generative mechanisms which enable such a world to arise. Reality-as-it-appears is not reality-as-it-*is*, but this is not a cause for despair because reality-as-it-appears gives clues which, if interpreted correctly, can uncover reality-as-it-*really-is*. As such, Bhaskar claims that reality can be divided into the "real", the "actual" and the "empirical" (Bhaskar 1978, 12–17). The "real" comprises the realm of generative mechanisms which suffuse the natural world and which is the "object" of scientific analysis; the "actual" comprises those events as they manifest themselves as the world unfolds; the "empirical" comprises the observations made by humans of the actual through which the operations of the real can be discerned. Mistakes, in the form of human error, can, of course, enter at this empirical level – as can other "social factors" (such as the need for research funding). These levels imply a hierarchy to reality, for it is a tenet of Critical Realism that whilst these levels of reality have their own degree of self-sufficiency their interrelation is best explained in terms of the actual emerging out of the real, and the empirical out of the actual; for it is such emergence of one realm out of another which ultimately characterizes the structure of reality.

Once such emergence has occurred, we are dealing with new forms of self-contained, effective reality which exhibit their own causal mechanisms. In this respect Critical Realism attempts to deflect some of the problems of linear accounts of causation by asserting that whilst there are causes in nature, these causes are not of a uniform, unidirectional character. They have to be understood in terms of generative, nondeterministic properties which can be isolated within closed, experimental situations (in a laboratory, for instance), in order to establish their operation. But such isolations are an abstraction from the more complex and interdependent character of the full reality which is comprised by the autonomous "real". Furthermore, Critical Realism claims that each level of reality can retroactively effect downwards or backwards onto a previous level, once elements or objects have emerged into efficacy. For example, the panic instantiated in a human or a rabbit by the sight of a car approaching toward them can cause the production of hormones which affect the composition of the biological body and enable the human or rabbit to flee or cause them to freeze in the middle of the road. Critical Realism thereby attempts to develop a multiform account of reality and causality which avoids some of the problems inherent in naïve post-Humean or positivist accounts of cause and causation.

The above analysis does not claim to offer a full account of all the subtleties of the positions which have been developed by Bhaskar or by subsequent writers working in this field. Instead, it is offered as an overview of some of the overarching conceptual premises which inform Critical Realism. Accordingly, the following analysis and critique is not intended as a wholesale assault on the detailed arguments of Critical Realism. Instead it is offered as an indication of the limitations and presumptions which this approach both inhabits and prolongs. To stay *within* this mode of argumentation would run the risk of accepting some of the basic positions of that argument. The relevance of the work of Whitehead for both Critical Realism and social theory more generally lies in his suggestion that we reapproach such questions from a different angle. This change of position will involve a questioning both of the status of the human and the transcendental within Critical Realism, and of its resolute retention of a necessary distinction between the natural world and the social realm. Insofar as Critical Realism emphasizes the importance of recognizing that science is a process of abstracting and abstraction, Whitehead would agree. The problem arises when such abstraction and its relation to transcendence is regarded as implicitly a production of the human enquirer, be they a scientist, philosopher or social theorist.

Realism and Transcendence

This question of transcendence is one which has occupied thought since Kant established it as tool of objective critical thought in the late eighteenth century. Quentin Meillassoux (2008) and others in the loosely-titled school of "Speculative Realists" have returned, as have Critical Realists, though in a different manner, to the problem of accounting for a real which is independent from human cognition, language and thought. For Meillassoux, the modern culture of thought (although he does not use this term) is infected by what he calls "correlationism" and which he defines as 'the idea according to which we only ever have access to the correlation between thinking and being, and never to either term considered apart from the other' (Meillassoux 2008, 5). That is to say, through a critique not entirely different from Bhaskar's notion of the "epistemic fallacy", Meillassoux outlines the modern, post-Kantian difficulty of designating a reality which is independent from humans, as such a realm of being is ultimately only conceivable in terms of human cognition, language, statements or thoughts about such a realm. To simply state that there is a reality which is independent of humanity would be to resort to a stringent and unacceptable dogmatism which misunderstands or forgets that all statements about reality or all thoughts about reality are mediated in, through and by human language or cognition. The insidious character of "correlationism" is that it would seem to make it impossible ever to make a statement about, or even think about, an independent reality without acknowledging that such statements and thoughts are, eventually, reducible or referable to human thoughts or words about reality rather than somehow immediately accessing that reality independently of such words or thoughts. In this way, Meillassoux outlines contemporary theory's important task of developing approaches to reality which evade this pervasive but pernicious reduction of reality to an aspect of human cognition. The call is to establish a strong concept of an independent reality consonant with the claims, practices and findings of science but not reducible to its concepts or presuppositions. In this respect, Speculative Realism is sympathetic to the aims of Critical Realism. It differs from the latter, however, insofar as it would suggest that Critical Realists do not take the problem that the concept of an independent reality offers natural science and social theory *seriously enough*. Whilst the arguments that Meillassoux makes to escape the "correlationist circle" of thought and being is not one that will be taken up here, the level of the challenge to contemporary thought will be. Perhaps surprisingly, it is the question of transcendence and its supposed relation to human thought which is the key.

It has been seen how Critical Realism identifies the transcendental with a mode of argument which can enable the discovery of deeper realms of reality. The implication of such arguments is that the transcendental refers to a mode of thinking rather than a mode of being; in this sense Meillassoux would suggest that they remain with the correlationist circle. Whitehead does not want to impose this limitation on his philosophy. For him, the great discovery of Kant, in his transcendental method, is that of the process of construction. 'Kant, and the philosophy of organism agree that the task of the critical reason is the analysis of constructs; and "construction" is "process"' (PR, 151). However, instead of seeing the genuine process of construction as the manner in which the world transcends itself, irrespective of human involvement or thought about such process, construction and transcendence, Kant reduces the operation of process, construction and transcendence to elements of human thought. Kant asserts that construction is limited to human thought about the world. Whitehead views this move as both arbitrary and unwarranted and as limiting the scope of Kant's "discovery" and analysis. On Whitehead's reading, within Kant's philosophy, "process" is mainly a process of thought...and [he] turns the "apparent" objective content into the end of the construct' (PR, 152). As has been seen, Whitehead does not view the thinking subject as the centre of reality or of humanity. The thinking subject is an occasional occurrence within reality. Hence, Whitehead views his approach as one which reorients that of Kant.

> Thus for Kant the process whereby there is experience is a process from subjectivity to apparent objectivity. The philosophy of organism inverts this analysis, and explains the process as proceeding from objectivity to subjectivity namely, from the objectivity, whereby the external world is a datum, to the subjectivity, whereby there is one individual experience. (PR, 156)

Whitehead does not disallow or disavow the notion of the transcendental as a process of thought; hence Bhaskar's notion of a transcendental procedure is not unwarranted as such. What is unwarranted, however, is the presumption that such transcendence is witness only to the operations of human thought as opposed to being an example of the wider, ongoing processes which inhabit and constitute the process of all existence. Kant's limitation of the process of transcendence (and Whitehead's redrawing of its boundaries) is extensively analysed by Shaviro in his recent, important work:[5]

> Kant risks limiting the scope of his own discovery of constructivism. "Experience as a constructive functioning" is reserved for rational beings alone. At the same time, those being are not themselves vulnerable to the vagaries of such experience. Kant's subject both monopolizes experience, and exempts itself from immersion in that experience. (Shaviro 2009, 50)

Thus one ongoing and limiting aspect of the legacy of Kant's philosophy for our modern culture of thought is its prioritization of human experience as the apotheosis of the experience of the constructive functioning which is emblematic of rational thought and, at the same time, is divorced from any other form of experience which might taint such thought. Whitehead's philosophical approach is less dogmatic and more democratic in that it does not prejudge the evidence and does not assume that human experience and human thought are primary. Transcendence is not simply a product of the human mind (though the human mind can be involved in transcendence). Objects can transcend themselves: 'An "object" is a transcendent element characterizing that definiteness to which our "experience" has to conform' (PR, 215). Whitehead assigns experience, in general, as the best mode of description of the constructive process of existence, no matter how surprising a claim this may be at first sight.

Such a philosophical manoeuvre might appear to have little relevance to social theory. However, Whitehead's account of the arbitrary limits that Kant places on his philosophy points to the severe consequences that these limits have had on contemporary thought. Not least, and as will be seen in the following chapter, it has made the question of the status of values and the value of the world solely dependent on the operation of the human mind and has made any description of the world as valuable in itself (as in some ecological visions) intensely problematic. For the moment, and in relation to the previous analysis of Critical Realism, the arbitrary limits which Kant places on his transcendental are replicated in the distinction that Bhaskar and Critical Realism draw between the natural and the social realm. The former is the province of science and scientific activity. Such activity is a human activity, and human beings alone are able and entitled to deploy the transcendental method, to uncover the real reality out of which, upon which, or within which, the later, emergent, quasi-efficacious social realm arises and operates. Cats can't do science. In Bhaskar's account '*realism…*regards the objects of knowledge as the structures and mechanisms that generate phenomena; and the knowledge as produced in the social activity of science' (Bhaskar 1978, 25; emphasis in original). Bhaskar assigns, *a priori*, a different mode of ontological existence to the natural world and to society, for example when he states that 'We can be sure that society exists and confident that it has certain general features… Its existence…is a necessary condition for any knowledge, including knowledge in the natural sciences of everyday life' (Bhaskar 1978, 186). The immediate question might be, how can we be so sure? – especially as Bhaskar seems to vitiate this surety by placing knowledge as inherently social ('reflection on natural science…is a social activity, prosecuted by people' (Bhaskar 1979, 18); 'the nature of scientific activity as *work*' (Bhaskar 1979, 20; emphasis in original). On this view, science and knowledge production in general are inherently human affairs concerned with developing accounts of both a natural and a social realm which are nevertheless resolutely different in kind. But what is it in the natural and social worlds that enables such a distinction to arise (both ontologically and epistemologically)? Given the premises of his transcendental account, what is it that produces the unmistakeable conditions of possibility of a distinction between the natural and the social? The simple point to be made here is that Bhaskar and Critical Realism attract more problems than they might by assuming such an irreducible distinction between the natural and the social. The former becomes truly real and the latter is beset with vagaries which theory then tries to overcome in ever more tortuous ways. As such, it may turn out that Critical Realism offers more as a philosophy of science than it does as a philosophy of social science and that it has overextended the range of its abstractions by attempting to deploy the former in the supposedly distinct realm of the latter.

A related outcome of this melding is the difficulty raised by the ontological status of structure and agency, and their causal interrelation. This becomes clear when, for example, Bhaskar defines society as a 'structure…irreducible to but present in the intentional activity of men [sic]' (Bhaskar 1978, 248). Subsequently, Critical Realism has engaged with renewed vigour in one of the oldest and thorniest of social-theoretical problems with some (Elder-Vass 2010) leaning toward the notion of structure whilst others (Archer 2003) emphasize the role of agency. Whitehead would not respond, in a deconstructive way, that the structure-agency question was simply an outcome of an acceptance of the bifurcation of nature and hence irrelevant or irrational. Yet, he would require that the very stanchions of the argument and the conceptual divisions be changed so that it is no longer a matter of accounting for which aspect of the structure-agency divide has primacy but, instead, of insisting that the mode of conceptual construction which produces this divide be interrogated and reoriented.

As such, Whitehead might argue that structure and agency are themselves abstractions which could have their place and point in certain analyses, but social theory has tended to give them an unwarranted authority and assumed that they are relevant to all "social" occasions and descriptions thereof. Structure and agency have been lifted from their specific operations and occurrences and granted a reality outside of these specific moments and analyses. Their status has been misrecognized through the assumption that they accurately reflect an ontological manifestation of all (social) reality and can and must be deployed as explanatory of all manifestations of (social) phenomena. That is to say, structure and agency may, on occasions, help describe the interrelation of moments of existence but they cannot and must not be seen as universally applicable, nor as a starting point for social theoretical reflection or empirical analysis. More real and practical work must be done to establish when and where such abstractions are effective rather than insisting that they correctly describe the manner of all (social) existence. Such insistence merely replicates the worst excesses of science when it insists that the sunrise is only explicable in terms of the operations of molecules.

The problematic status of structure and agency will be returned to in Chapter Five and it may seem that the present discussion is a long way from the stated aim of this chapter, namely to provide a discussion of Whitehead's notion of a 'thorough-going realism' (SYM, 10) through his specific elaboration of the twin notions of causation and conformation. The point of the previous discussion has not been to rehash or to overly criticize Critical Realism but to situate its concerns and problematics within a wider conceptual field, and to point out the moments of its assumptions and the limitations that these impose on its inquiries. The purpose of this has been to establish the parameters within which Whitehead's own philosophical constructions might appear the most effective and beneficial for social theory.

Cause and Conformation in Whitehead

Whitehead's insistence that apart from the experiences of such subjects there is "nothing, nothing, nothing, bare nothingness" entails that there are no objects in the world which are not, themselves, experiencing subjects. Existence is not made up of objects, or of objects and subjects, but is constituted by the experiences of subjects. And, contrary to the initial impression that such an emphasis on "subjective experience" might lead to some form of idealism, Whitehead is clear that the materialized location of all bodies is key to the having of an experience. In doing so he directly challenges the usual empiricist equating of experience with sense-data and the subject with a mind which collates such data. This is where Whitehead's difference from empiricist, positivist and Critical Realist accounts of causation lies.

Whitehead maintains that one major element of the problematic status of cause in contemporary theory comes from the mistaken belief that our senses alone provide us with data about the world. Such a belief applies not only to simple empiricism but to the operations of science as a practical activity involving technology, instruments and experiments, and to modern philosophy more generally, in so far as it emphasizes sense-perception as the royal road to contact with the world. 'My quarrel with modern Epistemology concerns its exclusive stress upon sense-perception for the provision of data respecting Nature' (MT, 182). Philosophy's overemphasis on sense-perception and especially visual perception has, Whitehead argues, been disastrous as it ignores the multifarious ways in which we gather information about the world. It is not that Whitehead rejects or denies the role of sense-perception. His point is that such approaches are not wide enough; they do recognize other important sources of data about the world. And it is here that the body becomes central to Whitehead's thought. The experiences which constitute subjects and bodies should not be envisaged as simply "perceptual", in the usual sense of the term. The experiences of the world which make up Whitehead's subjects are broad and varied and they include much which goes beyond everyday philosophical conceptions of information about the world. The manner in which information about the world is produced through the locale of the body also points to Whitehead's resituating of the concept of cause. There are two elements to his challenge to the limitations of theoretical approaches which overemphasize sense-perception at the expense of the link between the body, causation and conformity. These will be discussed in the following sections, "Presentational Immediacy" and "Causal Efficacy".

Presentational Immediacy

"Presentational immediacy" is the term that Whitehead uses to refer to that which has been taken by many theorists to be the sole mode of access to the world or to information about the world. It is 'the experience of the immediate world around us, a world decorated by sense-data dependent on the immediate states of relevant parts of our own bodies' (SYM, 14). Whitehead does not deny the part that such sense-data plays, it furnishes experience with its sense of immediacy, with its images, colours, sounds, smells and textures. It is that facet of experience which provides its vivid aspect. But it is important to note that, even at this stage, Whitehead links this to body. Such experiences are not created by a subject or mind but are reliant upon the operations of the body. Whitehead uses the phrase (which he appropriates from Hume) "the withness of the body" to explain how all perception must be understood not as a magical projection of some outer world onto some inner screen but as a process whereby the body, the eye, the ear, the skin, the palate, the nose, all partake in rendering elements of the world as bright, loud, near, bitter, or obnoxious. Hence: 'we see the contemporary chair, but we see it *with* our eyes; and we touch the contemporary chair, but we touch it *with* our hands' (PR, 62; emphasis in original).[6] The importance of the body as the vehicle of the data of presentational immediacy indicates a second crucial aspect of Whitehead's argument which has already been hinted at, namely the rejection of the usual notion of perception in terms of projection. 'There are no bare sensations which are first experienced and then "projected" into our feet as their feelings, or onto the opposite wall as its colour. The projection is an integral part of the situation, quite as original as the sense-data' (SYM, 14). Whitehead criticizes those philosophies which envisage data about the world as a projection by the mind back on to the world of that which it thinks to be "out-there" as a result of the reception of passive and inert data which has been received and interpreted by the mind or its concepts. This is how he avoids the Kantian position as well as the positing of grids of intelligibility. It is also how he moves away from the initial problem of empiricism and its associated inability to locate causation in the world, as he is clear that the data which empiricists (and much modern science) take as the sole mode of production of information about the world is only one element of this production. The world does not placidly manifest itself in a way which causes the perceptions of human subjects. The experiences of all subjects are the experiences of the world as a process, not as a set of objects. This is not to deny any role to causation but it is to re-place, to relocate it.

For Whitehead, the data that is originally directed toward the subject provides, in and of itself, information about its location, its nearness, thickness and spatial orientation. That the world is "out-there" is an integral element of a subject's acquaintance with it for 'presentational immediacy is that peculiar way in which contemporary things are "objectively" in our experience' (SYM, 25). The world and our experience of it are not two separate things or moments, the one is in the other in experience. 'We are in the world and the world is in us' (MT, 227). Presentational immediacy is that element of experience which provides the lively, changing aspect of such experience, the passing shapes, colours and clouds which punctuate our engagement with the world. There is no strict separation between our perceptions of the world and the world itself. Nature is not bifurcated. Nature does not have primary qualities which constitute how it really is, separate from the secondary qualities through which the perceiving subject renders and comprehends the world. Sense-perceptions are one of the ways in which we feel the world and in which the world actually is in us. This follows from Whitehead's view on actual entities as processes of feelings and his own notion of relativity (see Chapter Two).

For Whitehead, presentational immediacy is a mode of perception which only occurs in what he terms 'high-grade organisms' (see, for example, PR, 172) and it does not explain the manner in which information is generally distributed in existence. That is to say, presentational immediacy may be an important element of human perception but this does not make it the model by which perception, more generally, occurs. It needs to be recognized as a rarity, although one which accounts for numerous occasions of perception that populate existence, such as when a stone perceives (prehends) or encounters the cold sea which laps over it and the warm sun which dries it. He accuses philosophers, such as Hume and Kant, not only of taking the human level of sense-perception as founding or originary, thereby making them unable to account for the interrelation of nonhuman objects via perception, but worse, of ignoring those elements of human acquaintance with the world which precede that of presentational immediacy and which are integral to the subject and the body's experience and location, and upon which presentational immediacy depends. Whitehead insists that the mistake that philosophy has made is in seeing presentational immediacy as primary when it is actually a specific and derivative stage of our perception and acquaintance with the world. Such a mistaken view is not limited to accounts of sense-perception but also infects other philosophical concepts such as that of causation.

> One reason for the philosophical difficulties over causation is that Hume, and subsequently Kant, conceived the causal nexus as, in its primary character, derived from the presupposed sequence of immediate presentations. But if we interrogate experience, the exact converse is the case; the perceptive mode of immediate presentation affords information about the percepta in the more aboriginal mode of causal efficacy. (PR, 178)

In opposition to such a rendition of causation, Whitehead proffers the crucial concept of "Causal Efficacy".

Causal Efficacy

'A traveller, who has lost his [sic] way, should not ask, Where am I? What he really wants to know is, Where are the other places? He has got his own body, but he has lost them' (PR, 170). Despite the heavily gendered pronouns, these sentences again exemplify the centrality of some notion of bodilyness to Whitehead's philosophy. Crucially, the link is made between identity, the materiality of the body and other things and other places. To understand what one is, is also to understand where one is, and to be able to understand this requires taking into account one's relation to that which surrounds one but also, notably, to the past. It is the notion of causal efficacy which is the primary and novel way in which Whitehead weaves and develops a reconceptualization of causation.

'Causal efficacy is the hand of the settled past in the formation of the present' (SYM, 50). As opposed to presentational immediacy which acquaints us with the vivid and lively aspects of the environment which we presently inhabit, casual efficacy is another, distinct form of perception, as surprising as this might seem at first. Causal efficacy provides us with more solid, lasting, data which emerge at a different rate, a slower pace; it situates us in a more settled manner, and in relation to past events. The most important point to be made here, and to be stressed, is that causal efficacy is a form of 'direct perception' (SYM, 51ff.). Whitehead's insistence that there is more than one mode of perception, that presentational immediacy is only one aspect of the manner in which data is accumulated, is a major element of his challenge to modernist philosophy and he squarely sets up his account as 'controverting the most cherished tradition of modern philosophy, shared alike by the school of empiricists which derives from Hume, and the school of transcendental idealists which derives from Kant' (SYM, 31). His beguiling argument is that both sets of followers have ignored half of the data which makes up our acquaintance with the world and, even more damaging, they have promoted this data as being primary when it is, in fact, derivative of a more fundamental mode, namely causal efficacy.

The problem of cause as characterized in the work of Hume and which famously spurred Kant to leave his idealist reveries, thus became, within modern philosophy, a problem of how the human subject thinks of the world, and not one of how the world really is. 'Both schools find "causal efficacy" to be the importation, into the data, of a way of thinking or judging about those data' (SYM, 39), whereas Whitehead is clear that we think of cause because we are located in a world of cause (but a different kind of cause to that which is usually envisaged). 'The notion of causation arose because mankind lives amid experiences in the mode of causal efficacy' (PR, 175). Hence Whitehead is able to assert, against strict empiricists, that cause is of the world. And, against Critical Realists, he is able to assert that such an implanting of causation as being of the world does not then entail a necessary distinction either between natural and social causes or between a realm of real causes in nature which science uncovers and more temporary or even arbitrary, humanly created causes in the social world which social theory is sometimes able to describe.

Instead, Whitehead sidesteps such bifurcations through his elaboration of casual efficacy which points to the manner in which our material being *and* our beliefs and actions are always located within a realm of efficacy, of a passing-on of data, of reasons, of motion, of feeling. This is not to say that any of these are strictly caused by that which precedes them, but it does point to the irrationality and ineffectivity of those accounts which either deny cause altogether or locate it as merely a natural or human phenomenon. As such, causal efficacy:

> Produces percepta which are vague, not to be controlled, heavy with emotion: it produces the sense of derivation from an immediate past, and of passage to an immediate future; a sense of emotional feeling, belonging to oneself in the past, passing into oneself in the present, and passing from oneself in the present towards oneself in the future; a sense of influx of influence from other vaguer presences in the past, localized and yet evading local definition, such influence modifying, enhancing, inhibiting, diverting, the stream of feeling which we are receiving, unifying, enjoying, and transmitting. This is our general sense of existence, as one item among others, in an efficacious actual world. (PR, 178)

The sense-data which colours our immediate world – the bright sun, the traffic din, the cold wind, the bitter chocolate, the acrid smoke – do provide some information about the world, but it is partial and meaningless if it is not situated with regard to a past and a future. Too many theorists have fixated on the data provided in the immediate, presentational mode and passed straight from it to attempts to develop theories about how we can know or conceive of this world, based on such data. But this data itself is provided by our bodies which are themselves located in the world and, even more importantly, provide a link to the past and to the future. 'Our most immediate environment is constituted by the various organs of our own bodies, our more remote environment is the physical world in the neighbourhood' (SYM, 17–8).

Presentational immediacy is concerned with the present and whilst it may provide direct and precise information about that car's exact shade of blue, unless we also have more vague but continuing information about our location in the world and its relation to us and to possible future consequences, we would not be moved to get out of the way of the car and avoid being run over. This is not to assert that it is our bodies which rule us, which tell us to jump out of the way of the oncoming bright metallic-blue car, but it is to deny that we simply see the car and, based on our immediate sense-data of an oncoming bright blue thing, decide to jump out of the way. If we did not know where we were or where the car might hit us we would not know where to jump. We are not lost travellers, we are firmly located and oriented to an immediate world with a history and for which the future matters. The historical location of our selves as our bodies is usually ignored by philosophers with their fixation on sense-data and its relation to the human subject and also, until recently, by many social theorists. 'The world, given in sense-presentation, is not the aboriginal experience of the lower organisms, later to be sophisticated by the inference to causal efficacy. The contrary is the case' (SYM, 49). The body is thus the site of the process of existence. This locates the body as a mode of enduring existence which attains both continuity and exhibits change; the body acts as the fulcrum between the past and present. 'Thus the causal efficacy *from* the past is at least one factor giving our presentational immediacy *in* the present' (SYM, 58; emphasis in original). This interrelation between the two modes of perception make up what Whitehead terms "Symbolic Reference"; this notion and its importance for contemporary social theory's understanding of the material body and the problem of signification, especially with regard to the work of Judith Butler, will be taken up in Chapter Six. What is important, for the moment, is to emphasize the radical challenge that Whitehead is making to modernist accounts of data.

There is not a simple or straight division between data dealing with fact and the interpretation of such fact. Our present experience arises from the historical, natural and social environment from which we proceed. This applies to the experiences of all subjects (warming stones, scared rabbits, growth hormones and pigs awaiting slaughter in an abattoir) not just human ones. There is an integral and elemental link between "what" and "how" and no need to divorce the factual from the value-laden (this will be discussed in more detail in the following chapter). However, this is not to claim that science or objective statements about the world are impossible. For, to jump from one side of a belief system, namely that there is either pure (objective) data about the world which tells us how it is, to the other, that there is only impure (subjective) data about the world which therefore cannot tell us how the world really is, is to accept the modernist culture of thought's premise that there are facts *and* there are values, that there is science *and* there is the social, that there is matter *and* there is meaning. Such conjunctions are really disjunctions as they presuppose an originary distinction between the terms linked by the word "*and*". 'There are no components of experience which are only symbols[7] or only meanings… This is the foundation of a *thoroughgoing realism*. It does away with any mysterious element in our experience which is merely meant, and thereby behind the veil of direct perception' (SYM, 10; emphasis added). Whitehead is challenging any approach which divorces meaning and intention from the world, requiring it to lurk behind our actions and perceptions. In its place, he provides a mode of thought which enables the past to suffuse the present reality and thus to inhere, meaningfully, in experience; this is the role of the body and of causal efficacy which 'is heavy with the contact of the things gone by, which lay their grip on our immediate selves' (SYM, 44). But this does not imply any form of determinism; it is simply to correct philosophy's overemphasis on perception by balancing it with the body's place and contribution to our selves and our ongoing adventures of existence. It should also be noted that Whitehead is not developing a theory of how such causes are to be known or described. We are at the ontological not the epistemological level. How causation, in terms of conformation, is later understood or analysed by humans is a different question, although it must be remembered that whatever means are adopted in developing such understandings, they will entail an abstraction from the fullness of that conformation and the body's implication in it.

Conformation

Whitehead's rejection of the primacy of sense-data as the sole provider of information about the world also entails a rejection of the notion of time as 'pure succession' (SYM, 34ff.). This has important consequences for the shifting of emphasis from the notion of cause as merely comprised of efficient causes whereby one object acts on another (a car causes a lamppost to bend) or one force generates certain phenomena in the world (gravity "causes" cannonballs to fall towards planets with the appropriate atmosphere). Any notion that there is a pure form of time which constitutes an uninterrupted flow *within which* such things occur is, according to Whitehead, 'an abstraction of the second order' (SYM, 35). There is no mere time which is filled up with events and happenings. There are simply events and happenings through which we experience and within which we find ourselves. Events do not simply cause each other externally, rather, there is causation immanent within events. We can, clearly, abstract from the passage of events to a concept of time as pure succession but to predicate such succession as primary is, Whitehead argues, a naïve assumption. 'The assumption is naïve, because it is the natural thing to say; it is natural because it leaves out that characteristic of time which is so intimately interwoven that it is natural to omit it' (SYM, 35). With an intriguing play on the word "natural" Whitehead, once again points out that that, far from encompassing or accounting for all that is pertinent to experience and knowledge, modern theory's tendency has been to narrow its inquiries and not to ask how time concretely is. 'Time in the concrete is the conformation of state to state, the later to the earlier; and the pure succession is an abstraction from the irreversible relationship of settled past to derivative present' (SYM, 35). This is the basis of causal efficacy, that there are distinct states which inform each other but do not simply cause each other. Such *in*-formation between events must have an element of *con*-formation.

If there were nothing in common between different occasions, experiences and events then communication or connection between two states would be impossible. Yet it must be stressed that this notion of conforming and conformation must not be seen as some kind of mechanistic approach. Whitehead is, in no way, advocating or expressing that determinism is the key to the universe. Such a version of conformation would undermine the whole project of his philosophy and his cosmology which are premised on the centrality of process and creativity to reality. Whitehead's discussion of the conformation of event to event should be taken as arguing against the notion of time as pure succession which arises from the overemphasis on sense-perception in the mode of presentational immediacy. Through his notion of "conformation", Whitehead treats time not as a pure mode of existence or of apperception but as an abstraction which arises from the more basic interrelation of events within which we are implicated: 'Our primitive perception is that of "conformation" vaguely, and of the yet vaguer relata "oneself" and "another" in the undiscriminated background' (SYM, 43). The notion of conformation is that which enables recognition and repetition as well as providing the possibility of evaluation and alteration; activities which are inherent and integral to the body and its relation to other bodies and subjects.

In his discussion of the problem of cause, as in his more general philosophical approach, Whitehead is clear in his insistence that there is a fullness to existence which is not captured by abstractions of knowledge. But this does not prohibit or exclude there being a "truth" of the world. However, this truth of the world, as exhibited in the process of conformation will be a very specific one. 'Universality of truth arises from the universality of relativity, whereby every particular thing lays upon the universe the obligation of conforming to it' (SYM, 39). That is to say, the necessity of conformation is an aspect of relativity, of history and of actuality. To paraphrase Marx, again, we find ourselves, and things find themselves, located in and at particular moments which are not of our (or their) choosing or making. The world up until now has happened and organized itself in a particular way, for particular reasons. We have no choice but to orient ourselves with regard to these happenings and reasons. But this does not mean that we have *no* choice. The principle of relativity, that each being is a potential for becoming, bears witness to this. The fact that we find ourselves, as do things, amidst specific occasions and events does not proscribe or rule out change and novelty in response to these occasions and events. But any such change, novelty or action can only occur if there is a degree of conformity of the present entity and event to those of the past. The creativity of the process of existence ensures that there must also be some degree of change and resistance. But this will not be effected solely by intentions or consciousness, though they may play a derivative part. The focus on the problem of cause in social theory has obscured such intricacies by suggesting that the only choice is between the efficacy of causal social laws and the primacy of human action (or a melding of specific elements of these in terms of some version of structuration – see

Giddens 1984 and Stones 2005). Stengers (2002, 566–7; 2009b; Pignarre and Stengers 2005) has discussed the importance of Whitehead's work in challenging the established position where there only appears to be such an either/or choice. Instead, the challenge is to take the problems, which have produced such ostensibly unavoidable dichotomies, seriously, but to rethink their generation and to develop new conceptual approaches. Theory's emphasis on the apparent facticity (one might even say reification) of either social laws or human intention has led to a misrecognition of the abstractive and selective aspects of these concepts. Whitehead does not flatly deny the partial efficacy of such abstractions but insists that they do not explain as much as they think they do, precisely insofar as they miss out certain vital elements, such as the body. Through his notion of conformation, Whitehead points both to a way in which more of reality can be accounted for and to the need for science and theory to pay more attention to the extent that their concepts and descriptions of reality are, in themselves, abstractions.

For example, a carbon molecule always exists at a specific place and at a specific time. The notion of a carbon molecule which is often offered by science as consisting of a certain number of electrons, protons, neutrons, and with a specific atomic mass, and so on, is an abstraction from the full reality of the real existence of real carbon atoms in the real world. 'Undoubtedly molecules and electrons are abstractions... an electron is abstract because you cannot wipe out the whole structure of events and yet retain the electron in existence' (CN, 171). This form of abstraction is a powerful and sometimes productive one, but it is an abstraction nevertheless. Science's neglect of the abstractive character of its "objects" and its attempts to render such abstractions as descriptive of real reality is a pernicious element of our culture of thought – where to deny the existence of molecules or electrons, for example, is to render oneself naïve or foolish. Much of the work of Stengers[8] (1997, 2000, 2002) is dedicated to explaining this abstractive character of science and the misplaced authority that it claims for its abstractions. Science abstracts from nature and thereby is able to make "discoveries", such as electrons; the problem arises when it attempts to reduce nature to this abstractive aspect of reality. When a scientist wants 'to convince us that electromagnetic radiation constitutes the sole type of entity which belongs to nature...it has found "more" in nature, but it proposes to reduce it to "less"' (Stengers, 2002, 52). To return to the specificity of a carbon molecule, it will always be located somewhere and somewhen. It may be deep under the desert in Iraq in an oil field, and to this it must conform. But it also has the potential to become the petrol in a car in France taking children to school, to be part of that oil which is set alight as troops retreat and attempt to make the oil wells unusable, or it may sit there for another thousand years contributing to the geological stability of the region.

The notion of a carbon molecule distinct from its environs is an abstraction. The definition of a molecule 'precisely because it seems self-sufficient, exhibits its abstraction, exhibits the rare success which constitutes the definitions of the objects of science' (Stengers 2002, 120).

The concept of the human, too, and of human subjects, is also a powerful abstraction which haunts modernity. For humans are, in actuality, always located. They, like molecules, must conform, to a degree, to their surroundings: to their education system, media, economy, but they must respond to these as well. The future is not completely open; it must conform to the past. But it is certainly not closed. 'The *how* of our present experience must conform to the *what* of the past in us' (SYM, 58; emphasis in original). Again, it must be insisted that conformation and reaction to the environment is not the sole provenance of human existence of action. Degrees of conformation are evident throughout the world.

> A flower turns to the light with much greater certainty than does a human being, and a stone conforms to the conditions set by its external environment with much greater certainty than does a flower. A dog anticipates the conformation of the immediate future to his [sic] present activity with the same certainty as a human being. When it comes to calculations and remote inferences, the dog fails. But the dog never acts as though the immediate future were irrelevant to the present. Irresolution in action arises from consciousness of a somewhat distant relevant future. (SYM, 42)

Thus, as opposed to Critical Realism, and many models within social theory, there is no need to distinguish between the realms of the social and the natural or to posit cause and purpose as being limited to one of these realms, or as existing in a different mode within these realms. Furthermore, the actions and responses of stones, flowers, dogs and humans are made in relation to enduring patterns to which they must conform but which do not *cause* their existence or actions. Such enduring patterns have been described by some as "structures" which exist either in nature or in society. There then arises the problem of addressing how individuals can be conceived as being distinct from, as elements of, or as subsumed within, such structures. As discussed above, Whitehead would have no truck with approaching the problem in this way. Indeed his whole philosophical system could be seen as an attempt to account for the complex interrelation between real wider forces and real individuals without prioritising or hypostasizing any of these elements. For, as Stengers has pointed out, it is possible to view his initial philosophical problematic as arising from his mathematical-physicist interest in the problem of how an electron (an individual) can occupy a field of force (its environment) without being reduced to it or separate from it (Stengers 2002, 205). For the moment, it is clear that Whitehead has reframed the entire question and attempted to posit conformation as the mode of relation of an individual to its past which informs its present status in its environment. There are causes in reality but not in the way that philosophy, science and social theory have usually envisaged. Whitehead's account of cause and conformation, whilst an important intervention in its own right, raises the question of the individual's relation to the future and also the status of value within this scheme. This makes up the topic of the next chapter.

Chapter Four

THE VALUE OF EXISTENCE

The question of the value of value is one which may be familiar to social theorists as deriving from Nietzsche and from more recent reappraisals of his work. The problem of value, however, is stubbornly embedded in the presumptions and assumptions of social theory. Most students of the subject will, at some point, be led through the distinction between positivism (with its emphasis on facts) and interpretivism (with its emphasis on meaning and value) as having, for many years, offered the two major approaches to studying and conceiving of the social world. As seen in the previous chapter, Critical Realism, in many respects, identified itself as an attempt to synthesize these into a more complete account of the world and the social world. There is something neat about such a division of both the history and the practice of social theory which then enables more "modern" approaches (such as postmodernism, feminism, postcolonial theory, queer theory etc.) to position themselves both within and as reactions to these conceptual legacies. The position of Whitehead would be to insist that what is needed is a thorough examination of the manner and extent of the very division between fact and value. What was it that led to this division and how far does its reach still extend to, and inhabit, our contemporary concepts? Only then will it be possible to refine the conceptual strategies which still tacitly support this dichotomy.

This chapter will, therefore, review the post-Kantian legacy which attempted to solicit value as an inherently human affair, divorced from the factuality of scientific knowledge. In laying bare the roots and reasons for this split, it will outline the extent to which the problems which the fact-value distinction was meant to solve still lurk within the sociological imagination. Before proceeding to this, and in order to establish just how modern and surprising the nineteenth-century conception of the differentiation between fact and value is, a very brief and somewhat schematic account of the status of value within Greek philosophy will be offered. This is not meant as a complete analysis of this field but as an indication of its difference from the notion of value which haunts our culture of thought and whose status is, all too often, taken for granted.

Within Greek philosophy, value was real but was not defined in opposition to fact; instead it was regarded as that which had worth. For Plato, value, insofar as it resided in the Forms, preceded fact. These Forms made sense on their own terms and they had their own intrinsic "value", indeed they were value, in a sense quite distinct from its modern usage. The separate reality of value is also true of Aristotle's notion of value as virtue. For him, virtues were not generated within humans but were that at which humans aimed, in order to make themselves all that they could possibly be (and as "happy", in the sense of *eudaimon*,[1] as they could be). It is in this way that virtues had value. Values, as virtues, were examples of 'that which is in itself worthy of pursuit more final than that which is worthy of pursuit for the sake of something else' (Aristotle 1954, 11) and were separate from humans. Values were not seen as creations or elements of humans: 'Neither by nature, then, nor contrary to nature do the virtues arise in us; rather we are adapted by nature to receive them, and are made perfect by habit' (Aristotle 1954, 28). There is much that Whitehead borrows, remoulds, rejects, and returns to within the approaches of Plato and Aristotle. However, the context that he is writing in is not Greek but that modern, post-Kant world where fact and value have become specifically separate in that they are now apparently implacably opposed. This raises the question of why and how such a distinction came about and managed to inhabit modernity so fully. One important element of this is the development of neo-Kantianism in nineteenth-century philosophy and theory and the divisions that it offered and which were taken up by many conceptual protagonists within social theory.

Facts, Values and the Nineteenth Century

In the nineteenth century, many philosophers viewed the great success of Kant's work as being that it had, especially in the *Critique of Pure Reason*, established the basis for objective, scientific knowledge of the world. He achieved this by describing the categories of thought invested within the human mind, which both produced and underscored the possibility of such knowledge. The intricacies and accuracy of his account are not important here, it is the impact that the supposition of his success had on social theory which will be examined.

For writers such as Windelband, Rickert and Dilthey, the problem was not the stanchions of Kant's argument but that his work did not provide a basis for analyses of the social and cultural world. That is to say, Kant's three critiques (of Pure Reason, of Practical Reason and of Judgement) seemed to offer foundations for knowledge of the natural world, morality and aesthetics, respectively, but did not provide a conceptual basis for the burgeoning "sciences of the social". For Windelband (1848–1915), the problem was most acute with regard to the question of history (see Oakes 1986, ix–xiii). According to Windelband, and in contradistinction to the axiological approach of Plato and Aristotle, the problem of value for the modern West was located in the need to identify and explain the individual value of specific historical phenomena. Science would seem to be concerned with those things that happen repeatedly or can be made to repeat in laboratories with the relevant conditions measured, changed and governed. In this way, tests can be done, observations made, hypotheses developed. But historical phenomena, by definition, occur only once. That is precisely why they are of interest and why explanations of such phenomena are so important and require a different methodology to that of science, according to Windelband. So, he said that the role of the study of history is to identify and explain the very particularity, meaning and value of specific historical events rather than to explain different events as mere examples of a more general term, form or value (such as revolution, democratization, decline, or decadence). For Windelband, individuality is the bearer of value as it is the very specificity and unique character of individual historical events which give them their importance and meaning (Oakes 1986, x–xi).

The manner in which such individuality is conceived is one which points to a specific element of the conceptual milieu of modernity, namely Christianity. For, within Christian theology, as opposed to Greek theodicy, there germinated the idea of value as adhering only to specific events. 'The Christian idea that values can be ascribed only to individual phenomenon has its origin in the conception of the Creation, the Fall, and the events of the life of Christ as unique events endowed with unprecedented significance' (Oakes 1986, ix). On this view, value comes precisely from the uniqueness and unrepeatability of a phenomenon. More generally, this bled into the notion that the role of history is to identify and explain the very particularity and hence the meaning and value of specific events rather than to explain the general course of events. Individuality became the bearer of value, and the Greek conception of value as inhabiting its own realm or having its own purpose was rejected. It also points to a surprising twist in the development of modernity's culture of thought insofar as that which enabled it to premise a distinction between facticity and the secular value-realm of human culture is predicated on a specific theological admission.

Rickert (1863–1936) took up Windelband's proposed approach to the problem of historiography and developed it into a more general philosophical point, one which had a significant influence on Weber. Rickert sees both the problem and the solution in terms of the distinction between concept and reality. For Rickert, concepts are needed for knowledge – as they 'recast and transform reality in such a way that its complexity is reduced' (Oakes 1986, xx); 'we unwittingly translate the content of perceptual reality into the content of general concepts'

(Rickert 1986 [1902], 39). The knowledge which natural science produces is an abstraction which moves from the individual phenomenon to the laws which explain such events and then to wider (and more abstract) generalizations so that the individual details and phenomena become less important, insofar as the laws which explain them become more extensive and hence more "scientific". In this way science 'brackets the unique and nonrepeatable properties of reality' (Oakes 1986, xxi) and becomes less concerned with the specific perceptions of individual humans in the world and, therefore, increasingly distant from the fullness of reality (that is, from reality thought of as an empirical experiential realm). There is, it will be noticed, something akin to Whitehead's analysis here, in that science is to be viewed as developing abstractions whose success relies precisely on their dislocation from specific, historical events. For Rickert, it is history, rather than science, which has the role of explaining the peculiarities of concrete, perceptual reality. The historian selects those elements of reality which are important to, or relate to, shared human values, as opposed to the "valueless" statements of science, and in doing so helps identify precisely what constitutes such values (Rickert 1986 [1902], 78ff.).

Consequently, the split between fact and value is sedimented, in that the theoretical task to be undertaken is the conceptual delimitation of those values which grant meaning to individual things and events in the human, social world. Values are utterly distinct from factual existence and become self-referential indicators of the very humanity of humans. On this view, knowledge comes from concepts, concepts themselves are not derived from reality, rather, reality is recast through concepts. Hence reality-as-it-is is not directly open to rationality as it cannot be given and understood in total and at an instant; it can only be approached through the abstractions of science: 'a science…can have nothing to say about what exists at a specific point in space and time, and what really and uniquely holds true here or there, now or then' (Rickert 1986 [1902], 47). Yet values, even though they have no factual existence, are directly accessible as they are not part of external reality but a necessary element of the sphere of the human mind:

> It is irrelevant why *all* persons are linked with values or are related to values and thus qualify as individuals in the strict sense of indivisibility. It is important to show only that our principle is truly *general*, and therefore that by its means any reality at all…can be analyzed. (Rickert 1986 [1902], 85. Emphasis in original.)

Whitehead would remark, perhaps, that the citing of "irrelevance" here is an admission of failure. Identifying the reason and way in which "all persons are linked with values" is an important theoretical task that must be undertaken openly and consistently. As will be seen later on in this chapter, this is precisely what Whitehead undertakes. Before proceeding to this, however, it is important to look at another, distinct, post-Kantian attempt to account for values which was made in the *Lebensphilosophie* of Dilthey (1833–1911) which also had a direct influence on sociology and social theory. In response to the problem of the status of history, value and meaning, Dilthey argued that in addition to Kant's categories (which furnish us with scientific knowledge), more categories (in the Kantian sense) are needed for a full understanding humans, history and life. Dilthey's categories include: "of part and whole", "of means and end", "of power" and "of value". Rickman (1976) summarizes Dilthey's approach as follows:

> While Kant's categories provide us with the means of knowing the physical world, Dilthey's enable us to grasp the meaning in human life. Things become meaningful to us because we see them as parts of a whole, goals we desire or means for achieving them, physical manifestations of mental states, products of human efforts, or sources of satisfaction or dissatisfaction. *What* they mean is, of course, a matter of empirical investigation. (Rickman 1976, 17. Emphasis in original.)

So, Dilthey argues that the categories which constitute knowledge are not fixed; they can change. Unlike Kant's version of categories, Dilthey's are not strictly *a priori*, they can be accessed via experience, and constituted (changed) via human experience.

> We interact with the physical world because we are physical creatures, evaluate things because we have feelings and purposes, understand history because we are ourselves historical beings and we are able to understand the expressions of others because we produce them ourselves. (Rickman 1976, 21)

Dilthey maintains that there is a need is to develop categories of understanding that will enable us to develop historical knowledge and grasp the meaning in and of human life. This form of understanding requires its own form of explanation in order to differentiate it from science which views particulars as instances of general laws. The method which enables such nonscientific understanding is that of "Hermeneutics" (the treatment and interpretation of history and social life as if it were a text where wholes and parts are interdependent). The interpretation of both wholes and parts are needed to develop the specific form of understanding at which Dilthey is aiming and which he terms *Verstehen* (empathetic understanding). The identification of the method and ground of this novel form of human understanding establishes a supposedly legitimate source of knowledge which Dilthey posits as the basis of the social and human sciences (Dilthey 1976, 226–8, 260). The study of value through understanding produced one cornerstone of social theory, as established in the work of Weber. Here the emphasis is on value-relevance, where that which is to be studied is the range of values which are instantiated or seen as important within various cultures (or subcultures). These can be identified through the (social) actions of the members of these groups, in that such actions must be premised on the orientation toward such values: 'only on the assumption of the belief in the validity of values is the attempt to espouse value-judgements meaningful' (Weber 1949, 55). This somewhat circular account entails that social theory has dislocated value and values from their Greek heights and reduced them to mere creations of human consciousness and subjectivity. Rickert, Dilthey and Weber all assume that humans are value giving entities: it is just a part of being human that we assign values and act on them, it is claimed. But, Whitehead would object, this is just an assumption; one which lacks justification and which falsely promotes humanity to the privileged position of the sole progenitors of value. Such assumptions need to be challenged.

All this may read as little more than a slightly diverting, if tendentious, account of a local problem of late nineteenth-century German quasi-idealist thought which no longer bears much relevance. But what is of interest is the way in which this concept of value has been taken up and still operates within contemporary social theory, most especially in terms of discussions of norms and values and their relation to questions of structure and agency. This latter dyad signals the inclusion of the work of Durkheim in such discussions, who might otherwise be seen as offering a distinct challenge to the idealist approach outlined above. Hence, it is perhaps not too far-fetched to suggest that, even today, the work and legacy of Parsons is still in partial operation as he attempted a synthesis of the supposedly structural and agential approaches of Durkheim and the German idealist school, as represented by Weber. Furthermore, he situated value as the prime motivating and explanatory factor of social life insofar as an orientation toward values became the underpinning guarantor of his theory of action[2] and subsequent variations thereof. For example, when he defines value as follows: 'An element of a shared symbolic system which serves as a criterion or standard for selection among the alternatives of orientation which are intrinsically open in a situation may be called a value' (Parsons 1991 [1951], 12). The ultimate reason for the performance or occurrence of an action is the aim at, or avoidance of, a value. The problem with such a position is that, unlike the Greek conception, such values are both the product of humans and external to humans. Therefore, they reinforce or repeat the parameters of the structure-agency divide and the repeated arguments over whether emphasis should be laid on the voluntarist element of human agency, or the effectivity of the structural-cultural value-systems which such agents inhabit.

The way in which the notion of value has been conceptualized as distinct from that of fact has led to one abiding problem of social theory and of social research, namely that of "how to put these back together again?" But it has led to a whole host of other questions such as: How to ensure objectivity in the research method given the inherent values of the researcher? How to establish an objective analysis of subjective phenomena? How to understand the relation of value-bearing agents to impersonal structures? How to view values as inherent in structure? And so on and so forth. The Whiteheadian approach would be to ask that we slow down and consider how we ever got into such a position. Why and how were fact and value ever rendered as distinct? This is not simply to reduce the division to a socially constructed concept which is then to be explained away. It is, rather, to demand that we interrogate the presumptions and assumptions which subtend the frames of our thought and enable us to view fact and value as discrete. Why do we value value as an inherently social and human affair? What does this mode of thought produce and what does it disbar? Most importantly, are we really paying attention to what we mean by "value" or are we taking it on trust and quietly acceding to the rather peculiar nineteenth-century roots of the version of this concept, which still abound today?

Even social theorists such as Fararo (1992, 2001, 2006) who declare that they adopt a processual, Whiteheadian approach to sociology, often neglect to stop and challenge the very concept of value. Fararo, like Parsons (1949 [1937]; 1991 [1951]), accepts the nineteenth-century settlement that viewed value as an inherently human affair which it is the task of social theory to investigate. This, clearly, is a step too far and too early for Whitehead. It replicates the bifurcation of nature. If values, along with norms, somehow reflect or indicate the shared ideas of a social group to which its members must conform or at least orient their actions, as it is possible to interpret both Durkheim and Weber, then values are no more and no less than utterly social and human phenomena. Whitehead would not want to deny that values play some role in social action or orientation to social structure. He would, however, deny that this is a necessary or sufficient account of value. Further, the more that value is rendered as solely a human creation, the more its disjunction from the facticity of fact is solidified. This leads to the utter divorce between the objective, social, yet unmaterial world, which is the province of social science, and the objective, natural, material world which supposedly falls under the aegis of natural science (see Fraser 2006 for a fuller discussion of this and the relation of the fact-value distinction to questions of reality and science in the work of Latour and Whitehead).

The question of the value of value and its relation to the question of facticity is therefore an important one for understanding and developing our culture of thought. It is one which permeates the work of Whitehead, which he treats of carefully and to which he returns again and again. His arguments are not immediately directed to the concerns of social theory but his philosophical attempts to explain the mutual implication of fact and value witness a mode of thought which might provide a way of avoiding the seemingly inevitable splitting that pervades our culture of thought.

Whitehead on Value

Various attempts (for example, Belaief 1975; Shindler 1983; George 2004) have been made to address Whitehead's conception of value and to explain his attempt to develop a metaphysics which moves beyond static conceptions of objects and facts which lack potential, purpose and aim. They outline Whitehead's refusal of the scientistic model of a universe composed simply of objects, and relations between objects, and describe his challenge to that 'tendency in modern Western philosophy to equate the "actual" with the "factual"' (Shindler 1983, 117). However, such accounts of Whitehead's placement of value into the metaphysical scheme take for granted what is meant when he deploys the term "value". They tend to assume that value has a generally accepted meaning or that it refers to something "concrete" or immediately understood; there is, supposedly, a specific content to value. In doing so they risk missing the radical character of Whitehead's approach, for he posits no such specific content to value and, instead, aims to account for the general status and role of value within existence. This is not to simply put fact and value back together or to make them equivalents; there is a distinction to be made between fact and value but this distinction does not presuppose them as being, or as ever having had, separate realms of existence or validity. Fact and value require to be thought together. On this view, to reinvigorate the object (or objective) world with value is not simply a matter of reintegrating or reimposing already existing values. The difficult task that Whitehead sets himself is, rather, to develop an account of the place of value in existence without either making value a solely human creation or readily assimilable to any preexisting examples of value that humans might hold dear. The key to Whitehead's integration of fact and value is his description of the essential role of potentiality in existence. In proposing such an approach, Whitehead does use the terms "value" and "valuation" at various points to express the integration of potentiality into actuality but he does so less frequently and much more carefully than some of his commentators suggest. Rather than simply enabling us to reassert our existing values and their content (be it in terms of generosity, selflessness, beauty, conservation, peace, sustainability), Whitehead develops a metaphysics of value in terms of valuation which accounts for its role within his philosophical framework but gives no indication of what such values are or how they might be ranked or judged. Such decisions are for us to make and for which to take responsibility. But the main point is not to confuse value with virtue.

Whitehead provides one clear description of the setting of value in reality, which signals a first move in avoiding reducing it to a notion of virtue or viewing it as human-based, when he states: 'Value is inherent in actuality itself. To be an actual entity is to have a self-interest. This self-interest is a feeling of self-valuation... The value of other things, not one's self is the derivative value of being elements contributing to this ultimate self-interest' (RM, 87). Schindler emphasizes this self-interest, which means that any concern for others is secondary, and this leads him to suggest that Whitehead's notion of value ultimately fails insofar as it is unable to move beyond this dangerously solipsistic position (Schindler 1983, 127–8). Such a conclusion appears to be too strong, especially as it is based on a misreading. It assumes that when Whitehead says "value" he means value in the post-nineteenth-century sense of values, expressed, for example, in notions such as truth, privacy, honesty and beauty. However, Whitehead has not defined value yet. Instead, he has simply attempted to describe the experience of an individual being itself. The importance of reapproaching the status of value cannot be overemphasized. "Value" is a loaded term, replete with connotations, and Whitehead knows that, in order to avoid the bifurcation of nature, it is incumbent on him (and us) to explicate the operation of value in reality without relying on, or assuming, that any of these connotations can be taken for granted as providing shortcuts to shoring up our theoretical positions. With this in mind, his "definition" of value, which comes on the next page, is as follows:

> There is no such thing as bare value. There is always a specific value, which is the created unit of feeling arising out of the specific mode of concretion of the diverse elements. These different specific value-feelings are comparable amid their differences; and the ground for this comparability is what is termed here "value". (RM, 90)

This definition is not as straight-forward as it might first appear. Unlike Plato, Whitehead does not want to posit an abstract and complete realm of value. Instead, there are always only specific valuations rather than a set of values or ideas about what is valuable and to which we orient our (social) action, as Parsons and others might hold. For Whitehead, values are therefore not values-in-themselves, rather they are value-feelings. That which exists comports value but is not, in itself, value. Value is that which enables, or grounds, the differences between feelings (or prehensions) as developed by individuals. In one sense this does sound reminiscent of a realm of prior values as envisaged by Plato but, again, this is not Whitehead's position. For, in his account, there are no values except those value-feelings which are realized in individuals. Value is simply that which enables valuation. It is not a set of principles or guidelines which permeate the social world and its structures and agents.

The most sustained of Whitehead's discussions of value, in terms of valuation, is to be found in *Process and Reality* (PR). However, the first thing to notice is that the term "value" (used as a noun) appears only approximately ten times in this text.[3] There are, however, extensive references to valuation throughout the work. It is an important element of Whitehead's metaphysics that it is the activity of valuation which is vital (as expressed in his deployment of the verbal form) rather than the notion of values as static things (nouns). Whilst it would clearly be a fundamental error to maintain that Whitehead's cosmology was not interested in accounting for value in some sense of quality and worth, it is also clear that Whitehead is not interested in (indeed does not believe in) the existence of a set of (moral or social) values which can be elicited, described or enumerated and against which our experiences and activities can be measured. It is precisely because of his desire to account for the very inherence of value in existence and to describe how value is not opposed to fact that Whitehead avoids the word "value" in *Process and Reality*. To put it simply, valuation, which is the activity that comprises the operation of value in reality, refers to the *manner* in which any process occurs. All reality is constituted by process but these processes are not inert, they always occur in different ways. There is a "how" as well as a "what" to existence. As discussed in Chapter Two, facticity always occurs in a certain way (quickly, warmly, greenly) and the expression of this manner of existence makes up the valuation which is an integral part of that entity and hence of that facticity and actuality.

To recap, Whitehead wants to avoid the problems associated with following Plato in separating off a static realm of value, from which the present, imperfect reality is derived. 'Plato found his permanences in a static, spiritual heaven, and his flux in the entanglement of his forms amid the fluid imperfections of the physical world' (PR, 209). Instead, Whitehead wants the process to be the reality. He also wants to argue against the neo-Kantian position (as also evidenced in various forms of realism) where concept and reality are seen as separate, so that facticity falls under the purview of science and, consequently, value becomes limited to, at best, an epiphenomenal realm fabricated by and for humans or, at worst, a subjective creation of individual humans which merely expresses unfounded sentiment and holds back science. For Whitehead, value and actuality must not be shorn apart. Indeed, accounting for their cohabitation is one of the major tasks that he sets himself. How to describe a nondeterministic process wherein stubborn fact is both an attainment and a ground for novelty and where experience is constitutive of subjectivity and objectivity? This is the role granted to potentiality in Whitehead's universe and this indicates the crucial link that Whitehead makes between potentiality and valuation (and hence value). But in order to fully explicate his position he cannot simply assert that potentiality *is* "value" and declare the fact-value split overcome (and nature as not bifurcated). The next step is therefore to explain how potentiality inhabits actuality without being reduced to it and without having to posit a separate realm of abstract, yet existing potentials. This crucial explanatory role is one that he assigns to what he calls "eternal objects" which, as will be seen, perform their task by incorporating potentiality into existence through the process of valuation.

This phrase "eternal object" is one of the most complex of Whitehead's technical terms and has caused much consternation on the part of Whitehead scholars. The following section will briefly, but densely, identify some of their key functions. However, it does not, of itself, stand as a proof of their legitimacy. Rather, it is an indication of the metaphysical moves that are required (by Whitehead) if the bifurcation of nature is to be avoided and valuation placed within actuality. In subsequent chapters, (especially six, seven and eight) which deal with specific topics and concepts within social theory, the efficacy and validity of Whitehead's conceptual apparatus and metaphysical framework will become more fully apparent.

What is an Eternal Object?

Whitehead makes it clear that 'eternal objects tell no tales as to their ingressions' (PR, 256). So, in one sense, the question "what is an eternal object?" is impossible to answer, in that eternal objects are never encountered as such but only as aspects of those occasions in which they find ingression into a particular entity. That eternal objects do not exist in their own terms or in a separate realm but only in their ingression into an actual entity may distinguish them from Plato's static forms, but it also makes them nigh on impossible to indicate in language (in the sense of denoting them, pointing to them, giving examples of them). This is why, although Whitehead does not state this quite so plainly, he believes that it is not possible to give names to specific eternal objects. The occasion on which Whitehead comes closes to a definition of them is through a discussion of Locke's philosophy:

> These "eternal objects" are Locke's ideas as explained in his *Essay (II, I, 1)* where he writes: *Idea is the object of thinking.* – Every man [sic] being conscious to himself that he thinks, and that which his mind is applied about, whilst thinking, being the ideas that are there, it is past doubt that men have in their mind several ideas, such as are those expressed by the words, "whiteness, hardness, sweetness, thinking, motion, man, elephant, army, drunkenness," and others. (PR, 52. Emphasis in original.)

Whitehead does not stop to analyse or explain this passage, he seems to take it as self-explanatory and simply moves on to a discussion of how Locke's work can help explain another of his technical terms, "nexus". This leaves a rather peculiar feeling that "man" and "elephant" and "drunkenness" are eternal objects! It is clear from the rest of *Process and Reality* that Whitehead does not intend this to be the case. Perhaps the simplest way of explaining what an eternal object is, is to set out the position as follows: Given Whitehead's resolute critique of any conceptualization of objects and subjects as static, as well as his emphasis on the process and creativity of existence, both of which are linked to his explicit aim to account for "stubborn fact", then he will have to explain how such facticity is not a mere self-sufficient object in the Newtonian tradition but partakes in the wider process of existence and yet is still an individual. Early on in *Process and Reality* (PR) he puts it as follows: 'The true philosophic question is, 'How can concrete fact exhibit entities abstract from itself and yet participated in by its own nature?' (PR, 20). One important aspect of his answer to this question is through "eternal objects". This notion may surprise us, or even confuse us, both in terms of the very words that he puts together to coin this term ("eternal" and "object") which, at first sight, look as if they go against the grain of the rest of his philosophy, but also with respect to the complex role that they play in his work. Yet to dismiss them as obscure, irrelevant or uncomfortable is to misrecognize that they are required by Whitehead to avoid falling back into the bifurcation of nature.

In *Process and Reality* (PR), Whitehead is clear as to the purpose, status, manner of interrelation, of eternal objects. They have various roles, four of which will addressed below: they provide definiteness to an entity; they constitute logical variables; they express the dipolarity of existence; they comport value into actuality through the process of valuation.

Eternal objects characterize the different manners of becoming, the range of options informing an actual entity, some of which must be incorporated within that entity in order for it to gain its individuality. Eternal objects thus grant definiteness to an entity by enabling pure potentiality to be actualized on given occasions (e.g. PR, 149).

Eternal objects perform the role of "logical variables" which underpin the whole notion of process: 'the characteristic common to all eternal objects, [is] that it introduces the notion of the *logical variable*, in both forms, the unselective "any" and the selective "some"' (PR, 114; emphasis added). Eternal objects thereby perform the role of guaranteeing, at a metaphysical level, the principle of process, via the notion of potentiality, within a general system of becoming punctuated by divergent moments of individual subjects. It is this sense that they are "logical" rather than actual. This is not to say that they do not occur, rather that they are never encountered as discrete individuals.[4]

Eternal objects, importantly, express the dipolarity of existence:

> Thus an actual entity is essentially dipolar, with its physical and mental poles; *and even the physical world cannot be properly understood without reference to its other side, which is the complex of mental operations.* The primary mental operations are conceptual feelings. (PR, 239. Emphasis added.)

As opposed to the neo-Kantian separation of concept from reality and the subsequent relegation of value to a mere consequence of the human mind, Whitehead allows conceptuality to suffuse existence. This is a crucial aspect of eternal objects. 'A conceptual feeling is feeling an eternal object' (PR, 239). The mental and the physical are two aspects of the concrescence and the existence of a material entity. Concepts do not find their origin in thinking or the human mind: conceptual feelings are an integral part of the coming-to-be of all entities; they refer to the manner in which an entity combines diverse elements into a unity on that occasion. This is not to say that stones think. But they do enjoy conceptual feelings, in Whitehead's sense of the term, as they always experience the world in a specific way. The description of this low-level form of conceptual engagement is achieved through the very notion of eternal objects. It is these which enable him to avoid the post-Kantian gap between reality and concept, because the conceptual is an integral aspect of all reality. Whitehead deploys eternal objects to explain how conceptuality and potentiality are integral elements of all existence (and to reinforce his argument that human consciousness is not the progenitor or guarantor of rationality, thinking and conceptuality). This perhaps difficult placement of conceptuality within all existence will be elaborated in later chapters.

There is, however, a further step to be made which is key to this chapter and this is to state that the inherence of conceptuality and potentiality is displayed and explained in terms of valuation; for valuation is the mode by which eternal objects gain specific ingression and help grant individuality and definiteness to an entity. 'By reason of the actuality of this primordial valuation of pure potentials, each eternal object has a definite effective relevance to each concrescent process' (PR, 40; see also PR, 21, 26, 31, 32, 53, 108). But this potentiality does not have free rein; it is not existent on its own. It is always, everywhere, displayed in actual things, in facticity: 'apart from things that are actual, there is nothing – nothing either in fact or in efficacy' (PR, 40). This is his "ontological principle". Hence, to attempt to separate fact from valuation is to rip reality apart. Now, an analysis of the world as if fact and value were separate may be possible, indeed desirable on occasions, in order to produce worthwhile or interesting abstractions. But to assert, as the neo-Kantian legacy invites us to do, that fact and value are separate in existence, or inhabit separate realms, is to make a serious error. It should be noted that this discussion might appear to have slipped from talking about valuation to value – but this is what the neo-Kantian legacy makes us do, and it is precisely this which Whitehead is attempting to enable us to reapproach. That is to say, post-Kantian and positivist distinctions between fact and value have misread the character of existence. But the answer is not simply to reassert value into fact, for the very distinction between these two does not, in itself, exist (except as a badly formed abstraction). Rather, for Whitehead, the task is to reassert the qualitative aspect of existence through a redescription of the enactment of potentiality as an operation of valuation. This is the role of eternal objects which, though unnameable, are a vital aspect of his philosophy of organism.

After *Process and Reality* (PR) Whitehead does not mention eternal objects again in *Adventures of Ideas* (AI) or *Modes of Thought* (MT), whilst he does retain other aspects of his terminology. One simple reason for this might be that he found that the term had been unhelpful for readers.

> There is one point as to which you – and everyone – misconstrue me – obviously my usual faults of exposition are to blame. I mean my doctrine of *eternal objects*. It is an endeavour to get beyond the absurd simple-mindedness of the traditional treatment of Universals. (Whitehead, from a letter written on 2 January 1936 to Charles Hartsthorne, cited in Kline 1963, 199. Emphasis in original.)

Or, it could be argued that Whitehead felt that the status of eternal objects as unnameable elements in his speculative system was not, ultimately, an adequate response to the demands of the world, of actuality considered as a contemporary and a historical realm. So, despite the unnameability of specific eternal objects in their role of explaining the inherence of potentiality in fact, Whitehead understands that is still a requirement to describe how valuation operates and has operated in the world (historically speaking). It is to this that he turns at the beginning of *Adventures of Ideas* (AI) when he provides an account of the development, dissipation and retention of a range of ideas in the West over the last 3000 years (AI, 1–127).

This shift from the metaphysics of *Process and Reality* (PR) to the "sociology"[5] of Part I of *Adventures of Ideas* (AI) might be explained by Whitehead's belief that, as distinct from the generalized descriptions of metaphysics (and yet in order to help confirm its descriptions), philosophy and theory must provide a description and response to the pressing needs of thought, experience, life, and the world. That is to say, history intervenes in our speculations and it demands that we respond and attempt to understand. 'The crash of the Great War marked its [the nineteenth century's] end, and marked the decisive turn of human life into some new direction as yet not fully understood' (AI, 358); 'the misery of the great war was sufficient for any change of epoch' (AI, 359). Without wishing to personalize the matter, Whitehead's loss of a son in World War I might have been one factor which sharpened his awareness to the need to account for the technological, social, economic, and political upheavals which surrounded him. The adequacy of a philosophy's response to such demands will both rely upon and confirm the adequacy of its metaphysics. *Adventures of Ideas* is therefore a test that Whitehead set himself after *Process and Reality*. It is a test that continues in his last major work, *Modes of Thought*, where he again returns to questions of fact, value, reality and nature, for example when he states: 'The potentialities in immediate fact constitute the driving force of process' (MT, 136–7). And: 'Fact includes in its own nature something which is not fact, although it constitutes a realized item within fact. This is the conceptual side of fact. But, as usual, the philosophic tradition is too abstract. There is no such independent item in actuality as "mere concept"' (MT, 168). There is no mere fact and no mere concept, just conceptual facts and factual concepts, as will be discussed in later chapters on the body and sexual difference. Whilst Whitehead is no longer trying to account for such conceptuality in terms of eternal objects, existence for its own sake (or the sense of existence for its own sake) is still not to be rendered as a value on its own.

Hence, in *Modes of Thought* (MT), Whitehead continues his rejection of the primacy of objects and subjects and, instead, focuses on the process of experience:

> Our enjoyment of actuality is a realization of worth, good or bad. It is a value-experience. Its basic expression is – Have a care, here is something that matters! (MT, 159)

From the whole edifice of *Process and Reality*, through the historical sweep of *Adventures of Ideas*, Whitehead fixes on his point. "Something matters". If there is to be a value in existence, then this is it. That something matters. However, it is important not to then run too quickly from this point and simply reassert that which we already consider valuable into our accounts of existence. This would be to betray the extent of the conceptual reappraisal that Whitehead is asking of us. 'The main point of this description is the concept of actuality as something that matters, by reason of its own self-enjoyment, which includes enjoyment of others and transitions towards the future' (MT, 161). It is in the relation of self-enjoyment to otherness, with others as constitutive of existence, that value is seeded and the individual both validated and superseded. But, again, this is not a theory of value.

It could be argued that Whitehead's philosophy is encapsulated in the phrase "something matters". To claim that the phrase "something matters" is a metaphysical one might appear to be a rather weak point. But it is not. Given the history and influence of the fact-value distinction which has dogged philosophy and social theory, it was never going to be as simple as just declaring that fact and value are not really separate. The bifurcation of nature (as exemplified in the fact-value dualism) cannot be rectified or healed simply by saying it is not so or "it isn't like that". Whitehead's "something matters" is that moment of condensation of his philosophy to the inclusion of fact to value and value to fact.

The stipulation that Whitehead makes, and as evidenced in Latour's insistence on the irreducibility of things (e.g. Latour 1993a, 153ff.), is that reality is, of and in itself, enough of a resource for analysis, as it is replete with actuality and potentiality. There is no need to invoke extra realms of explanation such as the values of a society, its enduring structures, its ideological underpinnings. There is, however, a need to be prepared to take seriously those things which do populate the world: trains, matches, schools, oil, children, hostels for the homeless, sex-workers, detention centres for "asylum seekers" and to trace the manner and connections which constitute and enable their continuing existence. For, Whitehead is clearly involved in important battles as to what constitutes reality in his refusal of the modern culture of thought's division of reality into natural and social realms, facts and values, objects and subjects, structures and agents, humans and nonhumans. This is the requirement that Whitehead makes of social theory through his emphasis on the primacy of those things which "matter" and which incorporate the value and facticity of the world. There is, as such, no fact-value division but attention needs to be paid to the way that things and facticity are rendered, their qualities, their modes of being. That is to say, Whitehead describes the world in terms of an utter reality which is nonetheless not innate, essential, or fixed, but instead, is premised on the coming-to-be, the construction of facticity. It is this notion of an actual construction, which has led Stengers (2002 2008a) to consider Whitehead as exemplifying a constructivist approach to the world which moves beyond the limitations of linguistic constructionism and discursive production. Such a concept of productive constructivism (as opposed to any form of deconstruction) and its relation to the specific topics in social theory will make up the remaining chapters of this book.

Chapter Five

SOCIETIES, THE SOCIAL
AND SUBJECTIVITY

Sociology studies society; social theory analyses the social. These seemingly straight-forward statements mask a nest of conceptual and practical difficulties. The extent, dynamic and locale of societies have proved problematic. The status of the social, indeed its very existence, has proved hard to pin down. Such questions are well-rehearsed nowadays and are often presented in terms of "the end of the social?" Proponents of such a thesis adopt a range of positions and have variously argued that new forms of globalized, networked, complex, mobile societies have emerged which bear little resemblance to the stable nation-states which social theory has tended to assume (e.g. Castells 2000, Urry 2000) and upon which it was originally predicated. Others have questioned whether the concept of the social was ever adequate to describe the development and existence of the modern world (e.g. Latour 1993b). It has also been suggested that the social was always some kind of a simulacrum (Baudrillard 1983). Another slant has been offered by those who argue that the notion of the social was itself some kind of a historical, discursive, if not social, construction (e.g. Rose 1996). Some of the major concerns which animate such debates over the status of society and the social are evident in the following:

> While our political, professional, moral and cultural authorities still speak happily of "society", the very meaning and ethical salience of this term is under question as "society" is perceived as dissociated into a variety of ethical and cultural communities with incompatible allegiances and incommensurable obligations. (Rose 1996, 353)

There is a mixture of empirical and theoretical concerns over the very reality of society. As a concept and as a word it still has much currency and force and it would be naïve to suggest that it should be jettisoned and pronounced dead, theoretically and practically. There is a requirement to reapproach the very notion of society and the social. However, the very meaning and legacy of the term "society" makes such reanalyses problematic.

> One further issue that this raises concerns what we might call the nature of social edges, of how to think through what happens when social processes meet, and with how they are traversed. To use the terminology of "society" criticised in the last chapter, how should we conceptualise through metaphor where one society stops, how do we know that it has stopped, what is over the edge, what is the nature of non-society and what is society's "other"? (Urry 2000, 48)

In his attempt to develop a theoretical framework which can account for the novel complexity of societies which are no longer like those supposedly stable societies in relation to which social theory arose, Urry finds it hard to abandon the force of the term "society" but now reduces it to some kind of metaphor. The point of the metaphor is to account for that which both is and is not a society and thereby demarcates the lines of mobility which exceed the static conception of societies as nation-states. This, however, creates a bit of a muddle; it invokes the term "society" as a metaphor to explain that which might once have been a society but now exists differently. Rather than elucidating the contemporary character of societies, the reliance upon metaphor seems to disavow, not clarify, precisely what it tries to explain.

For Whitehead, this indicates that the premises and assumptions which inform discussions of the character and status of the social and society have led to contradictions and incoherence. There is a need for an investigation of the concept of both society and the social. This chapter will, very briefly, outline the notion of the social as developed in classical social theory in order to situate the conceptual concerns and legacies of this debate; in doing so it will also outline the notion of the individual as conceived within such sociality. The discussion will then turn to Whitehead's description of societies as consisting of those enduring entities which make up the world but which are not predicated on the human or the social realm. This will not be to "solve" the problem of the concept of society but it will throw fresh light on the manner of the construction of the concept of the social. The second half of the chapter will then return to the notion of subjectivity, and Whitehead's specific understanding of this term, in order to develop an account of the interrelation of subjectivity and sociality which might evade the problematic disjunctions between the individual and society and between structures and agents. Before proceeding, it may be worth outlining the general argument or position which the rest of the chapter will attempt to substantiate. This will give a taste of both the critical analysis and the conceptual construction for which the chapter aims.

Since its inception in the early nineteenth century, social theory has looked at the relations between people, and the changing forms of these in industrial societies; it has taken such relations as comprising the basis of sociality. This is, perhaps, quite understandable, but it has misconstrued the status of that which comprises such sociality as it prioritized human forms of relations as explanatory of all other forms of sociality. In this respect there is an irreducible emphasis on the social as a solely human affair. This limited conception of the social sedimented the gap between science and social theory in that the former was viewed as that which dealt primarily with things rather than relations. More importantly, any relations between things were to be seen as different in kind from relations between humans. The point to be made is that the associations between humans which are assumed to be indicative of the specific concerns, objects and subjects of sociology were a limited and limiting abstraction. The misrecognition of the status of this abstraction has had severe consequences as witnessed by contemporary debates over "the end of the social" as these are based upon an assumption of the death of that which was only ever a partial element of the wider field of sociality.

The Birth of the Social

It would be unwise to insist or even suggest that all contemporary social theorists think of the social in the terms bestowed upon us by Durkheim, Weber and Marx. Yet, the writings of this trio do constitute important elements of social theory's culture of thought and describe moments and modes of conceptualization within which and through which contemporary thought still moves. The following brief outlines are intended as indications of a tone of thought which might be recognized even if not fully subscribed to by current commentators. This is not intended as a complete description of the birth of the concept of the social; the aim is to identify the prevalent notions of sociality which run through social theory and to outline the problematic status that this sets up for thinking about the relation of the individual to such sociality. This will set the scene for the later discussions of Whitehead's concepts of the social and of sociality, and of the relation of subjectivity to these twin concepts.

The strangeness of the challenge which Durkheim offered nineteenth-century thought is often underestimated. His continuing advocacy of his primary statement that 'social phenomena, although immaterial, are nevertheless real things, the proper objects of scientific study' (Durkheim 1964, lvii) and that such social facts 'have a nature of their own' (Durkheim 1964, lviii), tends to blind us to the very peculiarity of his claim, namely that the social is *immaterial*, yet real. Furthermore, he is clear that the social has a nature of its own. Social reality is, by definition, as real as the natural but is distinct from it. The immateriality of the social does not preclude investigation of it, as its effects are as real as those of the natural world.

Sociology is a science of the unseen; a strange beast indeed. Whilst Durkheim shifted his emphasis with regard to the status of collective representations as constituting such social facts, it is still the case that this unseen, causal sociality is one that proceeds utterly from humans yet, once established, moulds the individuality of the humans which inhabit (or produce) such collective representations. On this view, the humans of a society are utterly human creations as their individuality is premised solely on the inhabitation of a space and time which is instantiated within the effective operations of the sociality of collective representations.

There is an interesting tension within the work of Durkheim as witnessed by his notion of the duality of human nature (e.g. Durkheim 2008 [1915], 16–17; see also Lukes 1992, 432–4). This tension expresses the very problematic which Durkheim's all-encompassingly human version of sociality produces. As the social is only ever and immediately human, it prioritizes the unseen immaterial aspect of existence – the social, over what would normally be taken as the true reality – nature. It is important to note here that there is not a strict corollary between the two terms 'social' and 'nature'. The former has an adjectival aspect to it whilst the latter is a substantive noun. However, it would seem that both Durkheim, and readings of Durkheim, have precisely taken the social as substantive rather than as a description of a mode of existence. In this respect, there is a hypostasization of the social which belies its descriptive character. As will be seen later, Whitehead is extremely clear in his distinction between the noun-based substantive notion of society and the adjectival description of the social as indicative of a form of relation.

The work of Weber, by contrast, seeks not to substantiate the social. He emphasizes the process, the activity of the social through the notion of social action. 'By "social" action is meant an action in which the meaning intended by the agent or agents involves a relation to *another* person's behaviour' (Weber 1978, 7; emphasis in original). Here sociality is not to be envisaged as some kind of substratum but as a kind of activity. What makes this activity social is the relation between the agent, another agent and their interrelated behaviour. Sociality, once again, but in a very different manner from that envisaged by Durkheim, is utterly human. It is constituted in and through the complexity of relations between human actors who, by virtue of their status as meaning-giving animals, are to be credited as conscious agents. As discussed in the previous chapter, it is clear that Weber is indebted to the German neo-Kantian school for his positing of humans as those specific entities which, amongst all creation, are able to grant meaning and value to their thoughts, actions, life and the world. And it is this debt which establishes the different mode by which sociality is rendered as entirely human without being as substantive as it is in the work of Durkheim.

Although not always seen as a social theorist who was interested in the social in the same manner as Durkheim or Weber, and despite the competing characterizations of his work, it is clear that Marx had a clear conception of the operation of the social which also has its influential legacy. In his later works, and especially in *Capital* (Marx 1990), the social is presented as that arena wherein humans manifest their specific mode of interrelation within different forms of society. Hence, within capitalism it is the commodity *form*[1] which takes precedent.

> It thus becomes evident that because the objectivity of commodities as values is the purely "social existence" of these things, it can only be expressed through the whole range of their social relations; consequently the form of their value must possess social validity. (Marx 1990, 159)

It is striking how many times Marx uses the term "social" here in order to account for the very specificity of the form of society which is capitalism. There is some similarity between this rendering of the concept of the "social" with the one found in the work of Durkheim, in particular, but also in Weber, insofar as the social is rendered as utterly human and as inherently distinct from the material. As Marx puts it elsewhere:

> The commodity-form, and the value-relation of the products of labour within which it appears, have absolutely no connection with the physical nature of the commodity and the material (*dinglich*)[2] relations arising out of this. It is nothing but the definite social relation between men themselves which assumes here, for them, the fantastic form of a relation between things. (Marx 1990, 165)

Whilst it might be possible to render Marx's account as one which is able to account for the very materiality of the social relations, and the sociality of material relations which are imbued in commodities, this is not the line which has been taken within much of traditional sociological theory. Instead there has been a tendency to subsume Marx's notion of the social as equivalent in kind, even if different in quality, to those of Durkheim and Weber. That is to say, it is an utterly human affair, distinct from the world of physical nature and of the thing-like (*dinglich*) relations between natural objects.[3]

To bring things a little more up to date, this distinction between modes of material reality is also evident in Althusser in his discussions of the thorny problem of the question of the relationship of the individual to the social in Marx's work, a position which has often (though incorrectly) been envisaged as one which almost eradicates the level of agency which Weber later wants to reassert. One aspect of Althusser's attempt to solve this problem of the relation of the individual to its society, and the need to overcome the notion of the social as simply a human affair, is to grant a materiality to ideology insofar as 'an ideology always exists in an apparatus, and its practice, or practices. This existence is material' (Althusser 1984, 40). However, Althusser then goes on to distinguish between such "modes" of materiality: 'the material existence of the ideology in an apparatus and its practices does not have the same modality as the material existence of a paving-stone or a rifle' (Althusser 1984, 40). This distinction between levels of materiality becomes especially problematic within Althusser's elaboration of the place of the subject within his scheme. Following the Durkheimian emphasis on the social as external to, and yet constitutive of the individual, Althusser explains subjectivity in terms of its instantiation through ideology. Hence: *the category of the subject is only constitutive of all ideology insofar as all ideology has the function (which defines it) of "constituting" concrete individuals as subjects* (Althusser 1984, 45; emphasis in original). Thus, although Althusser does discuss the relationship between materiality and subjectivity and thereby suggests a concept of sociality which is not solely predicated on the human realm, he does so at a level of materiality which is divorced from the "physical" modes of matter of "paving-stones or rifles". This engagement with materiality is, thereby, limited to addressing only those modes of matter which are tied up with human subjectivity. This, once again, reasserts the primacy of human relations for defining and understanding sociality. Overall, the point remains the same. Divergent writers in nineteenth-century social theory, as well as their subsequent interpreters and commentators have tended to posit sociality as a purely human affair. This has had some major consequences for the culture of thought of modernity. It has made it nigh on impossible for social theory to talk about material things. It has rendered the relation between such sociality and the individual and subjects which populate it, problematic. It has divorced nature and society, the natural and the social. The following account of Whitehead's concepts of societies and sociality will attempt to offer a fresh perspective on these concepts and their possible deployment within contemporary social theory.

Sociology and Sociality – Defining the Terms

Within Whitehead's texts there is only one lengthy treatment of the topic and concept of sociology and that is to be found in Part 1 of *Adventures of Ideas* (AI). Yet, whilst this section is titled 'Sociological' (the others being 'Cosmological', 'Philosophical' and 'Civilization'), it would scarcely be recognized as contributing to the canon of sociological thinking as usually envisaged. Instead it reads like a rather specific or even peculiar version of the history of ideas, depending on your standpoint. It is not clear how far Whitehead followed the development of the discipline of sociology, a discipline which rose to prominence concurrently with his own life span – 1861–1947 (he therefore "overlaps" with two of sociology's founders namely Durkheim, 1858–1917, and Weber, 1864–1920). However, he does discuss societies, the social, and sociology across a range of his texts and he intends a very particular sense to all of these terms.

In Whitehead's post-1920 texts, the two in which the terms "sociology" and "sociological" receive most attention are: *Symbolism. Its Meaning and Effect* (SYM) and *Adventures of Ideas* (AI). Here they have very specific roles to play in Whitehead's lexicon.[4] Whitehead was a very precise thinker and a very precise manipulator of language and throughout these texts he uses two pairs of words which, although clearly related and often used interchangeably by others, are, for Whitehead, to be granted specific and precise roles. The most important point to be made, and to be insisted upon, is that Whitehead makes a sharp distinction between the noun *sociology* (and its associated adjective *sociological*) and the noun *society* (and its associated adjective *social*). This is not a distinction that he discusses in itself or upon which he himself comments. Yet, it is there within his writings and has implications for social theory which this chapter will attempt to draw out.

Briefly, for Whitehead, *societies* refer to the achievement of groups of entities, of any kind, in managing to cohere and endure and thus to constitute some kind of unity. The term *social* refers to the manner and milieu in which such endurance is gained. Rocks, stones, amoeba, books can, thus, be considered to be societies. 'I draw attention to this lowly form of society to dispel the notion that social life is a peculiarity of the higher organisms' (PR, 76). Whitehead thus immediately and absolutely refuses to partake in the nineteenth-century settlement whereby the social and sociality are envisaged as primarily a human affair, and human relations and interrelations are posited as the unquestioned and unquestionable model for such notions. For Whitehead, such a limitation of perspective, whilst understandable, is both regrettable and unwarranted. Just as he extends experience so that it is to be seen as integral to all entities, Whitehead extends sociality to all enduring entities. Humans and human relations may well constitute exempla of such relations but there is no need to found such relationality on the specific and limited examples of human interrelation. (As will be seen later, Whitehead uses the same procedure in his extension of subjectivity to all entities; another maximization[5] of a concept.)

So, the term "sociology", although rarely used by Whitehead, refers only to the manner and mode of the endurance (or otherwise) of groups of entities which involve the inter-relations of humans, as opposed to nonhuman societies which are simply "social" rather than "sociological". On one occasion he mentions 'the sociology of the Western World' (AI, 10). On another he uses "sociology" in order to describe elements of Plato's work: 'his sociology is derived from his conception of what man [sic] can be' (AI, 13). However, Whitehead much prefers the term *sociological*, which he uses when discussing the manner, concerns, and modes in which specific human societies manage or fail to endure. For example: 'In neither case did the leaders intend the sociological effects which followed from their efforts' (AI, 35); that is, their effects in the "humanly" real world. Although these terms can occasionally incorporate the usual sense of sociology and sociological, it is important to note that they have a different slant within Whitehead's texts, which describes the historical and actual state of specific forms of mentalities, institutions, things, events, and modes of life of human societies. His notion includes more than many social theorists might allow. Also, it should be noted that Whitehead refuses to develop an abstract sociological theory of how such (human) societies function, as no such theory can be adequate if it takes human societies as the starting point. So, the important point to stress, and to repeat, is that any discussions of sociology and of the sociological (at the human level) can only be embarked upon after accounting for the wider notions of society and the social which characterize all existence, for Whitehead.

Whitehead on Societies

As has been seen, Whitehead's theory of actual entities is designed to account for the reality of 'stubborn fact' (PR, 129) within a universe which is characterized by continual process. As such, it is an abstract theory of the conditions of existence. It is therefore necessary for Whitehead to relate this high abstraction to the contemporary world. He needs to explain the existence of larger, longer-lasting elements within the universe, such as rocks, plants and mobile phones, as well as that which is normally termed "human". In order to account for such entities he introduces the term society. The conditions for the existence of a society are as follows:

> (i) there is a common element of form illustrated in the definiteness of each of its included actual entities, and (ii) this common element of form arises in each member of the nexus by reason of the conditions imposed upon it by its prehensions of some other members of the nexus, and (iii) these prehensions impose the condition of reproduction by reason of their inclusion of positive feelings of that common form. (PR, 34)

As Debaise (2006, 139) points out, this form is not imposed from outside that society; these are not Platonic forms and a society does not fulfil a category defined prior to its existence. Rather, just as the manner in which an entity prehends helps to define what it is, so a society is an outcome of a mutual mode of prehension by a collection of actual entities. And crucially, this is not a limited one-off prehension, it is a mode of prehension which is carried on and through the society. 'A minimal definition of the concept of society could be found in that of duration' (Debaise 2006, 136). Whitehead's approach is to see those objects that endure in the world, be they rocks, dogs, cheeseboards or galaxies, as societies in his specific sense of the word. And this entails that it should not be asked what *is* an object? (or what *is* a society?) for this is to frame the question incorrectly. Existence insofar as it 'is', is some kind of a duration of a manner of becoming which will be enabled by and will rely upon that in which it consists. As Debaise makes clear, it is one aspect of Whitehead's specific understanding and deployment of existence, that it involves both having (in the sense of possession) and holding together (Debaise 2006, 145). So, again, such societies endure but the reason that they do is not because they conform to a specific pattern, type, or ideal (a degree of complexity of the division of labour, for example). Rather, they endure as long as they manage to ensure and keep their mutuality together, in a specific manner. 'Each task of creation is a social effort' (PR, 223).

Hence: 'For Whitehead it is always societies that we study. All is sociology' (Stengers 2002, 363): as long as it is remembered that such societies are neither human creations nor are they limited to humans. They explicate the manner in which aspects of existence manage to cohere and endure. Such coherence and endurance is predicated on the interrelation of that society with its environment: the continual feeding of one off the other; the novelty that this implies for such endurance; the interconnections and processes between the living and nonliving elements of that society and its milieu. This is what Stengers refers to as a 'culture of interstices' (Stengers 2002, 367). With reference to traditional sociological theory, this suggests that there can be no theory of human society in abstract which would apply to all societies, either historically or at present, as societies cut across the human and nonhuman realm. There is no point in trying to define human society in terms of the interdependence of its parts, or in terms of a necessary evolution or progress, or through the development of rationality, or in terms of class conflict or economic laws. There is, according to Whitehead, no necessary or self-sufficient reason why one society should exist or follow another (PR, 46–7). Societies are their own reason, just as actual entities are (this is a result of the ontological principle, PR, 18–19). On this view the task of sociological theory is neither to predict nor to simply collect data on societies, but to investigate the reason and manner of the existence and endurance of a given (human) society. Again, such societies are not to be envisaged in terms of, for example, British society between 1918 and 1948, subcultures such as punks, mods, emo, death-metal, etc., or diverse communities within a society. For Whitehead, such labels are really abstractions. Real societies are of a different kind of status and importance. One intriguing example that Whitehead gives of a society is that of knowledge of the Greek language in an individual human.

> For example, the life of man [sic] is a historic route of actual occasions which in a marked degree…inherit from each other. That set of occasions, dating from his first acquirement of the Greek language and including all those occasions up to his loss of any adequate knowledge of that language, constitutes a society in reference to knowledge of the Greek language. (PR, 89–90)

This surprising, even perplexing, example indicates the extent to which Whitehead is challenging usual conceptions of society and the social. Societies exist, they are real, they endure, they pass. Furthermore, they can be delimited and identified. But they are not passive, static, material objects and nor are they simply the collective or individual representations, ideas, or orientations to norms and values of an individual located within a wider "society". A society incorporates localized facts, such as Greek grammar and vocabulary, which are sustained and maintained in a certain locale and over a certain period of time. They also have a manner of existence which comprises a unity for that society. Greek is spoken often or rarely, with or without an accent, in shops, streets, universities or museums. Such a society is a real thing but it is not an object, as usually conceived.

Sociality is not something which is added on, it is a necessary element of the materiality of anything which exists. This applies to all individuality, to everything – to *every* thing:

> Every actual entity is in its nature essentially social; and this in two ways. First, the outlines of its own character are determined by the data which its environment provides for its process of feeling. Secondly, these data are not extrinsic to the entity; they constitute that display of the universe which is inherent in the entity. (PR, 203)

At its core, Whitehead's notion of the social and of sociality is an attempt to describe how that which comes to exist does so by combining elements which were not previously combined. Sociality is the process of incorporating elements of the environment into an individual, thereby changing both the environment and the individual. (This has important consequences for understandings of the interrelation of the individual and the environment which will be taken up later in this chapter.) Whitehead's notion of sociality has been taken up by Latour (2005) in his account of a "sociology of associations" where he directly compliments Whitehead's extension of the concept of society beyond its usual human limits. 'If we could retain this vastly expanded meaning of society, then we could again understand what Tarde meant when he said that "everything is a society and that all things are society"' (Latour 2005, 218).

That sociality is implicit within all existence and is not limited to the human level has clear ethical and political implications. One thing must partake of other things to be constituted as individual. Individuality presupposes commonality. The relation of the individual to society and of society to the individual is not one of internality and externality. Neither of these constitute discrete units, nor even make sense, without the other. Society is not derived from humans and humans are not derived from their specific society. We are neither creators of our social world nor puppets of an all powerful and indoctrinating sociality. A specific example of Whitehead's approach to societies and the social will be given later on in an analysis of the public-private split, as will further implications of Whitehead's concept of sociality. But before proceeding to this, a detour will be made through Whitehead's own discussions of the status and remit of sociology in the sense of it referring to human society alone.

The Individual and Society

> ...our traditional doctrines of sociology, of political philosophy, of the practical conduct of large business, and of political economy are largely warped and vitiated by the implicit assumption of a stable unchanging social system. With this assumption it is comparatively safe to base reasoning upon a simplified edition of human nature... For example, we can all remember our old friend, the economic man. (AI, 118–9)

Influential traditions within the social sciences, sociology included, have made much of their models of humans as either rational or based on consciousness, or as intentional, or meaning-producing, or value-oriented, or as simply choice-making. For Whitehead, to start with such conceptions, such abstractions, is to start from the wrong place, and it is to oversimplify. Human society is not a product or effect of human nature. Human nature (insofar as such a concept has any legitimacy) is to be understood as a product of a society which itself is not solely human. That is to say, social stability is produced at a different level to that which sociologists and other social theorists normally assume. Human society is not simply the human replication of the norms, values, traditions of the past. Nor is human society to be defined as a substratum of social facts, economic systems or cultural values within which and in relation to which individuals are socialized and through which their identity as an individual is constituted.

Thus the very division or conception of the individual as distinct from society (or of a disjunction between structure and agency) is, for Whitehead, a misnomer which misrepresents the character of existence. There are not individuals *and* society. There are societies which are individuals. Admittedly, such societies inhere and cohere in a wider environment, but to conceptualize such a situation in terms of a separate structure or realm of existence is to fall back into old categories of our culture of thought and to rely upon a Newtonian concept of individualized objects with only external relations to each other. One of the main points of Whitehead's philosophy is to challenge such an approach and to describe the world as an integrally processual and eventful milieu in which the grasping or prehending of the world, in specific ways, constitutes the real potentiality and facticity of existence, and also constitutes the manner of endurance of societies.

It might seem reasonable to ask, at this point, as to exactly what methodology Whitehead would advocate for sociology in order to investigate, challenge, or critique common sense? Yet, Whitehead's work would not appear to offer any easy answer to such a question.[6] The solutions to our (theoretical) problems are not easy to come by. And we should not look for or expect them to come to us ready-made. Whitehead's work points to the manner in which elements of history, science, concepts, emotions, animals, bodies, farms, satisfaction, literature, steam engines, poverty, quarks, decisions, operas, racism, rocks, electrons and galaxies, are all immanently connected. But he does not tell the sociologist how to identify such interrelations or to investigate or report them. However, he does point us toward a framework for thinking, researching and writing which is not constrained by the shackles of envisaging the universe as separated into a variety of dualisms such as: objects and subjects; agents and structures; gods and puppets; rational action and determination; necessity and choice. For, it can be argued that all of these dualisms proceed from the bifurcation of nature. Yet, rather like the existence of a society, the reasons and manner of the coming-to-be of each dualism (e.g. structure-agency, fact-value, body-language), their ability to endure, as well as their consequences and implications, will each have their own reasons (again as a result of the "ontological principle", PR, 18–19). It is, hence, an understanding of the specific construction of each dualism which is needed. Each discipline must trace the character of its dualisms, for Whitehead has not swept them all away in advance, he has not provided a magical, logical solution (a belief in such things is itself a symptom of a falling back into the bifurcation of nature, Stengers 2008a, 98–100). One such dualism might be that of "the public and the private".

'The sociological imagination enables us to grasp history and biography and the relations between the two within society. That is its task and promise'

(Wright Mills 1967, 6). For Wright Mills this involves, or should involve, not only developing accounts and understandings of the wider sweep of economic, cultural and historical change, but also their implications within the real lives of real people who are both subject to, and the acting subjects of, history. Many of the works of the traditional sociological canon might be claimed to fall within the scope of such a definition. Marx on how historical changes in production elicit new kinds of lives – the real lives of the new nineteenth-century wage-labourers, for example. Durkheim on the new kinds of individual enabled by the historical shift to a society based on (or created by) a qualitatively more complex division of labour. Weber on the development of the new mindset associated with Calvinist Protestantism and its emphasis on rational planning, as well as the influence of such a cultural shift on the development of Western capitalism. Du Bois on the historical developments and consequences of slavery and "freedom" and their legacy for the real lives of individuals in twentieth- and twenty-first-century USA (Du Bois 1994 [1903]). De Beauvoir on the social, political and existential consequences and possibilities of the becoming of woman (de Beauvoir 1972 [1949]).

Wright Mills goes on to elaborate the need to distinguish between "personal troubles" and "public issues".

> A trouble is a private matter: values cherished by an individual are felt by him [sic] to be threatened. *Issues* have to do with… the ways in which various milieux overlap and interpenetrate to form the larger structure of social and historical life. An issue is a public matter: some value cherished by publics is felt to be threatened. (Wright Mills 1967, 8. Emphasis in original.)

This is not just a rephrasing of the old question of structure and agency which has dogged so much sociological thinking. The structure-agency debate involves the questions as to whether social structures (such as institutions or economic forces) determine, produce, or create living human subjects *or* whether it is active human subjects who, through their collective decisions, practices or actions, create, produce or imagine the institutions, economic conditions or social expectations which are taken to make up the social structure. As stated earlier, one crucial lesson to be drawn from Whitehead is that we cannot simply explain away all examples of the bifurcation of nature by a sweeping philosophical *fiat*. And the structure-agency problem is clearly an example of a dualism arising from the bifurcation of nature which concerns the distinction that is made between the lived experiences of individuals and their social and historical locale. It is telling that Wright Mills renders this discussion in terms of the private and the public for it suggests that there is a rift between these terms, and that it is the task of sociology, out of all the disciplines, to breach or shore up this rift. Again, this is not the solution that a Whiteheadian sociologist would offer. The first step must surely be to rethink the private-public distinction and what is involved in the problem.

The distinction between the public and the private is one that, like sociology, is often associated with modernity. That is to say, the specific version of the distinction between the public and the private that is played out in contemporary society only came about with modernity. 'Before the 19th Century, the realm close to the self was not thought to be a realm for the expression of unique or distinctive personality; the private and the individual were not yet wedded' (Sennett 1977, 89). The model of the public-private split, that still survives today, was established, it is often argued, with the rise of capitalism. New relations of production, new employment practices, and the establishment of factories, led to the production of a new mode and sphere of social existence. The production of goods shifted from the small-scale domestic (or community based) level to the large-scale, anonymous level, which occurred away from the living-place of those involved in such production. People go *out* to work, in factories. All this helped establish a new conception of what constituted the public realm. Concomitantly, the dwelling-place becomes, in distinction to the world of public work, the private world and hence the modern notion of domesticity was created. This has implications at the level of class composition and stratification and serious implications in terms of gender relations. 'The bourgeois family was idealized… the family became a refuge' (Sennett 1977, 20); though this became more true for men than for women.

It is precisely the distinction between the public and the private, as established with the coming of modernity, that produces the invisibility of the domestic sphere. As with many dualisms, there are exceptions. But there are also connotations and consequences that go beyond this. For example: the linking of the private realm to the home, cleanliness, morality and women; of the public realm to work, education, pollution, immorality and men. To pass from one to the other would seem to be the prerogative of men who have equal access to both. The reason they have such access is predicated, historically, on the very distinction between the public and private which entails that women must not have equal access; they have to be associated with the private for the whole conceptual and practical machine to work. It is also has a cross-sectional relation to the notion of structure and agency, in terms of limiting what kinds of agents are related in what ways to what kinds of structures.

Some of this analysis obviously chimes with already existing sociological accounts. However, what is often missing in such analyses is the notion of process. There is still a gap between the public and the private, between the individual and society, both conceptually and practically. That is to say, either one or the other becomes the focus of sociological study – for example, the personal lives and documents of an individual (as representative of a group) or of a small, specific group, viewed as a self-contained entity. Yet, the study of the wider historical sweep is, ontologically and conceptually, divorced from such an individual. This is not to say that attempts have not been made to suture the individual into the wider social explanation or to descend from the peak of the wider social structure to explain the motives of an individual or small group. But the very conceptual starting point inhibits, indeed prevents, the successful reconciliation of these two camps. And, according to Whitehead, no amount of theoretical sophistication will manage to bring the two back together. Instead, what is needed is a recognition of the problem itself; that is, that the dualism of the public-private will always echo and resound with the problems associated with the bifurcation of nature until it is recognized that they are both elements of the same process. As de Beauvoir says of the distinction between male and female (de Beauvoir 1972 [1949], 14–29), there is no symmetry between the terms public and private. One always takes priority or subsumes the other, to a greater or lesser extent. In this way, studies of the personal are not seen as equal or equivalent to studies of the public. The distinction between them is loaded. The public inhabits the realm of the objective, the impersonal, the major, the transcendent – it is thereby consequential; the personal inhabits the realm of the subjective, the private, the minor, the immanent – it is thereby subsequent.[7]

Whitehead also discusses the distinction between the public and the private, but his analysis does not immediately map onto the distinction as usually conceived and as discussed so far in this chapter. For him, the public and the private refer to the different moments in the becomings and objectifications of actual entities or societies, through prehensions and should not be seen as some kind of immediate description of the humanly social world.

> The operations of all organisms are directed *from* antecedent organisms and *to* the immediate organism. They are "vectors" in that they convey the many things into the constitution of the single superject. The creative process is rhythmic: it swings from the publicity of many things to the individual privacy; and it swings back from the private individual to the publicity of the objectified individual. (PR, 151. Emphasis in original.)

In the usual accounts, the separation of private and public into two distinct realms hinges upon the delimitation of space as prior to the instantiation of entities. Instead, Whitehead sees entities as instantiating space; the privacy and publicity of prehensions are moments in this ongoing process. The public, for Whitehead, is an "extensive continuum" (PR, 61–82), which presents itself as that set of completed actual entities from which a novel actual entity may arise. The process of combining a certain number of prehensions into a unit creates a new subject, and it is this becoming which is "private". But this privacy is only a moment, and this moment is that which constitutes its subjectivity. Once this moment is over it becomes public and is now a possible datum for novel actual entities. 'Prehensions have public careers, but they are born privately' (PR, 290). There is, therefore, no solid interiority to the subject as usually defined; for once subjectivity is achieved it becomes a public fact. 'All origination is private. But what has been thus originated, publicly pervades the world' (PR, 310).

Through this description of prehensions Whitehead also develops a more general account of the meaning and status of extension and solidarity which links his discussion to a range of questions relevant to sociology, such as: What is it that links the world, that makes us both individuals and yet a part of a wider field? How are individuals linked to society? Can public issues and private troubles be reconciled? Attempts to answer such questions have been limited in so far as they have seen the private and the public as separate realms. Either the interiority of the subject takes priority in producing the individual, through autonomous self-creation of the will or reason, or the (social) world takes absolute priority and "we" are mere products of our culture, our language, or our genes (which in a bizarre conceptual twist are alien to us as subjects!). For example, in terms of gender, we are supposedly constituted as men and women either because biology (or God, or some such) makes us so; or because our society (or our culture) makes us so (Stengers 2008a, 93). And, in the end, it amounts to much the same thing as both are external and prior to us as individuals. For Whitehead, these are more consequences of dualisms associated with the bifurcation of nature. They result from a misrecognition of the very character of existence.

The prehensive aspect of existence (see Chapter Two) thus comes to the fore in enabling a reconceptualization of the public and the private. 'The theory of prehensions is founded upon the doctrine that there are no concrete facts which are merely public, or merely private' (PR, 290). This immediately differentiates Whitehead's position from the usual distinction within much thinking, philosophy, psychology and sociology, namely that there is a fundamental distinction between the objective (public) facts of the world and the subjective (private) experiences of such a world. Rather than seeing them as dichotomous, Whitehead differentiates between the public and the private as moments in the passage of prehensions from subject to subject. Exactly what Whitehead envisages by such a subject and its relation to individual (human) subjectivity will be returned to shortly.[8] For the moment it should be clear that prehensions are that which express how contemporary existents are constituted through relations which are not limited to such existence. They go beyond their implication in any particular existent to become an element within another and another and so on. They are constantly iterated within actuality but are not limited to any instance of it. According to Whitehead, the very character of existence involves, relies upon and creates interrelation. This interrelation constitutes extension, and it constitutes the world. The manner in which it does this, in terms of the public-private distinction, makes it important to realize that there is no qualitative distinction between the two. They do not involve two separate or different forms of relation. They are different aspects or moments of the same relations. It is in this sense that external relations are internal relations.

If the distinction between the public and the private leads to the necessity to describe the interrelated character of all existence, as just discussed, then there is also a need to analyse how this interrelation occurs not simply from moment to moment, in the passage from the public to the private, but in the enduring entities which constitute the world as encountered by humans and in which humans come to be. This is, or should be, one of the tasks of sociology.

Subjectivity and Individuality

It will be clear from previous analyses that Whitehead's concept of subjectivity will differ markedly from those held by most within social theory. Having demonstrated the specific and productive challenge that Whitehead makes to usual conceptions of society and the social, as well as the notion of the public and the private, this chapter will now turn to a related aspect of this field of thought, namely the status of subjectivity (and by implication, its relation to the social). The most striking aspect of Whitehead's departure is that he refuses to limit subjectivity to the human body, mind, rendering of concepts or discursive production. The confining and confinement of subjectivity to the human realm is, according to Whitehead, a prejudicial and unjustified procedure. If experience, and the experience of subjects is the primary element of his philosophy then this will entail that all items of experience must be rendered as subjects. In this way he is able to avoid the bifurcation of nature, in that there is no separation between the dead matter of science and the live subjective elements of the human realm. Instead, there is the process of existence which is solely constituted by the experiences of subjects. For some this may seem a little strange – that he envisages subjectivity as a maximized concept which suffuses the most significant and the most insignificant elements of the universe. Whitehead's response would be, perhaps, that it is stranger to assert, as does our modern culture of thought, that there is an utter disjunction between the internally related and self-sufficient objects which comprise the world and those subjects which magically and subjectively experience these objects. In this sense, the granting of subjectivity to all elements is less peculiar than assuming and retaining an unjustified primary division between two incompatible worlds.

Yet, there is still a requirement for Whitehead to relate his notion of subjectivity to more common-place understandings of the actions and lives of humans. Indeed, this is an ongoing concern of Whitehead from *Concept of Nature* at least, and the task of responding to this led him to move from an exposition of the character of perception to the description of the experiences of that which is disclosed in such perception (see Stengers 2002, 103, 221). In one of his most famous passages, Whitehead gives the example of the Ancient Egyptian obelisk known as "Cleopatra's Needle" which was originally constructed in Egypt in approximately 1450 BC and moved to the Embankment on the Thames in London in 1877, during Whitehead's lifetime; it was not an aspect of London when he was child (CN, 166). This seemingly permanent object is the occasion for one of Whitehead's most descriptive rejections of the concept of permanent self-identical items of matter and his alternative description of the process of existence and the status of human perception within this eventful world.

> As you are walking along the Embankment you suddenly look up and say, "Hello, there's the Needle." In other words, you recognise it. You cannot recognise an event; because when it is gone, it is gone. You may observe another event of analogous character, but the actual chunk of the life of nature is inseparable from its unique occurrence. But a character of an event can be recognised. (CN, 169)

Human perception is one element amongst the events of existence. There is no enduring subjectivity which enables or subtends human perceptions. Human perception is simply one experience of the world, within the world. It is an event like any other which goes to make up the world. Whitehead's discussion here is clearly set out as an attempt to make sense of the world and of human perception with regard to Einstein's work on relativity (see CN, 164–5). Just as Whitehead insists that the notion of an enduring subject needs to be given up, so does the notion of an enduring object which subtends such perceptions. Cleopatra's needle which Whitehead chose as an example precisely because it appears so weighty and enduring an object is, in actuality, implicated in a whole series of materially, historically, politically and environmentally significant events. It was not always what and where it appears to be and nor will it be. Indeed it is not what and where most people think it is now.

The static timeless element in the relation of Cleopatra's Needle to the Embankment is a pure illusion generated by the fact that for purposes of daily intercourse its emphasis is needless. What it comes to is this: Amidst the structure of events which form the medium within which the daily life of Londoners is passed we know how to identify a certain stream of events which maintain permanence of character, namely the character of being the situations of Cleopatra's Needle. Day by day and hour by hour we can find a certain chunk in the transitory life of nature and of that chunk we say, "There is Cleopatra's Needle." If we define the Needle in a sufficiently abstract manner we can say that it never changes. But a physicist who looks on that part of the life of nature as a dance of electrons, will tell you that daily it has lost some of its molecules and gained others…Thus the question of change in the Needle is a mere matter of definition. The more abstract your definition, the more permanent the Needle. (CN, 166–7)

The notion of Cleopatra's Needle as a weighty, permanent, physical thing is an abstraction. What is really real is its experiences and the experiences of those subjects which encounter it in the events which constitute their everyday lives. This includes but is not limited to, premised, or reliant upon the experience of those (human) Londoners and tourists who pass by it, with or without any care or concern for it. These experiences constitute the subjectivity of those events which comprise such experiences. This might suggest that Whitehead's conception of the universe and of existence is one of mere flux, flow and becoming. But this would be to overstate the case greatly. He is certainly attempting to express the utter relativity of the world (nodding to Einstein as he does) but this is not to make of him and his conceptions a simple celebration of the passing of time, things and subjects. Each event has an extension, a solidity, which constitutes the 'stubborn fact' (PR, xiv and passim) of existence. Yet, there is more to it than this. That which enables Whitehead to account for the individuality, importance and matter of such experiences, and to enable them to be differentiated and consequential rather than mere irrelevant moments of the passage of a meaningless world, is his insistence that purpose is inherent in all such events, in all moments of experience, in all items of subjectivity. This he introduces through his notions of 'subjective form' (PR, 19 and passim) and "subjective aim" which go to make up the concrete subjective experiences which constitute the real facts, the real events, of the world.

Thus an actual entity, on its subjective side, is nothing else than what the universe is for it, including its own reactions. The reactions are the subjective forms of the feelings, elaborated into definiteness through stages of process. An actual entity achieves its own unity by its determinate feelings respecting every item of the datum. Every individual objectification in the datum has its perspective defined by its own eternal objects with their own relevance compatible with the relevance of other objectifications. Each such objectification, and each such complex of objectifications, in the datum is met with a correspondent feeling, with its determinate subjective form, until the many become one experience, the satisfaction. The philosophies of substance presuppose a subject which then encounters a datum, and then reacts to the datum. The philosophy of organism presupposes a datum which is met with feelings, and progressively attains the unity of a subject. But with this doctrine, "superject" would be a better term than "subject." (PR, 154–5)

The manner of existence, the character of an event, its quality, its adverbial status, are integral to the formation, individuality, and actuality of all that exists (see Chapters Two and Four). There are no dead facts or objects out there waiting to be experienced. There are only the experiences of the world. Carbon molecules are not simple abstract entities but are always implicated in their existence, in a specific mode, for example, as diamonds, coal or carbon. The "quality" of their existence may be miniscule to human eyes but it is there. It is not to anthropomorphize to state that coal experiences warmness, or diamonds adamantineness, or charcoal flakiness, though it is to stretch language and thought beyond its normal bounds. The point is simply to acknowledge that that which experiences, and hence exists, always does so in a certain milieu and in a certain way. This "certain way" is integral to the full existence of that item, and is what grants it its character and its specificity. Thus its very subjective side is what makes a thing what it is amid the passage of relativity.

Subjective Aim

Insofar as the individuality of experiences, and the events which constitute subjectivity, are not a blind reaction to the past, this subjective aspect introduces aim, purpose and the troublesome notion of final cause all of which are inculcated in and expressed by each moment of subjectivity. For Whitehead, there is always novelty of reaction, and this indicates an aim at something different in the future. This aim at difference constitutes the operation of creativity, the production of novelty and the inherence of aim and purpose within all individuality. If there were no aim at the future and no purpose within subjectivity then the process of subjectivity would be no more than a reproduction of the past, it would only be an example of absolute efficient causation; the passing on of the world as it is now. This is not to deny the efficacy or operation of efficient causation in the world. Such causation is an element of existence (rendered in terms of "causal efficacy" – see Chapter Three) but science and positivism have overemphasized its role and neglected not only that of the body but also that of final causation.

Efficient causation expresses the transition from actual entity to actual entity; and final causation expresses the internal process whereby the actual entity becomes itself. There is the becoming of the datum, which is to be found in the past of the world; and there is the becoming of the immediate self from the datum. (PR, 150)

In other words, final causation and atomism are interconnected philosophical principles. (PR, 19)

With the rise of modern science (post-Galileo), the notion of nature or matter having in and of itself its own reason or purpose and at which it irrespectively aimed, that is, a final cause, was rejected and the concept of efficient cause came to the fore (see Fraser 2006). This abandoning of the Aristotelian concept and its theologically tainted siblings left science as the province of the explainer of the interrelations of inert and passive objects, as so explicitly advocated by Newton. The notion of any overarching purpose and aim was thereby, insofar as it were allowed, limited to the human realm in a fashion akin to the distinction between fact and value, as discussed in Chapter Four. Dewey, a contemporary and occasional commentator on Whitehead, puts it thus: 'purpose and contingency were alike relegated to the purely human and personal; nature was evacuated of qualities and became a homogenous mass' (Dewey 1958 [1925], 95). This is not to suggest that Dewey (or Whitehead) wish to return to some notion of ethereal final causes which exist separately from the material world and which draw the world ineluctably to its future. (Although it could perhaps be argued that the more extreme neo-Darwinian emphasis on "the selfish gene", for example, is witness to the irruption of an unrecognized attempt to return to such a severe version of the concept of "final cause"). Neither Whitehead nor Dewey is an advocate of such a fixed, separate realm of ineffable reasons, purposes or *telos*. However, they view the mechanistic version of science, which eliminates purpose from the world and instantiates efficient causation as dominant, as that which explains the movement, motion and reason of and for everything that happens, as both one-sided and mistaken. Such mechanisms merely take the generative aspect of the Aristotelian notion of final cause and re-place it within a different framework.

The view held – or implied – by some "mechanists", which treats an initial term as if it had an inherent generative force which it somehow emits and bestows upon its successors, is all of a piece with the view held by teleologists which implies that an end brings about its own antecedents. Both isolate an event from the history in which it belongs and in which it has its character. (Dewey 1958 [1925], 99–100)

That is to say, there is a misrecognition of the problem and status of cause and causation (see Chapter Three). By reducing nature to an inert and lifeless realm, mechanists have not rid themselves of the notion of generation, they have simply replicated the worst excesses of the deterministic element of old-fashioned teleologists who envisaged contemporary events and things as exempla of a wider pattern or plan which explained history, progress, and life. As opposed to such an outlook, both Whitehead and Dewey insist that both efficient and final causes must be located not in an exterior realm but as elements which make up the complex of historical, contemporary and future existence. In this respect, there are always ends and purposes implicated in all things and events. But such ends are temporary rather than absolutely final; they are expressions of the immediate concerns and aims of that which is experiencing and acting; they explain the manner or character of existence. Such "temporary-final" ends are not invented by humans, in the sense of being mere creations of their minds or value-oriented actions; aim and purpose are not to be considered as providing any such kind of overarching explanation. There are examples of purpose, ends, *telos*, but each of these is tied to specific occasions and objects and occurrences. Dewey refers to these particular purposes as "ends-in-view" which do exist but not as abstract, ideal ends comprising a separate, insubstantial realm.

> To a person building a house, the end-in-view is not just a remote and final goal to be hit upon after a sufficiently great number of coerced motions that have been duly performed. The end-in-view is a plan which is *contemporaneously* operative in selecting and arranging materials. (Dewey 1958 [1925], 373. Emphasis in original.)

Everything that occurs does so in relation to a historical and contemporary milieu which is "not of its choosing". The facticity of the historical comprises the realm of efficient causation. But the subjective response to this realm and the subjective aim at the future is both produced by and is productive of novelty. Such novel reactions are witness to the ingression of the future into the present and the role of immediate purpose as formative within the definiteness and actuality of immediate existence.

> In this sense, the future has objective reality in the present, but no formal actuality. For it is inherent in the constitution of the immediate, present actuality that a future will supersede it. Also conditions to which that future must conform, including real relationships to the present, are really objective in the immediate actuality. (PR, 215)
>
> The end-in-view is present at each stage of the process; it is present as the *meaning* of the materials used and acts done. (Dewey 1958 [1925], 374. Emphasis in original.)

This reintroduction of purpose, aim or teleology is not a recourse to outdated theology or Aristotle or bad metaphysics, but another way of challenging the fact-value distinction and is another aspect of Whitehead's refusing to allow nature to bifurcate. It also helps explain and emphasize the processual character of the subjective experiences which constitute the real things of the world. Whitehead's approach stresses that such subjectivity, such aims, purposes and ends are not solely located in the human realm. (This is also Dewey's position even though his texts have often been misinterpreted as granting a primacy to human interaction.)

Whitehead's insistence on the operation of aim and purpose within the world might, at first sight, seem problematic. Within recent social theory, teleology, purpose and the notion of final cause in terms of historical covering laws or quasi-biological explanations of the development of societies (as in Herbert Spencer and some renditions of functionalism) have been rejected wholesale. Instead, the notion of purpose has been envisaged as a creation and moment within the designs and desires of agential, conscious human subjects. On such a view, purpose is denied to the world as it smacks either of theological left-overs or scientific determinism. Whitehead's philosophy of organism is a stringent attempt to reconceptualize the notion of organisms and their inherent purposefulness. At first sight it might appear that there is a danger in his approach of advocating a form of socio-biology. However, Whitehead's notion of an organism is one which envisages such entities as neither completely living nor nonliving, "social" nor biological, material nor conceptual, but as indicative of the process whereby matter, potentiality and purpose come together to produce eventful moments of completely real existence. One major problem which might stall attempts to render this notion of the organism within social theory is a trepidation toward the implantation of biological "metaphors" in analyses of the social, especially since the demise of functionalism.

There are two main aspects to this problem which Whitehead overcomes. First, his notion of "organism" is not a metaphor; it is an attempt to produce a mode of thought which is able to describe the whole of reality without bifurcating nature into the living and nonliving, the material and conceptual, and so on. Second, the metaphor of biological organisms, so beloved of functionalism, was based on bad biology. The key terms it employed were homeostasis and equilibrium; it was, therefore, an inherently conservative approach which viewed existence (both natural and social) as a balancing act between self-contained entities which aimed for similarity and replication as opposed to novelty, vitality and change (see Shaviro 2009, 93–4). More recent moves within biology have undermined such homeostatic approaches where existence is viewed as an aim at unthinking reproduction and stability (see, for example, Kupiec and Sonigo 2000; Noble 2006). In doing so they elucidate those elements of developmental biology which reject the deterministic, atomistic assumptions of neo-Darwinism, in order to emphasize the active contribution and decisions made by cells, bacteria, organs in their interrelation with their environment. This mode of thought within the field of developmental biology takes its influence from two major twentieth-century figures in this area whose rejection of biological determinism is now seen as so fruitful, namely, Joseph Needham and C. H. Waddington. Significantly, both of these writers are explicit in the debt that they owe to Whitehead's philosophy of organism for enabling them to think beyond the limiting boundaries which the Newtonian concept of objects and relations forced upon biology through the dominance of physics and its methodology.[9] Not only do such intersections of critical analysis indicate the importance of Whitehead's work beyond the confines of social theory and toward the retexturing of all aspects of modernity's culture of thought, they also indicate the positive aspects of his attempt to reassert a nonreductionist notion of purpose within existence.

Conclusion

As suggested throughout this chapter, the work of Whitehead helps to reframe the discussion and debate over the "end of the social" by refiguring the very constitution of the social (and the individual). As has been seen, for Whitehead, sociality is inherent in all existence. As such, sociality is not limited to humans; indeed the very existence of human society presupposes a prior expression of nonhuman sociality. Furthermore, Whitehead has addressed some of the fundamental concerns and problems, both conceptual and practical, of sociological thinking. For him, social intercourse does not preclude the philosophical or scientific concepts of matter and individuality. The actual enduring entities (or societies) which comprise houses, farms, rocks, cells, factories, institutions, human bodies, are not excluded from the social. Unlike those who maintain that such material elements are the concern solely of the natural sciences, for Whitehead they must play an integral part in any full understanding of the world. And this is perhaps what Whitehead ultimately asks of sociology – that it renounce its claim to be able to explain the whole world in social terms, in order to be able to provide fuller accounts of the matters and concerns of the contemporary world (and that which we used refer to as societies). Sociology is not to be defined or practised in accordance with, or in opposition to, science. It does have a specificity in that it deals with human society, but the very boundaries as to what constitutes such societies and the manner of their constitution must be widened. Sociological analysis is not of a higher or lower level than that of science or humanities. It is one aspect of existence which is not divorced from the rest.

Whitehead's work is also productive in both diagnosing and reapproaching specific dualisms which have haunted and limited sociological thinking. It is not a question of making the private into the public, for example, and of opening all aspects of so-called personal life to the gaze of society. The point is to recognize that the personal and the private are both actual moments in the ongoing process of the creation, maintenance and reproduction of the social environment in which we find ourselves. This is one element of a thoroughly Whiteheadian sociology.

> The stubborn reality of the absolute self-attainment of each individual is bound up with a relativity which it issues from and issues into. The analysis of the various strands of relativity is the analysis of the social structure of the Universe. (AI, 376)

The social structure of the universe involves the interrelation of all individuals via an ongoing and thorough relativity. However, this is not a relativity in which things, ethics and politics dissolve. Indeed, it is only through this relativity that the "stubborn reality" of objects, subjects and our (human) selves are made possible. In this respect, we are implicated in all the social arrangements (good and bad) that enable or disable the lives of those around us. Private concerns are the momentary instantiation of the world, as are the inequalities which permeate our lives. And we are responsible for the manner in which we respond to these, in that we are resultants of the manner in which we have previously responded to the social environment. But we are not wholly and solely responsible for ourselves; others are reciprocally responsible for us. The personal is political because the personal is actual and we cannot absolve ourselves from the actual situations of others. We might try and abstract both ourselves (and others) so that we all appear to inhabit an equal plane. But such abstractions which aim at mere equality will flatten out and adumbrate social inequalities which themselves do not come from inside us but which are actualized within us. The sovereign individual is an abstraction. The actual situation of the actual individual is not. Individuality is the experience of the environment from which it proceeds and to which it will return. Social inequalities are all our faults. For: 'the community as an environment is responsible for the survival of the separate individuals which compose it; and these separate individuals are responsible for their contributions to the environment' (SYM, 93). The location of such actualized and actualizing individuals, the status of the body, and the notion of sexual difference will be taken up in the following two chapters.

Chapter Six

LANGUAGE AND THE BODY – FROM SIGNIFICATION TO SYMBOLISM

The body, deemed as an object proper to social theory, arrived late on the scene. This field has since burgeoned into an important area of research and theorizing, and it now seems surprising that the body and bodily life received such scant attention for so long (albeit with some honourable exceptions, e.g. de Beauvoir 1972 [1949] and Elias 1982). However, the success of this new realm of study also masks a problem. The further that social research uncovers and describes the very sociality of the body, the further such analyses both empirically and conceptually distance themselves from the "biological" body. As a result the "natural" body is viewed more and more rigidly as either some kind of a fiction (paradoxically, a fiction created by science yet not simply a "science fiction"), or as an irrelevance to the varied levels of social and cultural meanings which are somehow attached or written upon such a body. As Fraser points out, in many accounts of gender 'the "naturalness" of the biological body is hardly challenged' (Fraser 2002, 610) so that the "cultural" body becomes the object of study for the social sciences and the "biological" becomes the concern of the natural sciences. Such divisions are not only unhelpful but replicate a way of thinking which itself is historical (and gendered) in that they reproduce the subject/object, active/passive binaries of modern Western thought. They are a prime example of the bifurcation of nature. Such bifurcations have significant consequence with regard to the body that not only infect conceptual practices, but also create disciplinary divisions within universities which consequently reinforce the appearance of apparently different kinds of bodies in different areas of study. Such divisions arise from the professionalization of thought which Whitehead describes as an essential but regrettable element of the development of the modern university. The danger of professionalism is that it:

> Produces minds in a groove. Each profession makes progress, but it is progress in its own groove. Now to be mentally in a groove is to live in contemplating a given set of abstractions. The groove prevents straying across country, and the abstraction abstracts from something to which no further attention is paid... Thus

in the modern world, the celibacy of the medieval learned class has been replaced by a celibacy of the intellect which is divorced from the concrete contemplation of the concrete facts. (SMW, 245)

Such celibacy might be seen in the extreme postmodernist who feels free to play in a world constituted solely in, through and by signs or language, thereby treating the body as either an illusion or an impossibility. Whilst celibacy is not, of itself, to be decried, there is a danger that the monasticism of modern social theory might lead to its findings and abstractions regarding the body as being too easily dismissed as, at most, interesting but unreal reportings on an epiphenomenal realm which is subsequent to and less consequential than the supposedly real reality of cells, genes, blood vessels, enzymes and so on.

Of course, to suggest that social research is unaware of such problems would be to overstate the case greatly. A number of writers, for example Barad (1998), Fraser (2002), Kirby (1997, 1999), Sandford (1999), Stone (2006) have all addressed the need to confront head-on the status of the biological body with regard to and within social analyses. Thus, the time is right to develop a theoretical account of the complex status of the body within existence, an account which is able to describe both the materiality of the body *and* its sociality. This chapter will use the work of Whitehead to develop such an approach through a reading of the work of Judith Butler in terms of the problem of the relationship of language and the body. It will do this by suggesting that social theory's account of language and its relation to the body is one which is haunted by the notion of a primary and irreducible gap between the two; language and the body are envisaged as different in kind. It will, therefore, be suggested that what is needed is an approach which is able to describe how one thing can evoke another, an approach which is not predicated on any primary gap or foundational difference, as is necessarily the case with the concept of language as a form of signification. Such a framework is to be found in Whitehead's notion of "symbolism".

The Problem of Language and the Body – The Problem of Signification

How can one thing ever really refer to another? Can words really denote, capture or create the body? The character and status of language, and its relation to the world, have long been a concern of philosophy. As early as Plato's dialogue *Cratylus* (Plato 2008), addressing the problem of names and language's supposed ability to refer to the world was posited as an important philosophical task. Yet, it was only with the twentieth century that language, considered as a discrete object of analysis, took centre-stage in the work of, for example, and amongst many others, Frege, Saussure, Russell, Wittgenstein, Carnap, and Quine. For analytic philosophers the main concerns are ultimately the truth values or consistency of statements about the body, and the possibility of such statements being meaningful or actually referring to anything. These approaches also presume an utter distinction between language (or statements) and the body, which is the object of such reference. The body simply poses a "simple" philosophical problem (akin to that of proper names). Can we actually refer to it? Hence, whilst the reality of the body is certainly not denied, its material character is left as an object for and matter of concern of science, and is thus seen as none of the modern philosopher's business. Nature bifurcates once again and the monastic celibacy of analytic philosophy is established.

The second half of the twentieth century witnessed the development of discrete modes of the analysis of language which followed on from the work of Ferdinand de Saussure on linguistics in the early 1900s. Such positions blossomed into full-blown structuralism and poststructuralism, postmodernism and deconstructionism, where the primacy of the sign, the signifier, and the linguistic came to the fore. This twentieth-century intellectual settlement roundly rejected the naïve belief that language simply and plainly referred to a reality which is "out-there"; it denied that language refers to a simple reality and insisted that language is itself a social production which generates meaning through labyrinthine modes of social, historical and political forces. In such accounts signs, language or discourse are taken as their own all-encompassing systems, and that to which they refer is not the real world but the concepts and discursive subject and object positions which humans, as bearers of such language, inhabit. The problem is that such self-referential signifying systems are, by definition, precluded from the possibility of actually referring to any reality which is not created by or signalled by that system. There is thus the nagging doubt that the real material body is somehow ungraspable or beyond our reach or ken. 'It is the world of words that creates the world of things' (Lacan 1977, 65). Lacanian influenced accounts therefore make it impossible to even think, let alone act, outside the symbolic realm. This makes it possible for him to claim that there is no such thing as "woman" and to treat any ripostes to this declaration as exhibiting the unfulfillable desire to somehow jump out of the symbolic realm into the real (whatever that may be), to return to the safety of a home which never was (see Mitchell and Rose 1982, 48–51). This is why Irigaray had to set about setting up a whole new cultural imaginary in order to corrupt Lacan's system from within, as will be discussed in the next chapter. In a different context, Badiou argues that the folding-in of the problems of language and the body has led to the peculiar situation where much modern thought believes there to be only bodies and language, a position which Badiou has termed "democratic materialism" (Badiou 2009, 1–8). Such a limitation on thought and on philosophy needs to be challenged. The task is to assert that, yes, there are bodies and there is also language, but there is more than that to existence, and there is more to their relation than signification. Whitehead's notion of symbolism will be outlined as providing a response which accounts for language, the body and the "more than that". It is a conception of the interrelation of things which does not have its roots in signification and which does not assume or predicate a gap or hierarchical relation between that which symbolizes and that which is symbolized. The role that the body plays is fundamental to Whitehead's ability to develop such a system.

Judith Butler (1990, 1993, 2004a, 2004b) has developed some of the most important and influential attempts to reconceptualize the relation of language to the (real) body. *Bodies that Matter* (1993) most especially helped to set out what is at stake in the accounts, analyses, and living of the relation between real bodies and real language. Her starting point is the need to reconceptualize the very concept of matter and materiality and to challenge prevailing notions of social constructionism with regard to sex,[1] gender, nature, culture. There are resonances between her thoughts on materiality and those of Whitehead; however, it is with regard to the emplacement of language that they differ, as will be discussed later on.

In *Bodies That Matter*, Butler clarifies how various forms of social and discursive constructionism tend to see the social as acting upon a passive nature which, with regards to human sexual difference, is epitomized via the anatomical. Hence, the physical body is viewed simply as the substrate upon which the social and cultural meanings of gender are built. There are thus different kinds of bodies (for example, man and woman or male and female – depending on the severity of the constructionism that you adopt), yet such distinctions only gain importance through the granting to them of significance by a specific society, culture or discourse; they could thus be otherwise and there could also be more kinds of bodies if cultures, language and discourse were differently arranged. In such frameworks, culture, language and discourse are designated as active agents and, consequently, the physical body is reduced to a lifeless, inert receptacle. It is thereby rendered theoretically invisible and impossible to grasp through language (although medicine has been happy to accept such a fixed, yet invisible, body as its own).

As opposed to such accounts, Butler aims to demonstrate that sex has a history, as does the concept of nature (see Laqueur 1990, for another version of the history of sex). In doing so, she argues that linguistic (gender) constructionism is caught in a double bind. If language is a cultural phenomenon which is separate from the world, as is the case with the social constructionist distinction between the material body and its cultural meanings, then either language cannot gain access to sex as a site upon which it acts (thereby demonstrating the limits of constructionism) or sex is a prediscursive fiction which entails that everything is already only linguistic. To put it another way, social constructionism either makes it impossible to get to the body through language (or any other means), or a different kind of subject must be posited elsewhere (discourse must be granted a form of subjectivity) in order to account for the social body and to create the human subject. Butler reduces the various strands of this problematic to one succinct question: in what way is it possible to talk meaningfully about the body? Her short answer is: through a reconsideration of the materiality of matter:

> What I would propose in place of these conceptions of construction is a return to the notion of matter, not as site or surface, but as *a process of materialization that stabilizes over time to produce the effect of boundary, fixity, and surface we call matter* (Butler 1993, 9. Emphasis in original.)

The key words here are "process", "time" and "effect" as they indicate the interweaving of the notions of materiality and temporality in the coming-to-be of the body. However, there are two types of time operating within Butler's notion of materialization which she does not clearly indicate as separate. In the quotation given above, she forefronts time as a general, historical mode in which matter sediments within the normative requirements which induce certain forms of matter and subjectivity. This normativity makes up the environment where all further subject formations occur. In this regard, time is not just an aggregation of separate moments of time for 'the "past" will be the accumulation and congealing of such "moments" to the point of their indistinguishability' (Butler 1993, 245). This is a broad view of time. This is the time of discourse in its efficacy as the producer of normative effects; this is time as the macroconfiguration of the sedimentation of these effects and their continuing influence in materialization. But within such congealment there must also be those "acts", those moments within the process, that go to make up that process.

This is a crucial point and one which indicates both the value of Butler's approach and a problem inherent in it. Butler's work is a bold attempt to account for the general, abstract conditions which envelop and produce the individual occasions of materiality, yet is always aware of the machinations of power: she aims to account for "performativity" as an abstracted, limiting and enabling process *and* to describe individual, separate, momentary manifestations of performativity. The Whiteheadian question at this point would be "what is the ontological status of these momentary acts?" "Are they individuated within this process or are they false entities which are merely *thought of* as atomizing a more general flux?" Butler recognizes this distinction but does not make it explicit within the text: 'Construction not only takes place *in* time, but is itself a temporal process' (Butler 1993, 10; emphasis in original). She also maintains that 'an act is itself a repetition, a sedimentation, and congealment of the past which is precisely foreclosed in its act-like status' (Butler 1993, 244).

So, according to Butler's argument as set out in *Bodies That Matter,* there is a reconciliation to be made between the exterior temporal process which is exemplified in the inculcation of gendered subject positions (for example masculine, feminine), and the actual, individual renderings of these subject positions on different occasions by specific bodies and subjectivities. 'The bodies produced through such a regulatory enforcement of gender are bodies in pain, bearing the marks of violence and suffering. Here the ideality of gendered morphology is quite literally incised in the flesh' (Butler 2004b, 53). The detailing and confronting of such violence and suffering is clearly a major concern of Butler's oeuvre and is a thread which runs throughout her work. The need to describe, explain and revalorize modes of existence and kinds of bodies which have been refused and abjected is of critical importance. In responding to this need, Butler also points up the depoliticized character of much philosophy and the need to challenge such unengaged approaches.

> It is not a matter of a simple entry of the excluded into an established ontology, a critical opening up of the questions, What is real? Whose lives are real? How might reality be remade? Those who are unreal have, in a sense, already suffered the violence of derealisation. (Butler 2004a, 33)

In order to reapproach the question of lives, bodies and ontology, Butler is clear that it is necessary to challenge the orthodoxy of a certain strand of poststructuralism which appears to grant all power and agency to the linguistic or the discursive.

Thus, there are, for the purposes of the argument being made here, five main issues that are clarified within *Bodies That Matter.* These are: first, the questioning of the sex/gender binary as being able to account for the relation between the natural and the cultural, and the consequent need for a reappraisal of the status of matter. Second, the description of matter as a result of a process of materialization. Third, the importance of the concept of time as part of such a process. Fourthly, the need to theorize language (or the linguistic) as utterly material. Finally, the need to engage at a philosophical level with the concepts of matter and subjectivity. For, as Butler has shown, contemporary analyses of their interrelation both rely upon and invoke a theoretical field which has its own history, stretching back to Aristotle. (In this way her insistence on the importance of tracing the legacy of philosophical concepts chimes with Whitehead's approach.) Overall, Butler has opened up a whole field of inquiry and debate and established the need to engage, at a philosophical level, with the concepts of matter, language, subjectivity and the body. This marks an important shift in theorizing the body, and Butler's work stands as an important intervention as well as an injunction to question and develop new modes of analysis within this politically charged arena. Her work, however, has not been unanimously accepted.

One of the most sustained analyses of both Butler's texts and her ideas surrounding the notions of matter, corporeality, power, and subjectivity is to be found in Kirby's *Telling Flesh* (1997). Like Butler, Kirby is striving to think of another way through the nature/culture dichotomy with all its accompanying philosophical baggage. And Kirby is also aware of the pitfalls of overexuberant linguistic or discursive constructionism. 'I am critical of an empiricism that perceives data as the raw and unmediated nature of the world. However, I am just as critical of postmodern correctives that regard the apparent evidence of nature as the actual representation of culture' (Kirby 1997, 2). One of the main criticisms that Kirby makes of Butler is that in her attempt to describe how the materiality of signification must be rethought, in order to explain the process of materialization, there is a latent rendering of the signifier solely in terms of psychoanalysis. She states that this 'reliance upon a psychoanalytic understanding of the sign, or a reading of "the discursive" that subordinates itself to an unproblematized category of "the social," returns us to the very nature/culture, mind/body divisions that are so politically insidious' (Kirby 1997, 5). That is to say, by focusing upon the relation of language to materiality in terms which privilege the constitution of language in terms of signification, and more specifically through the analysis of such signification in terms of the symbolic, the imaginary and the "real", Butler stays within the limits posted by psychoanalytic theory, albeit the most sophisticated and poststructuralist version thereof, where the symbolic is both productive and regulatory. Such a symbolic is not an ideal realm in itself but a coalescence of social practices (and thereby alterable): 'the symbolic itself is the sedimentation of social practices, and…radical alterations in kinship demand a rearticulation of the structuralist presuppositions of psychoanalysis, moving us, as it were, toward a queer poststructuralism of the psyche' (Butler 2004b, 44).

The symbolic realm is, in such definitions, the human realm; the realm of signification is allied to the (human) linguistic realm. Both of these constitute or are constituted by culture. On such accounts culture is still not nature. This leads to Kirby's description of Butler's version of the social and the cultural as "unproblematized". By remaining within the ambit of the psychoanalytic approach to questions of signification Butler is constrained by the possibilities already inscribed within such analyses. A limit to the theoretical radicality is set, in that the very "nature" of nature is still regarded as either out of bounds, beyond signification, or simply impossible to talk of meaningfully. And the social tends to be rendered as that which is not natural. Thus Butler would seem to have replicated rather than avoided elements of the problematical relations between language and the body and has fallen back into unhelpful, human conceptions of the social which could be avoided by adopting Whitehead's distinctive approach to this concept.[2]

Further critiques of Butler's *Bodies That Matter*, such as Cheah's *'Mattering' in Diacritics* (1996) and Grosz's *Volatile Bodies* (1994), further point up the pressing political implications involved in contemporary discussions of matter, nature and culture:

> [The]…obsessive pushing away of nature may well constitute an acknowledgement-in-disavowal that humans may be natural creatures after all. Furthermore, as a theoretical position, antinaturalism itself is produced by the polemical energy that strives to keep nature at bay… Consequently, antinaturalism works with a conventional philosophical definition of nature…the concepts of "nature" and "the given" are, in fact, neuralgic points, the contested sites around which any theory of political transformation is organized. (Cheah 1996, 108)

So, it is the refusal to take on the "natural" as a contested term, as a term which is not necessarily explainable solely in relation or opposition to the cultural, which, they argue, leads Butler to produce analyses that end up simply as restatements of an entrenched philosophical position. The task is, therefore, to provide an engagement and conceptualization of existence, of nature, of bodies which is not predicated on any form of essentialism and which also avoids prioritizing the human.

One notion which runs through all critiques of Butler is her ultimate reliance upon some version of human priority. 'In her syncretization of Foucault/Aristotle, matter is invested with dynamism and said to be open to contestation only because the matter concerned is the product of sociohistorical forms of power, that is, *of the human realm*' (Cheah 1996, 113; emphasis in original). By identifying how Butler situates changing forms of matter only in the "human realm", Cheah, like Kirby, uncovers the anthropocentric aspect of Butler's account. This leads to the assigning of a primary dynamism to the cultural, at the expense of the depth of the materiality of matter. Thus, Butler's commentary is reduced to describing the surface of bodies rather than their "weightiness": 'the materiality of the body now designates its contours of intelligibility' (Cheah 1996, 114). Again, Cheah identifies this position as one ultimately *within* rather than challenging established philosophical discourse. 'The specter of Kantianism returns precisely because materiality becomes present, is given body, materializes only in being named or signified in language, which cannot quite avoid the role of being an epistemic grid of sorts' (Cheah 1996, 116–7).

There is, therefore, a recourse to an approach which is more concerned with explaining the significance of matter or nature for human subjectivity, rather than asking the question "what is the significance of matter for itself?" – as Whitehead consistently asks. There is also an unquestioned acceptance of that which constitutes the social in that the social is regarded as solely a human question and affair. Thus, Butler is in danger or allowing nature to bifurcate: matter always has to be distinguished from the truly social operations of the humanly social rather than allowing the social to suffuse all reality, as Whitehead would hold. 'What is never once posed in Butler's debate…is the possibility that matter could have a dynamism that is neither the negativity of the unsymbolizable nor reducible to a function of productive form' (Cheah 1996, 119). Here, there is evidence of a shift from a critique of Butler to the need for a theoretical reassessment along ontological lines. 'Philosophically speaking we need an account of the political agency of bodies that no longer respects the form/matter or nature/culture distinctions' (Cheah 1996, 121). It has been seen that Whitehead's work can be considered as a sustained and important attempt to develop lines of thought wherein matter is considered as neither fixed, nor given. Moreover, any definition of humanness, if such a thing is desired, must proceed from a wider understanding of the activity of matter, and not be predicated upon the agency of humans. As Wilson (1999) provocatively puts it: 'Matter (human, nonhuman, living, technological) does not simply *have* the capacity to convert, it *is* the capacity to convert. All matter wanders' (Wilson 1999, 16; emphasis in original).

To recap this discussion of Butler, it is clear that many of the criticisms of Butler's work on materiality and language, and Butler's response to these, have focused on the role of some notion of (psychoanalytic) signification in her work. They point to a tension in the work of Butler generated by her recognition of the importance and primacy of the body, the bodily and processes of incarnation, as well as her attempts to describe these in terms of norms which are utterly social. This distinction assumes a gap between the sociality of the enactment of norms and that which is enacted via these norms, a gap which is best expressed and problematized in terms of signification. This tension is something which Butler has explicitly addressed in her more recent texts. For example when she states:

> Every time I try to write about the body, the writing ends up being about language. This is not because I think that the body is reducible to language; it is not. Language emerges from the body. (Butler 2004b, 198)

If this were simply a terminological matter, one of signification (Butler) vs symbolism (Whitehead), then this would be of little concern, as long as the body were given its central role. But there is more to it than this. For, within the very concept of signification there is the positing of a gap between the social and its incarnations, between the norm and the normative act; these gaps are productions of the conceptualization inherent in signification and which Whitehead refuses in his democratic account of symbolism and his rejection of the bifurcation of nature. Signification always claims to establish a founding distance which enables it to operate, but there is then the apparent need for such a distance to be broached or healed. For example:

> The distance between gender and its naturalised instantiations is precisely the distance between a norm and its incorporations… In fact, the norm only persists as a norm to the extent that it is acted out in social practice and reidealized and reinstituted in and through the daily social rituals of bodily life. The norm has not ontological status, yet it cannot be easily reduced to its instantiations; it is itself (re) produced through its embodiment, through the acts that strive to approximate it, through the idealizations reproduced in and by those acts. (Butler 2004b, 48)

So, whilst Butler, quite rightly, critiques Lacan and Lévi-Strauss for separating the symbolic from the social (the symbolic position of the father does not directly refer, they claim, to the actual fathers of the social world) (Butler 2004b, 43–8) she is unable to account for the *process* through which norms are instantiated in the body and then return to the realm of an external sociality which constitutes a realm of putative idealizations. This process is just assumed to occupy 'the field of reality produced by gender norms [which] constitutes the background for the surface appearance of gender in its idealized dimensions' (Butler 2004b, 52). Again, a gap appears between the reality and the idealized dimensions; a gap which both produces and sustains the operations of signification, but which in itself ultimately fails to appear, operate, or explain. It is this gap, which imitates the bifurcation of nature and which needs to be avoided. It is not a question of healing or bridging this gap but of providing an approach which does not presume the founding gulf of signification, yet which still enables communication between and about bodies. The remainder of this chapter will outline Whitehead's notion of symbolism and will argue that it provides such a framework, thereby bolstering the immediate and politically important interventions on contemporary manifestations of violence, in all its forms, that Butler describes.

Symbolism and Symbolic Reference

Chapter Three outlined Whitehead's specific conception of causation. In doing so, it indicated the centrality of the body to our experience of the world and its causal character through his notion of "Causal Efficacy". This was distinguished from the realm of "Presentational Immediacy" which expressed the vivid character of the realm of sense-perception. Although conceptually distinct, these two fields of perception of the world operate together through what he terms "Symbolic Reference", and it is in relation to this that much of the symbolism of the human realm occurs.[3] Whilst causal efficacy and presentational immediacy make up the manner in which the objects of the world are directly perceived by us and thereby become a part of us, it is clear that these two elements of perception are not and cannot remain indefinitely separate. The interrelation of these two modes will furnish the crucial path by which Whitehead instigates his notion of symbolism (as opposed to signification). As will be seen, a crucial element of this is that the body gives rise to the very possibility of such symbolism and is not merely that which is symbolized, or that which is impossible to symbolize. It is in this way that Whitehead manages to side-step the problems of the relation of language to the body which have haunted so many writers. This is not to reduce symbolism to an operation of the human body but is to stress the ongoing process of bodily experience of the world. This enables Whitehead to develop a position which allows for no irreducible gap between language and the body, the signifier and the signified, that which is a symbol and that which is symbolized. It should be noted that one reason that he is able to avoid such a foundational gulf is that he recognizes that "Symbolic Reference", as it operates and is experienced at the human level, is not the starting point. It is a complex example of the operation of symbolism. In this way, symbolic reference should be seen as a subset of the wider notion of symbolism. Hence, as with his extension of experience throughout existence, of subjectivity to all items of existence, and of sociality to all enduring objects, Whitehead refuses to take the human level of symbolism as primary. Instead, he aims to produce an account which is able to explain and include modes of symbolism which are not predicated on the human, on consciousness, language, discourse or ideology but on the process whereby any thing *could* evoke any other thing. Again, Whitehead is shy of immediate definitions as these would limit the scope of his argument, so it is necessary to follow and consider the moves which he makes and their intertwining with other elements of his philosophy.

  With regard to the most general case of symbolism that is witnessed throughout existence (and which applies to the interrelation of all objects and not just to humans and things), the closest that Whitehead comes to a definition is when he states that such symbolism is the process by which a symbol 'evokes' or 'elicits' some response (PR, 181; SYM, 8). This might appear to be a rather weak definition of symbolism; that one element of experience can evoke or elicit another. However, this very generality will turn out to be to Whitehead's advantage, for nothing is ruled in or out, nothing is assumed by it. Symbolism does not rely on consciousness, subjectivity, culture, meanings, humans; furthermore, it is not bound to notions of representation, correspondence, or reference. Symbolism simply refers to the fact that elements in experience tend to evoke or produce other elements within experience. Experience is not flat or uni-linear; one experience sparks off another. For example, when a dog sees its lead being taken out of a cupboard it may elicit excitement, in that it presumes it will be taken for a walk. This does not entail that the lead signifies or refers to a walk. Questions of truth, and hence also of ideology, are also irrelevant at this stage of Whitehead's account. All he is positing, for the moment, is that it is possible for one item or element of experience to provoke a response beyond the immediacy of that item. There is nothing "natural" or necessary with regard to the relation of symbol and meaning. 'Considered by themselves the symbol and its meaning do not require *either* that there shall be a symbolic reference between the two, *or* that the symbolic reference between the members of the couple should be one way on rather than the other way on' (SYM, 9–10; emphasis in original). Whitehead insists that symbols and their meanings are not bound together in perpetuity (in one sense they are "arbitrary" as Saussure (1983, 67–9) maintains). There is a democracy inherent in symbolism insofar as anything which is a symbol could have been a meaning, and anything which is a meaning could have been a symbol.

The concept of signification implies a one-way relation between that which signifies and that which is signified and, simultaneously, a disjunction between that which signifies and that which is signified. The process of signification endlessly tries both to maintain and bridge these relations. In opposition to this view, Whitehead states that both elements enter into experience as equals:

> Why do we say that the word "tree" – spoken or written – is a symbol to us for trees? Both the word itself and trees enter into our experience on equal terms; and it would be just as sensible, viewing the question abstractedly, for trees to symbolize the word "tree" as for the word to symbolize the trees. (SYM, 11–12)

This lack of a hierarchy removes the need to see symbolism as inherently a form of domination whereby the inner reality of an individual item is either misrepresented or subordinated to the machinations of the operating system or structure which attempts to symbolize or capture such objects. Whitehead's version of symbolism also operates throughout existence and is dislocated from any reliance on consciousness or human intention. Footsteps on a path can be a symbol for a dog which awaits its owner. The meaning is not fixed however; they could mean a walk, food or a beating. Meaning is firmly placed *in* the world and not in the mind, hiding within a labyrinth of intentions or behind the screen of an individual will, or located only in the social realm.

Meanings are out there, they are as real as the symbols which invoke them. As has been seen, this 'is the foundation of a thorough-going realism. It does away with any mysterious element in our experience which is merely meant, and thereby behind the veil of direct perception' (SYM, 10). There is only ever experience, the experiences of subjects. This is again, the starting point and the end point for Whitehead. The provocation of experience by another is the operation of symbolism and hence there are real symbols which evoke real responses and reactions; they therefore have real meanings. Things are symbolic for each other without human intervention. The sound of the sea symbolizes life for turtles hatching on a beach. A large stone which has fallen into the mouth of a nest of a beetle symbolizes a problem for that beetle and evokes a specific, though not a determined, experience and response. This is not to dismiss or dilute the power or operations of symbolism; it is simply not to reduce it to a uniquely human affair. Symbolism is not to be denied to humans. It is just that their experience of it is simply a subset of this wider realm which suffuses existence.

Although Whitehead's account of symbolism entails that any thing could evoke any other thing, this does not mean that they do. To make such a claim would be to miss Whitehead's point and the level of abstraction which lies behind his seemingly innocent and sometimes seemingly banal statements. Whitehead is indicating that there is no metaphysical constraint on what might evoke or elicit what experience; in this sense his notion of the arbitrary character of symbolism is wider than that of Saussure, and many of his followers, and it is certainly not predicated on a narrow conception of the social or cultural as the arbiters of such arbitrariness. Although the number and manner of symbolisms are technically limitless, the actual symbolisms which occur at any given time will be limited, and to an extent, prescribed and proscribed. But the fact that the word "tree" tends to signify the concept of tree (to English speakers) or that Golden Arches tend to signify McDonald's (and in turn a specific form of capitalism) does not, in and of itself, explain signification. This is Derrida's (1976) crucial point regarding the failure of signification, with which Whitehead would concur. Derrida insists that signification can never itself guarantee or produce the means by which it operates, for the ability of a sign to signify is not self-evident or natural. The assumption that a sign can signify is, he argues, based on an outdated metaphysics which has its roots in Greek thought and medieval Christianity: 'one cannot retain the convenience or the "scientific truth" of the Stoic and later medieval opposition between *signans* and *signatum* without also bringing with it all its metaphysico-theological roots' (Derrida 1976, 13; emphasis in original). This neatly echoes Whitehead's critique (as set out in Chapter One) when he similarly argues that representation 'can never, within its own metaphysical doctrines, produce the title deeds to guarantee the validity of the representation of fact by idea' (PR, 54). The difference between Whitehead and Derrida might be that Whitehead takes this criticism of signification as a spur to develop a new metaphysics which can account for the evocation of one experience by another. His work and outlook are constructive not deconstructive; he insists on adding more to the argument and to reality. 'Adding, not deconstructing: this is a crucial point' (Stengers 2008a, 99).

Still, it might seem that Whitehead's account of symbolism is, at this stage, so vague as to lack any purchase. One crucial element which anchors Whitehead's account and enables him to avoid such a charge is the operations of the body as the carrier of symbolism. In order for a symbol to evoke that other thing which constitutes its meaning, there must be something in common between the two elements of experience; there must be a mode of connection between a symbol and its meaning. It has been seen that the meaning cannot come from a store of intentions or beliefs which hide behind experience and which magically appear when a symbol comes into view. Instead:

> Symbolic reference requires something in common between symbol and meaning which can be expressed without reference to the perfected percipient; but it also requires some activity of the percipient which can be considered without recourse either to the particular symbol or its particular meaning. (SYM, 9)

There is no need to refer to a specific individual speaker or hearer in order to express that the word "tree" symbolizes a tree. That is to say, acts of symbolism can be described without reference to those individuals involved in that act of symbolism. This might sound like straight-forward structuralism but it is not. To fully explain or understand symbolism and the mode of symbolism in which humans most often find themselves namely, symbolic reference, the role of the body is crucial. For, in the actual operation of symbolism, as opposed to a description of such an act, the body is required not just to hear, speak, read or write the symbol (i.e. in the mode of presentational immediacy) but to provide a continuity of experience within which the symbol and its meaning occur (i.e. in the mode of causal efficacy): 'the animal body is the great central ground underlying all symbolic reference. In respect to bodily perceptions the two modes achieve the maximum of symbolic reference, and pool their feelings referent to identical regions' (PR, 170).[4]

In the operations of symbolism, it is the body which enables the two experiences to combine and to elicit items in the other; it is the body which also experiences in the two distinct aspects of symbolism: Presentational Immediacy and Causal Efficacy. The body is thus the 'common ground' (PR, 168) whereby a symbol can evoke a meaning. No longer is the body to be seen as the passive receptacle which language tries to grasp, refer to, or write upon. Nor is the body an object of science or a cultural construction. Things are not inscribed on the body by either nature or culture. It is the body which enables the symbol to symbolize and the meaning to mean. As has been seen, Whitehead refuses both scientistic and culturalistic accounts of the existence of all objects and bodies (including the human body). He wants to provide a framework for thinking the materialities, ideas, lives and abstractions that have been included and excluded by those who attempt to situate and distinguish the body as either natural or cultural. In his refusal of the bifurcation of nature, Whitehead denies any purchase to those conceptual constructions which attempt to make a distinction between nature and culture. This is not some kind of limpid acceptance that human existence is a mix of nature and nurture, some banal, ineffective compromise which incoherently grants effectivity to both genes and the environment. It is, rather, the radical philosophical insistence that we must refuse to split the world into one of facts (nature) and one of meanings (culture, the social, humans); we have to learn to think them together (Stengers 2002, 74, 564; Stengers 2009a). The nature-culture division is simply not functional for Whitehead as it transgresses the extent of his realism. The symbols are real, the meanings are real, the body is real. There is no distinction, gap or hierarchy between these which needs to be bridged or overcome. There is, rather, a continuity which needs to be witnessed. 'There is thus a general continuity between human experience and physical occasions. The elaboration of such a continuity is one most obvious task for philosophy (AI, 244). One of the vital elements of this continuity is the body. This leads back to the work of Butler, but now on a different terrain, one which is not predicated on the natural or the social or the opposition between the two. For it opens up avenues of critical analysis as to how certain forms of the body are rejected and abjected and to the need to address the violence implicit in the accepted and extremely limited forms of bodily symbolism which inhere today, such as those of the "slender body" (Bordo 1995). It also leads the discussion back from the locale of the body to the operations of language.

Symbolism, Language and the Body

The great advantage of Whitehead's account of symbolism is that it does not have to be added on, it is not something separate from the activities of the body and, as such, there is no gap between language and the body or between a sign and reality. Symbolism and symbolic reference arise from the functioning of the body, the data it provides, and our enjoyment and rendering of it. Symbolism is not predicated upon or produced only by humans; it is occurs in any "high-grade" organism which has both presentational immediacy and causal efficacy. However, whilst causal efficacy is an integral aspect of all existence, presentational immediacy is not entertained at the same level of complexity by all entities. A stone feels the warmth of the sun causing it to dry. The flower turns to the sun. The greater the influence of causal efficacy over presentational immediacy, the more an entity will conform to its environment.

> A flower turns to the light with much greater certainty than does a human being, and a stone conforms to the conditions set by its external environment with much greater certainty than does a flower. A dog anticipates the conformation of the immediate future to his [sic] present activity with the same certainty as a human being. When it comes to calculations and remote inferences, the dog fails. (SYM, 42)

So, in those bodies which enjoy more developed sense-perception, in the usual understanding of the term, there is a mixed mode of perception which arises from the mingling of presentational immediacy and causal efficacy. This is the realm of Symbolic Reference. It is in this area of symbolism that human language and its operations can be found. 'The failure to lay due emphasis on symbolic reference is one of the reasons for metaphysical difficulties; it has reduced the notion of "meaning" to a mystery' (PR, 168). However, it must be stressed that symbolic reference is not divorced from other forms of symbolism, it simply demonstrates a greater degree of complexity. 'Symbolism is no mere idle fancy or corrupt degeneration: it is inherent in the very texture of human life. Language is itself a symbolism' (SYM, 61–2). Whitehead is clear that language is not a privileged form whereby humans are granted some form of supremacy within existence. This is not to deny the efficacy or importance of language either: 'this general relation of words to things is only a particular instance of a yet more general fact' (SYM, 13) and this fact is that of the reality of symbolism. Symbols and meanings are implicit in all existence and are not only produced by the specifically psycho-social existence of humans, whose language and concepts are the only mode of generating meaning. Language arises from and operates within bodily experiences. It is an aspect of bodily life. It must be stressed that this is not a form of biologism or socio-biologism, as Whitehead has completely altered what constitutes the body so that it is both material and conceptual, potential and actual, factual and interpretative: 'symbolic reference is the interpretative element in human experience' (PR, 173).

There is thus a continuum of experience but there is also complexity which characterizes the experiences of "high-grade" organisms, such as humans, and this is to be found in the operations of symbolism. When a detective, or a child playing at detectives, or an actor playing a detective, points to a footprint near a broken window and states that it is a "clue" they are not merely expressing an opinion but are calling upon the whole apparatus of symbolism whereby some thing invokes some other thing or some kind of response.[5] It is in this sense that Whitehead states that 'It seems as though mankind must be always masquerading' (SYM, 62). The term "masquerading" is intended to put his point forcefully, to jump us out of our complicity with the factual, and to make us realize the extent to which symbolism informs and infects our lives.[6] But there is an important distinction between Whitehead's approach and Symbolic Interactionism. For Symbolic Interactionism predicates and limits the operations of symbolism to the human realm, thereby replicating the bifurcation of nature. This sociological position is, therefore, still left with the problem of the disjunction between such human symbols and the body to which they occasionally refer. This is not to state that we are simply lying, or playing roles; it is to assert that our ability to communicate and to survive relies upon symbolism and, perhaps, might be linked to the notion of performativity as developed by Butler (1990, 1993). Whitehead's point is that any thing, action, word, image, object, or subject which invokes, evokes or elicits a response, is a symbol.

So, the Whiteheadian "sociological" task is to consider how some symbols manage to predominate, to take hold, so that the response to them can be predicted and certain groups or bodies included or excluded; the point being that such an understanding will help us to alter or change such modes of rejection. Whitehead's account may enable social theory to avoid having to prioritize language, to avoid the current position where it seems impossible to puncture its shifting meanings and associations in order to get to the real body. But he does not give an explicit account of why it is that despite his utter democratization of the bodily, both across and within different manifestations of bodily existence, the world that we find ourselves in is riddled with hierarchies of bodies marked in terms of size, colour, gender, sex, sexuality, age, to list a few imprecise yet evocative terms. And, to be clear, it was not his intention to do so, even though he is aware of the danger of the conservatism inherent within symbolism: 'when we examine how a society bends its individual members to function in conformity with its needs, we discover that one important operative agency is our vast system of inherited symbolism' (SYM, 73). Yet, he does not then go on to identify which symbols are good, which are bad, which are progressive and which are oppressive, but this should not be seen as problematic; it may be a boon.

It is not the task of Whitehead to tell us what to think, but he does suggest ways that we might think differently. As such, he clears a path which might help us to walk around and beyond the apparent gulf between language and the body, in order to enable us to rethink the empirical manifestations of symbolism in our current world (be they in the media, images, crimes, institutions, shops, bars, books or churches). For, as he states: 'In addition to its bare indication of meaning, words and phrases carry with them an enveloping suggestiveness and an emotional efficacy' (SYM, 66–7). The direct meaning of a word is only one aspect of its symbolism. The power of words is well known; the cruelty of symbolism is part of our history. 'A word has symbolic association with its own history, its other meanings…a word gathers emotional signification from its emotional history in the past' (SYM, 84). Those who state that language is an important and powerful tool of oppression and of liberation and that the purging and policing of language is an important element of social progress are half right. The problem arises when such language is seen merely as a cultural phenomenon which can either magically transform the world when it and its use are transformed or which ultimately does not "matter", as the truth of a person lies somewhere else, mysteriously hidden within their psyche, personality, subjectivity or even their body. For this replicates the gulf between the material and the cultural, the factual and the interpretative, the natural and the social, which plagues the modern culture of thought and which enables others to turn this argument on its political head. To view symbols and language as wholly social or cultural is to run the risk of implicitly positing their absolute separation from some "real truth" such as that we are all equal, natural beings, subject to the same eternal laws and duress. But it is precisely this striving for a supposed unseen, fundamental equality that can then be used to undermine or challenge the effects and import of the social and cultural level of language. In this manner the conceptual division between a realm of human meaning, language and signification and the real world of matter will always surreptitiously cede the argument to those who have laid claim to the right to speak of (or symbolize) reality. Whitehead's refusal to countenance such a division and his insistence that we in inhabit and think a single, but utterly multifarious reality, is the core of his political stance. It also returns the discussion to the tension in Butler's work alluded to earlier.

It has been seen how Whitehead's account of symbolism might be a way to avoid the need for any supposed reconciliation between the distinct realms of language and the body. The body and language are, and always were, linked in the most fundamental way. It is only through the bodily integration of the different modes of our acquaintance with the world that symbolism, and therefore language, can occur. The task facing contemporary theory is then 'to understand and purge the symbols on which humanity depends' (SYM, 7). Such a bold statement certainly challenges those who wish to reduce Whitehead's work to mere metaphysical abstractions. The status of the body is crucial for such an understanding and purging of symbols. No body, no symbolic. Butler too sees the body as central: 'the body that speaks its deed is the same body that did its deed, which means that there is, in the saying, a presentation of the body, a bodying forth of guilt, perhaps' (Butler 2004b, 172). This emphasizes the activity of the body, in what Whitehead terms the "withness of the body". It is a crucial step in both their work. The problem with Butler's approach is, again, the manner in which she envisages such bodilyness and the debt she owes to Lacan and signification. 'I follow Shoshana Felman's view...following Lacan, that the body gives rise to language, and that language carries bodily aims' (Butler 2004b, 199). Hence: 'Language emerges from the body, constituting an emission of sorts. The body is that upon which language falters, and the body carries its own signs, its own signifiers, in ways that remain largely unconscious' (Butler 2004b, 198). Whilst Whitehead would agree that language, in a sense, emerges from the body, he would not agree either that the body has its own signs or that language falters on the body. Instead, he would demand that we think both the body and its symbols together and interrogate the manner in which certain symbols are generated and deployed.

The point to be taken from Whitehead is that the symbolic is not something that is imposed on the body. Nor does the social exist as a distinct realm which somehow impresses itself upon the body. Human societies are full of symbols but this is not so special or so surprising, as all of existence is replete with the symbolic. As humans we find ourselves amidst competing cohorts of symbols. But these are not simply ethereal, ideological, or merely social. They are the past as it proposes itself to us and out of which, and with regard to which, we must form ourselves. Language, images, concepts, social symbols, stigmas are all rendered bodily by each of us. This is not simple iteration or reiteration, for the bodily is utterly implicated in the process. Nor is this simply a question of social or cultural norms which are enacted or to which we react. Whitehead moves beyond those accounts which tend to see the body as separate from, subject to, or constituted within, through or by the social. There is not a real body and a social body. There is not even a social realm distinct from any other realm. The social is neither constitutive nor limiting; it does not *exist*. Instead, the bodily (the natural-cultural body) must be envisaged as that series of events which constitute the possibility of the past issuing into the present and the future. Construing the body as a process does not somehow license or liberate the body so that it now becomes a set of self-generating and self-congratulating becomings. Our reactions and responses to other bodies and other subjects are elements of conformation to the predominant forms of symbolism in our society and societies. Such conformation is incorporated (literally) by the bodily events which go to make up the process that constitutes our lives. We are the vehicles through which equality and inequality, oppression and liberation, tolerance and hate, are comported. But such conformation does not necessarily imply acceptance or repetition. An essential aspect of the rendition of the symbolic through our bodily selves is the valuation or estimation of the relative worth of that symbolizing activity. As discussed in the previous chapter, it is in this way that value, through the process of valuation, is an integral aspect of all existence. To put it another way, all existence, and predominantly so in the case of human existence, is a matter of response, perpetuation or refusal of the modes of symbolism within which we find ourselves. It is up to us to dare to challenge the symbols which limit our being and becoming, whatever the cost.

> It is the first step in sociological wisdom, to recognize that the major advances in civilization are processes which all but wreck the societies in which they occur: like unto an arrow in the hand of a child. (SYM, 88)

Chapter Seven

THIS NATURE WHICH IS NOT ONE

Writing in 1920, Whitehead stated that: 'The history of the doctrine of matter has yet to be written. It is the history of the influence of Greek philosophy on science. That influence has issued in one long misconception of the metaphysical status of natural entities' (CN, 16). Previous chapters have examined some of the problems that have arisen with social theory's seeming inability to confront the status of the natural, and consequently the material, head-on. It has also been argued that one task facing social theory, and to which the work of Whitehead is especially fruitful in responding, is the development of *more* realistic accounts which encompass *more* of reality and which are not content with being limited to humanized accounts of social relations between human agents. One immediate problem which is encountered by these latter approaches is the very dominance in our contemporary culture of thought of the elision of nature with scientific conceptions thereof. This makes it hard to imagine or to conceptualize a return to questions of nature and of ontology which are not, in some way, philosophically, scientifically or biologically essentialist. Social theory's trepidation in the face of the natural and the ontological, especially with regard to the question of sexual difference, is well described by, amongst others, Fuss (1990) and Riley (1988). For example:

> Essentialist arguments frequently make recourse to an ontology which stands outside the sphere of cultural influence and historical change. 'Man' and 'woman,' to take one example, are assumed to be ontologically stable objects, coherent signs which derive their coherency from their unchangeability and predictability (there have *always* been men and women it is argued. (Fuss 1990, 3. Emphasis in original.)

Thus the concepts of ontology and nature are often viewed as essentialist, as opposed to the constructionist arguments deployed by social theory. 'Essentialists and constructionists are most polarized around the issue of the relation between the social and the natural' (Fuss 1990, 3). It is therefore possible to understand the antagonism that exists within social theory with regard to attempts to reclaim ontology as an important theoretical tool. The link between ontology, nature and a fixed realm of external nature has been used as a marker to differentiate the ground, procedures and epistemology of the natural sciences from those utilized in investigating the "social" aspects of humanity. Following such a distinction, any reclamation of ontology within social theory would seem to question its whole epistemological field, indeed its very purpose. At the very least, the inclusion of the ontological within social theory would put in jeopardy some of its most important conceptual developments. For example, in relation to analyses of sexuality, the success of social constructionism has been to: 'move us out of the realm of ontology (what the homosexual *is*) and into the realm of social and discursive formations (how the homosexual role is *produced*)' (Fuss 1990, 109; emphasis in original). That is to say, the importance of social theory has been its ability to make apparent the political and historical formations which have led to the appearance of categories such as "homosexual" and "heterosexual" thereby undermining normative moral and scientific claims regarding the status of those placed within such categories. Attempts to outline the importance of the ontological within the social are in danger of reasserting categories which would unpick some of social theory's most productive elements. Yet, this refusal or inability to take on the natural on its own terms, or in the terms designated to it by science, have proved problematic in themselves as they posit nature, things, materiality as being outside the remit of social analyses.

For Whitehead, such an impossibility is a result of the manner and efficacy of the conceptual constructions which inhabit and inhibit our culture of thought. They are, therefore, ripe for reappraisal insofar as they express the irrationality inherent in the modern settlement which implicitly accepts the bifurcation of nature, and which Whitehead is intent upon disallowing. This will involve an analysis and appreciation of the history and modes of the conceptual constructions of the relationship between the natural and the social. The problem is not so much nature as our concepts of nature and the limitations that they impose upon us.

That sociology and social theory have a testing relationship with nature and the natural (or concepts thereof) is both well known and well documented (see, for example, Eder 1996, 7–32, Bernard Cohen 1994, Haraway 1991, Soper 1995). Perhaps less immediately obvious is that sociology's specific rebuttal of the natural has led to a latent conflation of what could have been maintained as distinct problems. That is to say, the problem or question of materiality (as a philosophical or theoretical question) has been subsumed into, or reduced to, the narrower, and more limited question of *physicality*, as envisaged by the natural (or physical sciences). It has become difficult to talk of matter without finding oneself either trapped within, or in complete opposition to, the notion of matter as espoused by science (or, rather, the notion of matter as generally supposed to be espoused by modern science). So, attempting to discuss the material body has been envisaged as entailing an acceptance of the physical body as portrayed by science, and for a long time within social theory this was seen as stepping onto the slippery slope to reductionism, essentialism, and even socio-biology; it was to be inherently unsociological. Such problems become even sharper when it concerns the question of sexual difference. Once again, discussions of nature and of sexual difference are routinely assumed to be either *in* or *against* the scientific realm. If they are the former they are deemed to be essentialist; if the latter, they are viewed as mere social constructions. Clearly, questions around nature, sexual difference, materiality, the body, cannot deny the legacies from which they proceed and within which they have been situated. This chapter will argue that the answer is not to simply carry on either simply accepting or rejecting science's self-claimed authority to define what is meant by matter or physicality. It will sketch how Irigaray and Whitehead can be combined to help us not so much forget or ignore dualisms (such as that implied by the sexual difference between men and women or male and female, or the opposition of essentialism and social constructionism) but to develop new ways of thinking about them in order to avoid being trapped by them. As stated previously: 'A clash of doctrines is not a disaster – it is an opportunity' (SMW, 230).

Irigaray has herself, on occasions, been accused of essentialism and heterosexism. This chapter will try to deflect such accusations by suggesting that Irigaray's texts are an attempt to get to grips with thinking through the dualism of sexual difference, in the terms that it has been presented to us: historically, politically, socially and physically. That is to say – in reality. Rather than simply deny nature, Irigaray and Whitehead attempt to point out the specific manner in which science has constructed an abstracted concept of the natural which is only partial in its explanation and characterization of the complexity of existence. Such indications of the constructedness of scientific and philosophical concepts do not entail that these concepts, or that which they purport to describe, can be jettisoned, ignored or passed over. It is, rather, to refuse to accede to their claim to alone speak authoritatively of materiality and to provide complete accounts of the world and of nature. The task that Irigaray and Whitehead set themselves is to think through these abstractions and to provide novel modes of thought which include more of reality than these partial constructions. It may seem that the attention paid here to the status of man and woman is at the expense of questions concerning queer theory, a third sex or intersex. Whilst it is certainly the case that sexual difference in terms of man and woman makes up the core concern of this chapter, this is not to deny or diminish the importance of other such dualisms, rather it is to interrogate the conceptual frame within which the question of sexual difference has not only been posed but substantiated. Different dualisms will have different nuances, histories and outcomes which cannot be understood with the same categories that produce and infect concepts of sexual difference, although there will be shared conceptual developments. For example, it might be argued that intersex is not in itself a problem of biology but has been made into one.

So, in one sense, it is false to think of the dualism of sexual difference in isolation, as it is an abstraction from the "real" world where lived differences tend to overlap. Bearing this in mind, this chapter will remain with the question of sexual difference whilst recognizing that its parameters intersect with other abstractions and dualisms. This focus on sexual difference is not to prioritize it as an ontological or natural element which occupies a special place in any hierarchy of dualisms, but is to provide a coherent set of limits and possibilities in order to argue that the most important element to be drawn from Irigaray and Whitehead is the need for a new philosophy of nature, where nature is conceived not as pregiven, fixed and unified. But as *at least* two. And a process.

The goal is to develop a conceptual framework which does not immediately exclude anything and which can incorporate a "non-biological natural" (see Stone 2006, 94), and is therefore more "realistic". The challenge, which is evident in both Whitehead and Irigaray, is to refuse to view the natural as ontologically one and, instead, to assert a duality which is not reducible to the one. It is, perhaps, easy to jump from the one to the multiple, to state that existence and identities are multiple. The problem is that such an approach simply shatters the one into the many and returns to the old philosophical question of the relation of "the many and the one". It therefore remains within the problematic rather than shifting, avoiding or advancing it, as the "one" is still taken as primary and as that which is to be, or has been, dissolved. It is much harder to instantiate a thinking of duality as primary, as not premised on a one; to create a new culture of thought. As will be discussed throughout this chapter, it is important to recognize that this notion of the importance of duality is not a recourse to, or an acceptance of, any notion of binary opposition. Binary oppositions are predicated upon the existence of supposedly self-sufficient, oppositional individuals. Both Whitehead and Irigaray are resolute in their denial of any such version of individuality. At the same time, they also refuse to describe individuality as an aspect of the multiple or the manifold, as this tends to disperse rather than explain individuation.

Admittedly, this leads Irigaray, at points, to state that there is only the duality of male and female, and this tends to limit her argument as it excludes other forms of difference such as those described by queer theory, critical race studies etc. Hence, as will be seen toward the end of the chapter, it might ultimately be necessary to use Whitehead's work to go beyond Irigaray's philosophy of nature so as to explicate the complex manner of operation of other dualisms and differences of the world.

Reapproaching Sexual Difference

With an unenviable history (a history closely implicated with that of the doctrine of matter), one of the main markers of sexual difference has been conceptualized in terms of the possession or nonpossession of a penis or of the subject's relation to the phallus.[1] The anatomical organization of genitalia has been the cornerstone of most modern medical, scientific and legal understandings of the categories of man and woman (in the West at least). As such, sex immediately relies upon and invokes a concept of sexual difference, for if there were no difference there would be no sexes, or so this conceptual construction maintains. On this view, without such a distinction between the sexes, sexual reproduction would be *a*sexual, that is to say it would not be sexual at all – in the current understanding of the term. This demonstrates the intimate link between such scientistic definitions of sex as sexual difference and of sexual difference as tied to sexual reproduction. As will be seen, for both Whitehead and Irigaray, these links are in fact conceptual slippages. 'The obligation to have children or to keep a house does not constitute a female identity. It is a function or social role, no more' (Irigaray 1994, 18). Such slippages need bringing to the fore as does the conceptual apparatus upon which they rely. However, to then claim that because a conceptual problem has been identified then the problem itself has been solved is to be naïve, according to both writers. Given the philosophical, historical, political and social legacy, i.e. the reality of these conceptual distinctions and slippages, they cannot just be wished away or forgotten.

> The difficulties women have in gaining recognition for their social and political rights are rooted in this insufficiently thought out relation between biology and culture. At present, to deny all explanations of a biological kind – because biology has paradoxically been used to exploit women – is to deny the key to interpreting this exploitation. (Irigaray 1993, 46)

But these relations between biology and culture *can* be rethought and reoriented although, importantly, this is not to elide the two.

Some might hold that it is possible to claim that the biological plays a fixed but limited role and that in everyday life it is the cultural and social aspects (of humanity) which are more important and more malleable, so it is in these fields that progress has been and still can be made in terms of social research. It might even be claimed that that which constitutes humans is a mix of biological and social factors; we are complicated results of genetic disposition and environment. Often such positions simply fall back into forms of a simplified realism for, when pushed, they have to accept that practically and conceptually, the facticity of the (biological) body comes first. However, it is more often the case that there is an insistence on retaining elements of both. For Whitehead, such attempts to sit on both sides of the conceptual fence at once and are 'half-hearted and wavering' (SMW, 94) and they provide further evidence of how examples of the bifurcation of nature are lurking in the background of our culture of thought. That is to say, attempts to pick and choose elements from the natural and elements from the cultural in order to build up a more complex notion of humans is to fudge the issue and to misunderstand the conceptual apparatus upon which such definitions rely (Stengers 2009a, 33–5). Both Whitehead and Irigaray refuse to take this easy route and insist on the need to retrace these formulations and to produce new modes of thought.

Whitehead and Irigaray on the Problem of the 'One'

Throughout her major early work *Speculum of the Other Woman*, Irigaray (1985a) analysed and critiqued the abiding and influential concept of unity as a form of self-identity which claimed to explain the self-contained existence of subjects and objects. She traces the emergence and sedimentation of this concept in the texts of, amongst others, Plato, Aristotle, Plotinus, Descartes, Kant, Hegel and Freud. '*Unity, totality, entity of one who or that abstains from any conjunction whatever. That claims to take the place* of all conjunctions' (Irigaray 1985a, 312; emphasis in original): 'the subject is claimed to have always existed in that perfection of self-identity from before birth' (Irigaray 1985a, 355). Irigaray argues that in order for such conceptions to be developed they had to ignore unacknowledged presumptions and exclusions, which enabled such specific conceptions of unity and identity to arise. She maintains that that which constitutes such exclusions, presumptions and the unacknowledged grounds of the unity of subjectivity has been figured in terms of the feminine, of woman as the inessential substratum of the possibility of a unified subject. 'Is she unnecessary in and of herself, but essential as the non-subjective sub-jectum? As that which can never achieve the status of subject... Is she the indispensable condition whereby the living entity retains and maintains and perfects himself in his self-likeness?' (Irigaray 1985a, 165). That which is not figured within such a conception of identity, unity and subjectivity is a concept of relationality as comprising subjectivity and objectivity. There is an implicit denial of the possibility of an ontology which is not premised on the one, that is, an ontology which acknowledges existence to be primarily and always not one, or at least two.

Elements of Irigaray's critique resonate profoundly with Whitehead's attack on Aristotle's notion of "primary substance" and the adoption of the Aristotelian form of subject-predicate logic as expressing the ultimate character of existence (see Chapter One). Irigaray likewise identifies the presupposition of an unseen base which provides the ground for the existence of, and conceptualization of, a distinct and unified subject which distinguishes itself from such a base. She clarifies the extent of the infection of contemporary concepts by such presumptions when she points out that they, implicitly, yet silently, rely upon a figuring of maleness and femaleness for their very mode of operation. One consequence of this is that "woman" comes to occupy the role of constituting that which enables predication but can never itself be predicated as a genuine subject. Maleness and femaleness, man and woman, have become oppositional terms of thought and are deeply embedded in our language, abstractions, concepts and ways of life; their apparently real oppositionality is a prime element of our culture of thought. This has disallowed the feminine from assuming any objectivity in its individuality, as it is defined as that which is not masculine: 'Merely added to – or taken away from – essence, fortuitous, troublesome, "accidental," she can be modified or eliminated without changing anything in "nature"' (Irigaray 1985a, 167). Whitehead is even more specific, yet still in accordance with Irigaray, in his discussion of the problem of the term "one". 'The term "one" does not stand for "the integral number *one*," which is a complex special notion' (PR, 21). To divide the world up in terms of one table, two chairs, is to impose, *a posteriori*, a (rational) conception of the way the universe is divided up into objects. But such divisions of objects are not in themselves real, for these divisions rely upon a conception of the world as containing a class of self-identical, inert objects. 'The term "one"... stands for the general idea underlying the indefinite article "*a* or *an*," and the definite article "*the*," and the demonstratives "*this* or *that*," and the relatives "*which* or *what* or *how*." It stands for the singularity of an entity' (PR, 21; emphasis in original). Whitehead's notion of actuality is based upon a concept of individuality but differentiates his concept from those approaches to individuation which rely upon the internal consistency of objects (Newton etc.). As has been seen, Whitehead's interest is in how such singularity is premised upon the admission of, and the rendering of, the "external" world into one element or moment or singularity. This approach enables the description of individuation as real (though not numerically distinct) whilst also accounting for the operations of wider influences in such individuation.

The metaphysical aspect of *Process and Reality* entails that Whitehead's discussion of the process of individuation in his work is one which abstracts out to the conditions of all existence and, necessarily, ignores the specificities of any individual (in terms of maleness and femaleness, for example). This is not something that Irigaray believes to be possible. And it is here that the importance of sexual difference for Irigaray's approach becomes clear. It is not the positing of a primary, essential fact which subtends all existence. Initially at least, it should be seen as a way of confronting and disrupting a mode of conceptualization which has dominated western thought and culture. 'For if she were to shine, then the light would no longer, simply, belong to sameness. The whole of the current economic system would have to be recalculated' (Irigaray 1985a, 345).

It could therefore be said that Irigaray has provided a crucial chapter for Whitehead's proposed work on the history of the doctrine of matter. And she has not done this at a level of unwarranted abstraction; she has tied this to the conditions and cultures through which such concepts have developed and she has also tied the very development of specific aspects of such cultures to the production of such concepts:

> The fundamental model of the human being...one, singular, solitary and historically masculine, that of the adult Western male, rational and competent. Diversity was therefore still conceived of and lived hierarchically, with the many always subordinate to the one. Others were nothing but copies of the idea of man, a potentially perfect idea which all the more or less imperfect copies had to try to equal. These copies, moreover, were not defined in their own terms, in other words, according to a different subjectivity, but in those of an ideal subjectivity and as a function of their deficiencies with respect to it: age, race, culture, sex, etc. The model of the subject thus remained singular, and the 'others' represented more or less good examples within the hierarchy established in relation to the singular subject. (Irigaray 2000a, 122)

Hence, the premising of sexual difference is not a recourse to a biological given, it is an attempt to posit a mode of existence which is not reducible to the form of a unique, self-identical identity as constructed by Western thinking. That is to say, the way we think of objects and of subjects is not "how they really are"; it is an example of a mode of thinking which arises from the Newtonian concept of force and space and objects. Such an approach has been dismissed by much of modern science, yet we still retain its conceptual framework within other aspects of our culture of thought. So, when Irigaray is talking of nature, she is, like Whitehead, doing so in a manner which is not reduced or reducible to biology; such reductions, such limitations, are themselves historical inculcations of modernity. The reduction and limitation of nature to the study of science is a narrowing of focus which produces and relies upon abstractions which claim for themselves an unjustified and unwarranted authority when deployed outside of their original sphere, or when they are not recognized for the limited abstractions that they are really are (see Stengers 2002, 29, 52).

Irigaray and Whitehead thus recognize the power of abstractions and their abiding influence; they also pay attention to their modes of construction and their consequences. It is in this sense that they are immanently and continually aware of the ("political") importance of offering ways of rethinking nature. 'If we are to get away from the omnipotent model of the one and the many, we have to move on to the *two*, a two which is not two times one itself, not even a bigger or smaller one, but which would be made up of two which are really different.' (Irigaray 2000a, 129; emphasis in original.)

Nature is at least Two

As Stone (2006, 1–17) has pointed out, the importance of Irigaray's contribution to discussions of sexual difference has been misrecognized by those commentators who have emphasized her statements which insist upon the primacy and irreducibility of the difference between male and female, to the exclusion of an analysis of her work as a contribution to the philosophy of nature. It is within the scope of the latter that her discussions of sexual difference should be approached. As such, what is at stake is the development of a theoretical and empirical position where nature is not predicated on any unity of substance, on a conception and preconception of the *one* as originary. This is a theme that runs throughout Irigaray's work and which links her early critiques of the legacy of Western philosophy with her more recent investigations of civil (sexual) identity and rights. Irigaray points out the constructedness of what is normally conceived of as nature (without reducing nature to a social construction) and reclaims the right to define and discuss that which constitutes the natural, as against the (masculinist) and dominating appropriations of nature and the natural which have misrendered and limited its scope.

> The time of life has become a socio-logical temporality founded on a second (or double) nature of man that has caused him to lose his relation to the living world... What assures this torn and artificial temporality are logical structures founded in particular upon the principles of identity and resemblance, upon the principle of noncontradiction, that is to say upon the definition of a second nature the poles of which are no longer day and night, the seasons, the ages of life, but, at best, the oscillating from the true to the false. (Irigaray 2002, 47)

So, that which passes for nature in contemporary scientific, philosophical, environmental and sociological analyses is, according to Irigaray, an artificial nature which cannot, therefore, be truly universal. Like Whitehead, Irigaray points out that this nature is a logical construct as it exists only insofar as it relies on abstractions such as those of noncontradiction and binary oppositions. However, these only function as partial accounts and not as indications of the full reality of existence and of nature. They posit a somewhat limited and arbitrary nature which does disservice to the diversity and actuality of that which constitutes existence. This limited concept of nature excludes genuine differences of nature, such as day and night, which are not binary oppositions but part of a dynamic rhythm of the universe, its process. This is a form of duality which suffuses existence, but which is not constituted by supposedly binary oppositions; is not predicated on a notion of the "one"; is not the opposite of a many or multiple, but is genuinely dual. This is a provocative challenge to our culture of thought and to its envisaging of duality always in terms of a break, gap, opposition, bifurcation. Whitehead describes this genuine duality as follows:

> The universe is dual because, in the fullest sense, it is both transient and eternal. The universe is dual because each final actuality is both physical and mental. The universe is dual because each actuality requires abstract character... The universe is *many* because it is wholly and completely to be analysed into many final actualities... The universe is *one*, because of the universal immanence. There is thus a dualism in this contrast between the unity and multiplicity. (AI, 245. Emphasis in original.)

Thinking of duality as a *contrast* which does not prioritize either of its terms is a major demand that Whitehead makes to our limited culture of thought which stumbles with its notions of fixity, opposition, subjects, objects, matter, quality, inert facticity and agential humanity. Thinking of duality as a contrast enables actuality and potentiality to inhere absolutely; abstraction and facticity to be combined; unity and multiplicity to be mutually expressive of the process of existence.

The question now becomes, how is it possible to discuss or to develop such genuine differences within nature which are not circumscribed or limited by the concepts, facts and beings which populate the concepts of nature which predominate today? And the answer, for Irigaray, is to posit sexual difference as the key. Hence:

> The natural is at least two: male and female. All the speculation about overcoming the natural in the universal forgets that nature is not *one*. In order to go beyond – assuming this is necessary – we should make reality the point of departure: it is *two* (a *two* containing in turn secondary differences: smaller/larger, younger/older, for instance). The universal has been thought of as *one*, thought on the basis of *one*. But this *one* does not exist. (Irigaray 1996, 35. Emphasis in original.)

In order to challenge the philosophical presuppositions and errors which haunt us today in terms of the notions of unity and identity, it is sexual difference, figured in terms of male and female, which should be the prime mode and model, argues

Irigaray. Maleness and femaleness are deeply implanted in our language, concepts and world and cannot just be thought or explained away. The task is to refigure our conceptual inheritance and to boldly return to a philosophy of nature which goes beyond the unity of identity to a concept of duality.

As Stone points out, Irigaray envisages this duality of the world, its "bi-polarity", as inherently "sexuate".

> For Irigaray then, all natural phenomena have poles, which are placed in their polar relations to each other by the complementary rhythms at which they suck in fluids (expand) and expel fluids (contract). Insofar as this rhythmic bipolarity in all natural processes and phenomena makes them 'sexuate', this is because bipolarity approximates in structure to human sexual difference. (Stone 2006, 90)

Whitehead too insists that all existence is "bi-polar". But for him, this expresses the metaphysical character of the duality of all moments of existence as comprised of both actuality and potentiality (see Chapter Four): 'Each actuality is essentially bipolar, physical and mental, and the physical inheritance is essentially accompanied by a conceptual reaction partly conformed to it, and partly introductory of a relevant novel contrast' (PR, 108). The important element here is that there is a primary duality to existence which is best expressed, for Whitehead, in terms of materiality and conceptuality and, for Irigaray, in terms of sexual difference. Hence, the adverse reactions to her work, and the charges of essentialism and conservatism which are often proffered to her, could be seen as indicative of the depth of the challenge that she, like Whitehead, is making to the contemporary culture of thought. This culture is firm in its denial and refusal of the possibility of a duality which is not predicated on the "one", preferring as it does notions of unity or of the multiple. As Stengers puts it, the task for contemporary thought is to remain open to new ideas without imagining that we are free to think whatever we want. Openness always places a limit and a responsibility.

> Keeping the doors and windows open is a constraint on thinking. It does not only demand that the thinker leave the solid ground of agreed human conventions, which affirm the legitimacy of certain possibilities and condemn others. In order to leave this ground, it also demands that the thinker not aim at what would transcend the conventions that give its consistency to this ground. (Stengers 2009b, 18)

For Whitehead and Irigaray, "keeping the doors and windows open" entails a willingness to conceptualize nature as being *at least two*. The real task is to explain what it means and how it is possible to be not one, rather than simply asserting the bipolarity of existence or that two kinds of sexually different humans are

primary. Crucially, such duality cannot arise from the simple addition of ones as
this would simply be to try and create a multiple or diversity on the basis of the
model of the one: 'of one + one + one…juxtaposed and gathered together by
exterior and more or less artificial laws' (Irigaray 2002, 17).

To reiterate: simply stating that nature is not one and that it is multiple,
in the sense that it is some kind of (postmodern) free-for-all where there
is no unity or no identity, where everything is reduced to being merely
flux of flow, would be to miss the point. Positing a utopia of supposedly
democratic, multiple beings, would be to misconceive the actuality of
existence and it would enable the continuation of the status quo under
another name. So, Irigaray takes the harder road – that of rethinking the
overcoming of the domination of the "one" through a thinking of the
"not-one" as an "at least two".

> This *two* inscribes finitude in the natural itself. No one nature can claim to
> correspond to the whole of the natural. There is no "Nature" as a singular entity.
> In this sense, a kind of negative does exist in the natural. The negative is not
> a process of consciousness of which only man is capable. (Irigaray 1996, 35.
> Emphasis in original.)

Irigaray turns the usual formulation on its head by insisting that if you deny
sexual difference, then all individuals are forced into a supposedly "neutral"
society: 'an undifferentiated state of universality to be shared in a masculine or
neutral world' (Irigaray 2000a, 37). So it is the "at least two" which will guarantee
a form of identity which is not neuter, is not objectified, is not commodified
and reduced to the possibility of being exchanged in an economy of other
objects. Sexual difference, rather than referring to a biological category which
limits or fixes the possibilities of all individuals' being, capabilities and life,
becomes a mode of challenging dominant power structures.

There still remains the question of the status of the entities which constitute
sexual difference. It is clear that on occasions Irigaray insists that it is maleness
and femaleness, and men and women, which constitute a privileged site, to
the exclusion of other modes of difference (such as transgender or intersex).
In doing so, she apparently puts a primary ontological and social value upon
heterosexual relations.[2] But, whilst Irigaray does develop such positions within
her texts, they are not positions which necessarily follow from her critical
concepts and they do not invalidate her development of a novel version of the
philosophy of nature. It is possible to develop a faithful yet distinct reading of
her work which does not prioritize the masculine, feminine or the *sexual* aspect,
but emphasizes nonoppositional difference (which is, in her terms, "sexuate").
On occasions she does fail to allow for the possibility that there could be other

possible sexual differences which enable individuation to operate as a singular process without trapping such processes within fixed forms of individuals. And, perhaps it is through the work of Whitehead (despite his use of gendered nouns and pronouns) that alternative readings could be developed:

> Nature is plastic, although to every prevalent state of mind there corresponds iron nature setting its bounds to life... It is a false dichotomy to think of Nature *and* Man [sic].[3] Mankind is that factor *in* Nature which exhibits in its most intense form the plasticity of nature. (AI, 99. Emphasis in original.)

The first move in accounting for such a novel conception of individuation is not to limit the difference (whatever it is that constitutes this) to fixed human entities. Rather, it is to describe this plasticity and the forms that it adopts in the current world. Such plasticity is neither simply social nor natural; this would be to preemptively accept a division between the two and to reduce nature to a limited scene and mode of operation (as envisaged by post-Newtonian science). It is the delimiting of nature which has produced false notions of the status and role of the natural.

> But what by now we experience as natural immediacy is sometimes already distant from the natural. We have become fabricated humans. In order to reach something natural, we speak of the fact:
>
> 1) that the love between woman (women) and man (men) is "natural";
> 2) that reproduction is obligatory: it, therefore, is no longer an ornament of love, but a duty imposed by the State or by the Church in the name of nature.
>
> What nature leaves us is the instinct to violence... and the obligation to reproduce: two perversions of our being human. (Irigaray 2000b, 82–3)

In contemporary society, individuals are fabricated humans who mistakenly believe that the current alignments in terms of sex and gender somehow express something natural (when they are clearly constructions) and view sexual reproduction as a natural (compulsory) consequence of sexual relations. These explanations of "natural" behaviour, life, desires, are, says Irigaray, unnatural as they go against what we are and what we could be. Irigaray therefore makes clear the importance and possibilities offered by reconceptualizing sexual difference in terms of a novel philosophy of "a nature which is not one". This returns to the question as to whether the maleness and femaleness of sexual difference which Irigaray proposes actually exist (in a pregiven sense) prior to their elaboration in such relations.

We exist, we are born into a given set of relations (material and cultural) and these are often elaborated in terms of sexual difference. But could there not be a more elemental difference of which sexual difference, as currently conceived, is only a possible expression, not *the* expression? The following sections on sexual difference as relational, as comprising a contrast rather than an opposition, will attempt to respond to these questions more fully.

Difference and Opposition

One of the reasons that sexual difference is often seen as reductionist or essentialist within social theory is that it would seem to refer to a fixed, given set of properties which define what that entity is, and what it can be and do. In this way, an entity derives its being and purpose by acceding to an already established classification. Each thing is understandable on its own terms, as constituted by its own self-identity, and not in relation to other things; it is what it is and it is where it is. As has been seen, Whitehead and Irigaray have both contested this form of thinking about what constitutes an object (or a subject). In terms of sexual difference, this approach to understanding objects (and subjects) has further consequences.

Sexual difference is often conceptualized as involving a degree of exclusion of other properties and other characteristics in order for that entity to be what it is (and to not be something else). However, such exclusion is not mere noninclusion, instead it refers to that which is necessarily unnecessary for the definition and being of that entity. In this way, being is defined in terms of opposition. "What is a man?" "Well, whatever a man is, he is certainly not a woman". The so-called evidence to back up such claims is then premised on that which is specific to that sex, and not to the other. Whether this is done in terms of genitalia, hormones, chromosomes, the presumption is the same; identity proceeds from opposition, not from similarity or relationality.

As distinct from such approaches, Whitehead and Irigaray have outlined the need to understand being in terms which are relational, as well as the necessity of thinking in terms of contrast (see Stengers 2002, 566–72 for a discussion of the importance of the notion of contrast for "thinking with Whitehead"). As Irigaray puts it: 'Belonging to a gender represents a destination to the other more than it represents a biological destiny' (Irigaray 2000b, 33). Attempts to discuss sexual difference should not be seen as attempts to define what a man or a woman *is*, and certainly not to envisage such entities in terms of opposition, as has been the case with so many theorists, including Hegel: 'in order to overcome what he terms natural immediacy within the family Hegel turns to pairs of opposites. Hence he is forced to define man and woman as opposites and not as different' (Irigaray

1996, 20). Hegel fixes on the notion that oppositionality is constitutive of reality. Whitehead and Irigaray argue that there is a need to go beyond such simple oppositionality to rethink the interrelations of self and nature. For example: 'Her so-called passivity would not then be part of an active/passive pair of opposites but would signify a different economy, a different relation to nature and to the self' (Irigaray 1996, 38).

According to Whitehead and Irigaray, just because things are different does not mean they are opposed; the whole notion of binary oppositions relies on a notion of the one and lacks any thinking through of the possibility of a two (or an "at least two") which is neither secondary to, nor derived from, a unique "one". Instead, their notion of "contrast" enables there to be difference which is constitutive, in the sense of being productive, without being premised on the self-identity of any, or either, entity or concept (such as "Man" and "Woman"). Irigaray wants to be able to talk fully about difference and views traditional approaches to the dialectic as limited due to their reliance on a notion of opposition, which is unable to consider difference as nonoppositional. However:

> The rigor of Hegel can teach us that a third way is missing: a culture which corresponds to the objectivity of our destiny as sexuate beings. For this culture, there needs to be two subjects of different genders, not subjugated to the ties of blood. In this way, the natural can become culture without anything being missing from ethicality. This is the stage which Hegel could not realize... Hegel does not imagine that the relationship between woman and man can be a tie of culture. According to him, it remains uncultivated "natural immediacy". (Irigaray 2000b, 83)

As such: 'It is important to redialecticize the relations between nature and culture' (Irigaray 2002, 16).

It may appear that Irigaray is falling back into old categories and arguments about the relationship of nature to culture with all the dreaded connotations that they bring with them. Whilst there is certainly a danger of this within her texts, it is also possible to argue that Irigaray is resolutely refusing to claim more than is conceptually possible. She is aware of the efficacy, the history and the legacy of the nature-culture opposition (and its relation to the bifurcation of nature) but is also aware that it cannot be so easily dismissed. Instead, it has to be recast, rethought. Within this new philosophy of nature, the old meanings, associations and limits of the natural have to be shifted, as do those of that which constitutes the cultural. In this respect, sexual difference, the body and bodily sexual difference become the prime sites for a renewed investigation into our material and cultural constructions and abstractions. 'Sexual difference cannot...be reduced to a simple extralinguistic fact of nature. It conditions language and is conditioned by it...It's situated at the junction of nature and culture' (Irigaray 1993, 20). It is a preeminent yet dangerous aspect of our culture of thought which needs to be worked through thoroughly to provide new concepts and avenues for ways of being and acting.

Whitehead also critiques the prevailing division of the world into distinct classes of objects which can be defined and analysed in terms of their individuality and self-identity.

> Each substantial thing is thus conceived as complete in itself, without any reference to any other substantial thing. Such an account...renders an interconnected world of real individuals unintelligible. The universe is shivered into a multitude of disconnected substantial things, each thing in its own way exemplifying its private bundle of abstract characters which have found a common home in its own substantiality. But substantial thing cannot call unto substantial thing. (AI, 169–70)

Irigaray takes up this challenge of accounting for the difference between and also the interconnection of subjects: 'If a gesture of this sort were to take place, philosophy would have to recognize that two subjects exist and that reason must measure itself against the reality and the to be of those two subjects' (Irigaray 2000b, 36). In order to accomplish this, she posits the existence not of two primarily different kinds of subjects (men and women, or male and female) but of a twoness to the universe which is not reducible to a one, or explained away in a multiplicity. She characterizes this twoness in terms of a maleness and femaleness which permeates all existence but is not limited to their simplified manifestations in the bodies of men and women. On this account, sexual difference becomes the site of renewal of the discussion of subjectivity and politics. For: 'Hers is more an *inter-subject* economy than an economy of subject-object relations; it is thus a very social and cultural economy' (Irigaray 1994, 19; emphasis in original). Importantly, this does not predicate a purely human social. It is not an unthinking acceptance of the legacy of sociality as pronounced by nineteenth-century social theory. For such a sociality of solely human relations was itself, according to Irigaray, posited on the notion of supposedly self-contained conceptual and actual units which were the model of the individual man. So, 'man prefers a relationship between the one and the many, between the I-masculine subject and others: people, society, understood as *them* and not as *you*' (Irigaray 2000b, 17; emphasis in original). Hence Irigaray, with Whitehead, insists that establishing the notions of relationality and contrast as fundamental also involves and entails a rethinking and regrounding of the concept of the social as that which combines and brings together, at different moments and places, those historical, material and potential elements which constitute ongoing but changing experiences of the objects and subjects which populate the world. The notion of process thus comes to the fore.

The key, then, is to prioritize relations, relationality, contrast and process. This does not necessarily entail relativism or a dissolving of difference into mere diversity or a flattened notion of equality. Rather, it is to attempt to develop an account of the actual and potential relations within the contemporary world, given the construction of such relations as they have been, are and will be. One first move, according to Irigaray, is to recognize that existence and contemporary society are sexuate and relational. This would certainly suggest that these relations can change. In contemporary society and theory there pertain a specific set of relations, some of which we divide into natural and social (cultural) relations. The former are seen as fixed and given, and as falling within the realm of science. The latter are viewed as contingent and arbitrary, and they fall under the province of the social and cultural sciences. One consequence of this is a misconception of materiality and subjectivity as inhabiting distinct realms as do, supposedly, sex and gender. Materiality and facticity are once again delimited as permanent and set, rather than as relational. It is this misunderstanding of the nature of nature (and the refusal to see nature as relational) that has made the facticity of the body so contentious within social theory, doubly so when this is rendered in terms of sexual difference. Some possibilities of taking up the work of Whitehead and Irigaray to rethink the status of the facticity of the body will be addressed in the following and final section.

Gender and the Process of Becoming. The "Withness of the Body"

As set out in Chapter Six, Whitehead is insistent that there is no "gap" or lacuna between the body and the world (nor is there a gap between the subject and the world or thinking and the world). There is, therefore, an explicit continuation between the world and the body. But this is not to say that the body is simply a resultant of the world; it is not determined by the world. It is certainly *in* the world and is not merely a fiction or a pure social construction. 'We are in the world and the world is in us… The body is ours, and we are an activity within our body' (MT, 227). Whitehead describes this relationship of the body to the world in terms of '"withness"' (PR, 62 and passim). 'For instance, we see the contemporary chair, but we see it *with* our eyes; and we touch the contemporary chair, but we touch it *with* our hands' (PR, 62; emphasis in original). Perception of the world by a human subject does not just rely on bodily existence, it is an example of bodily existence. In order to avoid the notion of the bifurcation of nature, Whitehead resolutely imparts the body as that which enables perception: it is within and from this bodily experience of the world, of which it is an element, that the subject arises. 'According to this interpretation, the human body is to be conceived of as a complex "amplifier"' (PR, 119). Whitehead's notion of the "withness of the body" entails an utter interweaving of the body and the world and points out that all of the body (and all of the senses) are involved in the body's and the subject's acquaintance with the world. However, within Western philosophy and society, it is sight, as a disembodied faculty, that has been privileged, to the exclusion of the other senses, and has thereby become inextricably linked and reliant upon the prior existence of a mind. 'Philosophers have disdained information about the universe obtained through their visceral feelings, and have concentrated on visual feelings' (PR, 121). Sight, disembodied sight and the gaze have all been validated by western philosophy and science and the bodily aspect of existence, experience and knowledge have been ignored or denigrated.

In *Speculum of the Other Woman*, Irigaray (1985a) also explains the dangers of privileging sight at the expense of the other senses and of the body in general. This is associated with either denying or excluding the contribution of the body to the experience and existence of the human subject. The myth of the purity of the link between sight and thought is created and sustained, as such a subject has no body (this is the genealogy of the "male gaze"). In an interesting counterpart to Whitehead's notion of the *withness* of the body, Irigaray critiques this prevailing philosophical concept of a subject *without* a body.

> *Blind* except for the contemplation of his Ideas. *Deaf* except to the sounds of his soul revolving in harmony, and the soul speaks only to itself without the aid or assistance of any voice. Thought now capable of doing without "discourse" or "dialogue"... *Without hands or feet*, organs, unfitted to the movements of intelligence and reflection... *Taking care not to touch* any "strange things," also, and *deprived of legs* so that there can be no walking off toward something attractive outside the self. Completeness of one who is self-sufficient: this is the destiny to which the souls are called who have donned the nature of the living beings most able to honor the Gods. (Irigaray 1985a, 321. Emphasis in original.)

The ignorance of the body within social theory is not to be set to rights simply by outlining its social constructedness. There is more required than that. The very conceptual schemata which enabled the denial of the body need to be challenged through a productive conceptual account of the withness of the body in relation to subjectivity and being. This is what Whitehead and Irigaray provide. Yet it must be stressed that their emphasis on the need for a full account of the role of the body in experience and hence existence is not to resort to socio-biological descriptions. Conceiving of the body in terms of *withness* is not a positing of the body as an originator. Rather, the body is an exemplum of that system which characterizes how all that "is" relates to everything else that "is". Irigaray and Whitehead both refuse to accept any hierarchy between those things which are; they also refuse to predicate a distinction between the natural and the social or the factual and the cultural. They want to 'create a plane (*plan*) capable of welcoming the plurality of all that which we experience without establishing any privilege or hierarchy' (Stengers 2002, 74). In this respect, the human body, like any other body, is an "amplifier" but is not a substratum upon which the passing accidental changes of emotion, blood pressure etc., arise. The body is continually constituted and reconstituted through the reception, valuation, and passing-on of relations. Thus the world seeps into the individual and the individual seeps into the world. The definiteness of an individual is defined in relation to the manner in which it incorporates the world. Duration and materiality are real but only insofar as they manifest a complex arrangement of a specific and novel rendering of prior elements of the world.

It is in these terms that it might be possible to shift the focus of the relation of sexual difference and the body. Indeed, it could be argued that the possession or nonpossession of a penis is not that which defines the maleness of a man. The material penis is sometimes important, sometimes it is not. Sometimes it exists, sometimes it does not. Sexual difference is itself relational, materially and culturally. 'My body is not, therefore, a simple "facticity"; it is a relationship-with: with me, with my gender, with the other gender' (Irigaray 2000b, 33). For Whitehead, this relationality is an integral aspect of the existence of the universe. 'The creative process is rhythmic: it swings from the publicity of many things to the individual privacy; and it swings back from the private individual to the publicity of the objectified individual' (PR, 151); 'this pendulum of the universe that we are' (Irigaray 2002, 47). Reality is a process and process is the only reality. This is not to suggest that Whitehead or Irigaray dissolve existence into mere becomings, or ephemeral passings-on and passings-away in which actuality and materiality have a secondary place. Quite the opposite: what is so important about Whitehead's work is the demand to develop a theoretical approach which satisfies the demands of both a philosophy of becoming and the existence and effectivity of actual things (which he terms "stubborn fact").

> It is in respect to this "stubborn fact" that the theories of modern philosophy are weakest. Philosophers have worried themselves about remote consequences and the inductive formulations of science. They should confine attention to the rush of immediate transition. (PR, 129)

And this is part of the importance of the work of Irigaray in that she attempts to describe both the process and actuality of those elements of this "immediate transition" which constitute contemporary renditions of man and woman. 'Women and men must therefore be recognized as representatives or as incarnations of human gender. They have to be valorized for the sake of the becoming of their sexed *I*, for the relations between them and for the constitution of a spiritual dialectic of these relations' (Irigaray 1996, 108; emphasis in original). So, matter and materiality are not determinants and nor are they determined. The body is a quasi-stable material outcome of a whole set of processes and relations. Science has focused on a limited range of these and claimed the right to speak of all materiality. But in doing so it has overstepped the boundaries of its conceptual authority. Social theory too, in ignoring the importance of the materiality of the body, has rendered itself unable to address the sexed body adequately. Whitehead and Irigaray offer a way to reconsider such an impasse and to address the body's sexing. For example, for Irigaray, this will entail that: 'each man must remain a man in the process of becoming. He himself has to accomplish the task of being *this* man he is by birth and a model of humanity, a model that is both corporeal and spiritual' (Irigaray 1996, 27; emphasis in original). Being sexed is not pregiven, fixed and essential. It is part of a process which happens again and again, and in different ways. Tracing the manner and means of these ways might be one task of sociology.

Conclusion

Within his works Whitehead did not directly address the question of sexual difference but it is clear that his philosophical framework enables a reconsideration of the premises upon which such a distinction is set. For Irigaray, sexual difference is of the utmost immediate philosophical, political and practical importance. In her account, maleness and femaleness exist within nature, considered as the whole of existence, but sexed individuals do not exist, in that sexed individuals are not givens. Sexed individuals have to become, they have to become individuated individuals. It is perhaps possible to claim that when Irigaray states that there is maleness and femaleness "in nature" she is somewhat limited by the legacy and concepts of the language she finds herself within. Nevertheless, Irigaray is scrupulous and rigorous in sticking with the idea that maleness and femaleness invoke a difference which is not unitary and express a duality rather than a multiplicity. For:

> What must be surmounted for the becoming of our freedom is not only a natural pregiven but also a cultural one. We are born in a culture in which it is not always clear what belongs to nature and what belongs to a culture foreign to it. We must, therefore, interpret our culture as a determination which can possibly alienate our becoming. (Irigaray 2000b, 90)

To put it another way: maleness and femaleness do not really exist (in a pregiven sense) prior to their elaboration in the relations between sexed and gendered individuals in society as it is and as it changes.[4] That is to say, all humans are born into a given set of relations (material, natural, historical, political, social and cultural) and these are often embroiled and elaborated in terms of sexual difference. But sexual difference itself does not exist except in those actual individualizations which are expressed in contemporary society. As such, sexual difference is not foundational but is, rather, a limited and limiting expression rather than *the* expression of the difference which enables individuation as a material and social being. This is more of a Whiteheadian reading of the status of the *difference* of sexual difference than an elaboration of Irigaray's position. For Irigaray is ultimately more insistent on the primacy of maleness and femaleness as *the* difference rather than *an* expression of difference. However, her work does reiterate the importance of investigating why it should be that certain limited sexed positions are repeated with such disastrous effects and why the same tends to return rather than opening up new avenues of becoming sexed.[5] Irigaray's work also points to the importance and difficulty of challenging the prevailing culture of thought and of producing a mode of thought which is able to think of nature not as a one, or as a two premised on the existence of a one (or in the image of such a one), in order to think of a more-than-one which is exemplified in terms of contrast and not in terms of opposition. Genuine productive difference.

Combining Whitehead and Irigaray, it is therefore possible to reclaim discussions of materiality within social theory and to develop an account where material sexual difference would still not be a given, but does actually come to really be. Sexual difference does not subtend the existence of separate beings. But beings with sexual difference do come to be actual. And this is more than the coming to be of a sign or a signifying system; it is more than just developing ways in which we *know* the inclusion (and exclusion) of certain kinds of bodies as both mattered and mattering. It is both an ontological and epistemological matter. However, what it means and what it is to be a man or a woman (and indeed to be intersex or transgendered) is not to be predicated on the prior existence of sexual difference as a final fact, for 'it is the occasion characterized as completely concrete that is an abstraction' (Stengers 2002, 251). Being (becoming) *this* man and *this* woman is a material, historical, conceptual process. Whitehead and Irigaray both insist that the final fact will always be a becoming. And that, in our society, there is a becoming of both gender *and* of sexual difference. Man and Woman are abstractions.

Chapter Eight

CAPITALISM, PROCESS AND ABSTRACTION

Earlier chapters stressed the importance of abstraction for thinking, to the extent that thought is only possible through a process of abstraction. The previous chapter suggested that Man and Woman are abstractions. This raises the question of whether such abstractions are *only* abstractions in thought, some kind of conceptual device akin, perhaps, to Weber's Ideal Types? There are certainly some affinities between these two approaches but there are important disparities as well. Whitehead's culture of thought implies more than just a methodological approach to thinking about reality. He places abstraction at the heart of reality. That is to say, existence is itself a matter of abstraction. It is important that the term "matter" is emphasized here. Whitehead does not view abstraction as predicated on a fuller, more real, substratum of existence of which contemporary items, entities and societies are superficial reflections, representations or epiphenomena. Reality in all its fullness is exemplified and expressed by those things which populate the contemporary world: 'There is no going behind actual entities to find anything more real' (PR, 18). The notion of abstraction arises from the process of selection whereby some elements of the past are combined into a novel unity. This selection (or 'decision' (PR, 28 and passim)) cannot incorporate all elements of existence; instead, the positive selection of certain elements, their combining, the manner of their combining and the mode of mutual holding together which forms a society constitute a specific rendering of aspects of the world.

> The ultimate metaphysical principle is the advance from disjunction to conjunction, creating a novel entity other than the entities given in disjunction. The novel entity is at once the togetherness of the "many" which it finds, and also it is one among the disjunctive "many" which it leaves; it is a novel entity, disjunctively among the many entities which it synthesizes. The many become one, and are increased by one. (PR, 21)

This is what might be termed an additive abstraction. So, whilst Whitehead insists again and again that thinking is an abstractive process, this is not to limit abstraction to thinking alone. Once more Whitehead refuses to place human experience as central, originary or as constituting a complete explanation. He wants to break the seemingly inviolable link between abstraction and thinking which dogs much contemporary theory and philosophy.

> Thus "objectification" itself is abstraction... Abstraction expresses nature's mode of interaction and is not merely mental. When it abstracts, thought is merely conforming to nature – or rather, it is exhibiting itself as an element in nature. (SYM, 25–6)

In describing abstraction as a necessary element of material existence, Whitehead remains faithful to the etymology of the word "abstract". In the Collins (English) Dictionary, one definition of abstraction is 'the process of formulating generalized ideas or concepts by extracting common qualities from specific examples...an idea or concept formulated in this way: *good and evil are abstractions*' (*Collins English Dictionary* 1986, 6; emphasis in original). This invokes the primacy of the link between ideas and abstraction, as usually conceived. However, the dictionary also points out that the word "abstraction" comes, ultimately, from the Latin word "ab-trahere". This refers to the dragging off, or drawing off, of a thing; the moving of some thing from one place to another place. The meaning is, therefore, linked to that of "traction" adjoined to the prefix "ab-", which means "away from" or "off". Thus, it can be seen that abstraction is concerned with the movement of things and does not necessarily only have to refer to a process of thought or a thinking thing.[1]

Take, for example, the short piece of writing of 200–300 words that is placed at the start of many articles in academic journals and which is known as an abstract. It is supposed to be more than a mere summary of the article, it is supposed to contain all the vital elements of that article. It brings together what is most pertinent to that which follows. An abstract distils that which is new, the arguments made, the material to be covered and provides a concentration of what follows. Such abstracts are often written before the article itself. They are a combining of previously disparate elements, materials or ideas, they are a concentration of an argument. In what way can this be said to be either material or conceptual? It is both. It is a drawing or dragging off from one place to bring together in another place. It is an abstraction.

Another example: in the process of the distillation of alcohol, the aim is to bring together the best elements of the grains, water, etc., and to combine the key elements of these to provide a new product – malt whisky, for example. The process starts with barley which is made into malt and then into malt-flour to which water and yeast are added. This is then brewed and a kind of beer (wort) is made. This is then distilled and concentrated. It is then distilled again, and once this is done it is heated so that the "flavoured" alcohol evaporates (is separated) from the beer-like mixture; the result is malt whisky. A real abstraction.

Such examples and the metaphysical status of abstraction in the work of Whitehead might appear to bear little relevance to social theory. There is, again, a need to relate such concepts to its immediate concerns. One such aspect of this is the recent return within analyses of the work of Marx to the importance of abstraction for his attempts to understand the status and operations of capitalism (see Toscano 2008a and 2008b for a clear and detailed analysis and contribution to such a shift). This chapter will provide an analysis of Marx's description of the role of abstractions within capitalism and the mode of abstractive thought which is required to understand the operations of such abstractions. These two processes are interlinked. So, in response to Sohn-Rethel's question: 'Can there be abstraction other than by Thought?' (Sohn-Rethel 1978, 17), the answer will be in the affirmative (as it is for Sohn-Rethel and would also be for Whitehead). In this way it will be possible to move beyond the base-superstructure model to an account of capitalism as comprised of a certain quality of processes which infect contemporary society. It will be argued that, in a technical, Whiteheadian sense, capitalism does not exist; it does not subtend or determine the elaboration of social relations. Instead it is constituted in and through the manner of these relations. Hence process, facticity, potentiality, limitation, production are all interlinked as operations of the ongoing, ever-renewing dynamics which occur in a specific manner: the manner of capitalism. To claim that capitalism has no substantial existence is not to deny or lessen its pernicious effects. Rather it is to point to the insidious way in which it inhabits, inheres in, proscribes and prescribes contemporary existence.[2]

Marx on Capitalism

Marx does not, indeed he cannot, start the analysis of *Capital Volume 1* with a simple denouncement of capital and capitalism. He is trying to understand how it works. One problem of starting out on such a quest is that capitalism is a process with an alternating rhythm. The full character of this process will only become clear as the analysis unfolds. It is only toward the end of the volume that Marx is able to describe all the elements of the process of capitalism and the limiting manner of its operation:

> It is no longer a mere accident that capitalist and worker confront each other in the market as buyer and seller. It is the alternating rhythm of the process itself which throws the worker back on to the market again and again as the seller of his [sic][3] labour-power and continually transforms his own product into a means

by which another man can purchase him. In reality, the worker belongs to capital before he has sold himself to the capitalist. His economic bondage is at once mediated through, and congealed by, the periodic renewal of the act by which he sells himself, his change of masters, and the oscillations in the market price of labour. (Marx 1990, 723–4)

It is the rhythm, the process of the purchase and sale of labour-power by and through capital that expresses the specific mode of existence of capitalism. In order to get to this point of the analysis, Marx needs to get a grip, a foothold, on the process of capitalism in order to commence his analysis; he finds this initial foothold in the commodity, an analysis of which makes up the first chapters of *Capital*. Yet, he is always aware of the tension that inheres in this analysis as, in a sense, he is falsely rendering the commodity as an object, as a stable thing, when he is well aware that it is merely one element within the complex process of capitalism. Hence, the analysis of the commodity-as-a-thing is an abstraction from the reality which is the ongoing process of capitalism. Furthermore, and importantly, he wants to assert and explain how capitalism itself functions through the creation, sedimentation and operation of real abstractions. It is this complex interrelation of abstractions of thought and abstractions of reality which run throughout the programme of both *Capital* and his reflections on the method required for analysing political economy, as set out in some of his earlier texts.[4]

The positing of the commodity and the commodity form, as well as the consequent necessity of the notion of the equal exchange of commodities between free individuals, is one aspect of capitalism, but it is only one aspect; it is not its ground, even though Marx places it at the start of his text. The rest of *Capital Volume 1* introduces other elements of the analysis which are required to understand the real operations of commodity exchange, such as the valorization process and surplus-value. 'The exchange of equivalents, the original operation with which we started is now turned around in such a way that there is only an apparent exchange' (Marx 1990, 729). So, as he puts it right at the end of *Capital*, we are in a circle; the circle of capital accumulation in which the point is simply, and always, to accrue more value, as opposed to accruing more goods. It is this circular character of capitalism which might help explain the circular organization of *Capital Volume I* which shifts emphasis and trajectory throughout, moving from economic theory to social history to contemporary newspaper reports, back to history, now to theory, and so forth, as it grapples with the ever-changing fluidity that is capitalism.

Hence, one question that Marx is trying to answer throughout the whole of this text is: How does money make more money? It is this ever-expanding process that Marx is trying to explain: 'the valorization of value takes place only within this constantly renewed moment. The movement of capital is therefore limitless'

(Marx 1990, 253).[5] However, if capitalism and capital accumulation are *really* a process and a seemingly cyclical process at that, how can we find a ground or starting point from which to analyse, critique or understand it? How does it manage to continue? To put it another way – what is the ontological foundation of the process of capital accumulation? What are the moments within the process which make it move forward and which make it substantial? Two traditional and technically correct responses to these questions, as developed within Marxist thought, might be "surplus-value"[6] and "primitive accumulation".[7] Clearly such responses are not "wrong", but they are only partial answers. To over-rely on the explanatory power of either would be to take as real what is, in fact, relational. This point will be returned to later on. For the moment, one important element which is needed, in order to more fully respond to such questions, lies in the centrality of the notion of abstraction to Marx's texts and thought for his methodology and his ontology. Whilst the question of method and ontology do not appear paramount in the text of *Capital*, the very organization and order of the arguments in *Capital* reflect his method and his ontological concerns, for: 'in the analysis of economic forms neither microscopes nor chemical reagents are of assistance. The power of abstraction must replace both' (Marx 1990, 90). This power of abstraction should be used by theory to describe reality-as-it-is and not be manipulated in order to justify its own theoretical premises, against reality, by making a 'violent abstraction' (Marx 1990, 421), as Marx claims "bourgeois" political economy does. Such violent abstractions vitiate the reality that they purport to describe when they claim an unwarranted authority to explain the operation of the whole of the economic sphere but only include a portion of the relevant information required. It is then violent both in the manner of its birth and in the manner of its deployment.

Yet, it is not commonly held that Marx was interested in the efficacy of abstraction. Often it is presumed that Marx is opposed to the role and realm of abstraction, as he viewed it as too Hegelian, too idealist; it would appear to give primacy to concepts and not real, material, living conditions. Such readings would tend to support the view that Marx (or Marxism) provides a material and mechanical account of reality whereby the material (economic) base produces or determines the superstructure and the ideological (even if only in the last instance). Abstractions would seem to inhabit this superstructural realm and hence not to have the power to fully produce or determine the material. There are, however, a range of readings of Marx which contradict or complicate this view. As already stated, Toscano (2008a, 2008b) has recently demonstrated the centrality of abstraction to Marx's work. This is not to necessarily argue that abstractions have a material base (i.e. simply transferring the primacy back to the material) but is to suggest that things can, in themselves, be abstract. To argue that abstraction is either material or ideal is to start at the wrong place, as it is to start at the end of the argument. As Sohn-Rethel (1978) half-argues, the distinction between materialism and idealism is itself a consequence of more fundamental forms of abstraction. (This is an argument which Whitehead (SMW, 98–9) also makes.) These more fundamental forms of abstraction can be distinguished into two different modes which, although not ontologically distinct, can and should be differentiated. There are, therefore abstractions made "in the head";[8] and abstractions "in reality".

Abstractions in the Head

Marx, as an apparently thorough materialist, is consistent in stating that it is the real conditions, the concrete world, which must be the starting point of all analysis. 'It seems to be correct to begin with the real and the concrete, with the real precondition, thus to begin, in economics, with e.g. the population, which is the foundation and the subject of the entire social act of production' (Marx 1973, 100). But, he immediately couches this stance and introduces the centrality of abstraction to the analysis:

> On closer examination this proves false. The population is an abstraction if I leave out, for example, the classes of which it is composed. These classes are in turn an empty phrase if I am not familiar with the elements on which they rest. E.g. wage labour, capital, etc. These latter in turn presuppose exchange, division of labour, prices, etc. (Marx 1973, 100)

So, that which appears to be a concrete thing, something in the real world which political economy has assumed its analyses to be founded upon, turns out to be an abstraction. The notion of "population" is an abstraction in that it does not immediately represent a simple reality which is already out there and self-sufficient. This abstraction is problematic in so far as it does not indicate that which enables it to arise, supports it, as well as that which it requires in order to appear, namely its relations to other entities (and other concepts). However, this is not to denounce abstractions (such as that of population) nor is it to say that they are either unreal or ideological. Rather, it is to see an abstraction as only a starting point. If that which was allegedly concrete turns out to be an abstraction then it is necessary to follow this abstraction to confront that which informs and produces it.

> Thus, if I were to begin with the population, this would be a chaotic conception (Vorstellung)[9] of the whole, and I would then, by means of a further determination,[10] move analytically towards ever more simple concepts (Begriff),[11] from the imagined concrete towards even thinner abstractions until I had arrived at the simplest determinations. (Marx 1973, 100)

Once these simpler concepts, which are themselves abstract and which make up the elements which are combined in the more complex abstraction, have been isolated it is possible to return to the original abstraction with a fuller understanding of the manner of its construction, operation and validity. 'From there the journey would have to be retraced until I had finally arrived at the population again, but this time not as the chaotic conception of a whole, but as a rich totality of many determinations and relations' (Marx 1973, 100). The initial abstraction is now returned to, and through this process of analysis and return has been rendered more concrete. This is, for Marx, the process of the method of political economy (and *Capital Volume 1* is, of course, subtitled '*A Critique of Political Economy*'). Abstractions in the head are an important element of this process and methodology and are to be seen as, and treated as, concrete.

Therefore, the demand that both Marx and Whitehead make is that more attention is paid to that which constitutes abstractions. When abstractions are approached as units of the combination of previously diverse elements, they can be no longer seen as simple abstractions but as complexes which are neither easy to construct nor to dismiss. They are concrete abstractions (though Marx never quite puts it this way): 'the concrete totality is a totality of thoughts, concrete in thought, in fact a product of thinking and comprehending; but not in any way a product of the concept which thinks and generates itself' (Marx 1973, 101). At this point Marx is emphasizing the abstractive process of thought but this is not to venerate thought as the sole mode of abstraction for, as will be seen, this process of abstraction is only one example of the wider process of abstraction which infuses all existence. Abstractions can constitute concepts but concepts are not the only form of abstraction and, furthermore, such concepts are not in and of themselves generative (as Hegel would hold), for concepts are a product of generation. The fault of much political economy, according to Marx, is that it has taken for concrete that which is an abstraction. It has therefore misrecognized the ontological status of its foundations. It has treated as generative that which is in fact a result of thinking (such as the notion of population). This mode of abstraction is produced by the process of thinking, it is:

> A product...of the working-up of observation and conception into concepts. The totality as it appears *in the head*, as a totality of thoughts, is a product of a thinking head, which appropriates the world in the only way it can, a way different from the artistic, religious, practical and mental appropriation of this world. (Marx 1973, 101. Emphasis added.)

Hence, although it is often claimed that Marx stipulates and reduces modes of thought to a one-dimensional materialistic approach, he is aware that the mode of analysis of political economy is only one amongst other modes. Each thinker thinks and they think in a specific way: artistically, religiously, practically. Each manner of thinking is an appropriation of the world but such appropriation occurs in a specific head and in a specific way. The development of concrete categories is, therefore, a kind of possession, in that it is a taking hold, an appropriation of things. But this is not a possession which is enacted by an already formed subject. Rather, the process of thinking is the process of appropriation (and such appropriation is akin to Whitehead's notion of prehensions as a grasping of the world, as outlined in Chapters Two and Five).

This construction of concepts is not limited to science or the science of political economy. The construction of concepts is to be judged in so far as it produces abstractions which are concrete. The question remains of how the adequacy of such concepts is to be assessed (and how the danger of mediocre relativism or solipsism can be avoided if it is being suggested that each individual produces their own concepts). What is clear, at present, is the distance that Marx is putting between himself and Hegel and the notion of the idea as both the ultimate reality and that which is productive of reality.

> Hegel fell into the illusion of conceiving the real as the product of thought concentrating itself, probing its own depths, and unfolding out of itself, by itself, whereas the method of rising from the abstract to the concrete is only the way in which thought appropriates the concrete, reproduces it as the concrete in the mind. But this is by no means the process by which the concrete itself comes into being. (Marx 1973, 101)

So, Hegel has only told half of the story. He argued that the concrete arises out of the abstract, but this is to get things the wrong way round. As Whitehead puts it: 'The explanatory purpose of philosophy is often misunderstood. Its business is to explain the emergence of the more abstract things from the more concrete things… philosophy is explanatory of abstraction, and not of concreteness' (PR, 20; see Stengers 2002, 216–7 for a fuller discussion of this). For Marx, this concreteness goes on "in the head"; in the process of thought. Yet it is not a simple reflection of how the world is. This raises the question of whether such a distinction between the concrete thought and the concrete world means that Marx has created for himself an unbridgeable gulf between mind and the world, matter and consciousness, reality and ideology, science and fiction etc.? If so, he has bifurcated nature.

The answer to such questions will lie in how Marx conceives of reality. And, in the same passage he makes it clear that whilst thinking is distinct from that which it thinks about, both thinking and reality are themselves processes. Furthermore, they are processes whereby the diverse is concentrated to form something concrete.

> The concrete is concrete because it is the concentration of many determinations, hence unity of diversity. It appears in the process of thinking, therefore as a process of concentrations, as a result, not as a point of departure, even though it is the point of departure in reality and hence also the point of departure for observation and conception. (Marx 1973, 101)

The task now at hand is to explain further what Marx meant by the reality of abstractions and how these relate to both the concrete world and to concrete thought. 'The paradox is now established that the utmost abstractions are the true weapons with which to control our thought of concrete fact' (SMW, 41). This will entail an implanting of abstraction as a genuine element within existence.

Abstractions in Reality

Along with population, there are other categories which political economy has taken as providing both its real and conceptual foundation. Some of the others are exchange, money, and labour. It is the last of these which will be discussed in detail here.

Clearly, the concept of labour is an abstraction "in the head" as described above, but that is not all it is: 'Not only the category, labour, but labour in reality has…become the means of creating wealth in general, and has ceased to be organically linked with particular individuals in any specific form' (Marx 1973, 104). It is not that political economy invented the concept of "labour" and that it is, therefore, simply an abstraction which either does or does not correspond to reality. For:

> On the other side, this abstraction of *labour as such* is not merely the mental product of a concrete totality of labours. Indifference toward specific labours corresponds to a form of society in which individuals can with ease transfer from one labour to another, and where the specific kind is a matter of chance for them, hence of indifference. (Marx 1973, 104. Emphasis added.)

The kind of society in which it is possible to be a general labourer is a specific kind of society – but Marx means more than this. The dislocation of labour from any specific activity (such as weaving or digging or building or writing) is neither natural nor necessary. The fact that it is possible to develop such a concept indicates something about how the world is, and how the world is organized (see Sayer 1987, 127–9 for a very clear discussion of this). 'Indifference towards any specific kind of labour presupposes a very developed totality of real kinds of labour, of which no single one is any longer predominant' (Marx 1973, 104). Labour in abstract, *labour as such*, is labour emptied of any "concrete determinations", to adopt the terminology. *Labour as such* takes on its true effectivity not when political economists define it as a category but when this category becomes operative in the real world, that is to say, when it is possible not only to conceive of labour as abstracted from any particular kind of labour (weaving, baking, banking, teaching) but when individuals find themselves in a world where weaving, baking, banking and teaching are only secondary aspects of the fact that their labour can be bought and sold. *Labour as such*, the generalized notion that individuals have a certain amount of labour-power available for sale, becomes key to the conceptual and practical organization of the workplace where individuals can be moved from one task to another, laid off, redeployed, retrained, required to "multitask" precisely insofar as they embody *labour as such*.[12] This is then an abstraction in the head but also an abstraction in reality.

Marx is not arguing that the concept of "labour" is simply a modern invention and that it had never been thought of or employed previously:

> Labour seems a quite simple category. The conception of labour in this general form – as labour as such – is also immeasurably old. Nevertheless, when it is economically conceived in its simplicity, "labour" is as modern a category as are the relations which create this simple abstraction. (Marx 1973, 103)

As Althusser (1969, 193–7) comments, such simplicity is not the origin from which complexity develops. Simplicity arises out of complexity, it appears at a later stage and should not be premised as a starting point. Marx therefore decries those who provide a linear, historicist development of economic categories. There can be simple forms of production which have complex concrete categories, such as money, as elements within them, and there can be complex forms of production which do not have a monetary form, Marx argues (1973, 102). The point, for Marx, is not to understand history but to understand reality. And abstractions are part of that reality. And, interestingly, it was the modern United States, not the UK or Germany, which first exhibited the actual concretion of *labour as such*.

> Such a state of affairs is at its most developed in the most modern form of existence of bourgeois society – in the United States. Here, then, for the first time, the point of departure of modern economics, namely the abstraction of the category "labour", "labour as such", labour pure and simple becomes true in practice. The simplest abstraction, then, which modern economics places at the head of its discussions…nevertheless achieves practical truth as an abstraction only as a category of the most modern society. (Marx 1973, 104–5)

However, it might be argued that this is simply a description of the effectivity of an abstraction. As such, it merely demonstrates the materiality of ideas and is, therefore, little more than a sophisticated but fairly well-rehearsed materialist reading of the development of ideas. Worse, it might be argued that the effectivity of this abstraction is merely evidence of the ideological character of economics, which simply represents and furthers the interests of the bourgeoisie etc., etc. In order to avoid such an interpretation it will be necessary to provide a more detailed example of what constitutes a real abstraction. However, before doing so, a brief detour through the nonhistoricist manner of Marx's argument will be developed.

'The point is not the historic position of the economic relations in the succession of different forms of society' (Marx 1973, 107). Marx wants to explain reality – reality as it is now. Althusser, commenting on the passage in which Marx makes this statement, puts it as follows: 'where reality is concerned we are never dealing with the pure existence of simplicity, be it essence or category, but with the existence of "concretes" of complex and structured beings and processes' (Althusser 1969, 197). Marx believes that developing an understanding of capitalism is the best way of developing an understanding of reality; such analyses must start with what *is* now. The historical method cannot explain the present but the present can explain the past. Or, as Whitehead puts it: 'You can only interpret the past in terms of the present. The present is all that you have' (RM, 72). For Marx, 'Human anatomy contains a key to the anatomy of the ape' (Marx 1973, 105); it is not the other way around. Analysis of the concepts and categories of the present can help illuminate the past, and we might recognize elements or aspects of our current concepts and categories in the past but this does not make them identical; the historical and history are not concepts which have a quasi-evolutionary slant. There is no preordained purpose or logic either to reality, history or the development of concepts: 'No reason, internal to history, can be assigned why this flux of forms, rather than another flux, should have been illustrated' (PR, 46): so, this is clearly no recourse to dialectical materialism. Care must be taken when we are tempted to take our abstractions and simply apply them to the past as if they applied equally and immediately.

> This example of labour shows strikingly how even the most abstract categories, despite their validity – precisely because of their abstractness – for all epochs, are nevertheless, in the specific character of this abstraction, themselves likewise a product of historic relations, and possess their full validity only for and within these relations. (Marx 1973, 105)

This is not to completely bind abstractions to the present and, once again, it is not to limit abstractions to simply being reflections or constructions of society or language or culture. Abstractions have a force, a reality, once they are developed.

> As a rule, *the most general abstractions arise only in the midst of the richest possible concrete development*, where one thing appears as common to many, to all. Then it ceases to be thinkable in a particular form alone. (Marx 1973, 104. Emphasis added.)

It is this shift beyond the thinkable in a particular form which is, perhaps, the key to the reality and importance of abstractions within Marx, so that *labour as such* 'is not merely the mental product of a concrete totality of labours' (Marx 1973, 104). *Labour as such*, is a real abstraction and constitutes an important element of the character of the present. Marx thereby links the process of abstraction (in the head) with real abstraction in the world. He also indicates the importance of interrelations between abstractions themselves. For example, the abstraction which produces commodities as no longer simply items with use-value relies on the notion of abstract labour.[13] However, such abstractions do not just exist in the head, they partake in the operation of capitalism: 'it must not be forgotten that...modern bourgeois society – is always what is given, in the head as well as in the reality' (Marx 1973, 106). And, on the analysis being presented here, what is notable about modern society, about capitalism, is the preponderance of abstractions. For example, what makes capitalism possible is not just the economists' concepts of labour but the operation of abstract labour in the real world as that which conditions and permeates our world of work, leisure, survival – our lives. It haunts us. And there are other such abstractions. Indeed it is the proliferation and dominance of abstractions which characterize the contemporary world:

> Individuals are now ruled by *abstractions*, whereas earlier they depended on one another. The abstraction, or idea, however, is nothing more than the theoretical expression of those material relations which are their lord and master. (Marx 1973, 164. Emphasis in original.)

We are possessed by abstractions.[14]

To recap: it has been discussed how capital accumulation is an ongoing, almost circular process, the endless reiteration of value. The problem for Marx was to start out on his explanation of this process. In *Capital Volume 1*, he chose to start with the commodity. The character of the commodity does indeed seem central to the analysis but it cannot be the analysis in the whole. The very appearance of the commodity presupposes certain conditions which rely on other categories and other conditions. Here, Marx is simply carrying out his methodological principles. He starts out with what appears concrete – a commodity, but then explains how this is a chaotic whole which presupposes the distinction between use-value and exchange-value. He thus follows it to its simplest elements in order to build it back up and present it as fully concrete; as a real, capitalist commodity (which is also, therefore, abstract). 'The *commodity* that emerges from capitalist production is different from the commodity we began with as the element, the precondition of capitalist production' (Marx 1990, 953; emphasis in original). What makes the production of such a commodity possible is a diverse range of moments, concepts, events, laws, stipulations.[15] For example, as opposed to feudalism in which obligations and negotiations and the market were intertwined, the purchaser and seller in capitalism are "free".

> In the money relation, in the developed system of exchange (and this semblance seduces the democrats), the ties of personal dependence, of distinction of blood, education, etc. are in fact exploded, ripped up…and individuals *seem* independent…free to collide with one another and to engage in exchange within this freedom; but they appear thus only for someone who abstracts from the *conditions, the conditions of existence* within which these individuals enter into contact… These *objective* dependency relations also appear, in antithesis to those of *personal* dependence…in such a way that individuals are now ruled by *abstractions.* (Marx 1973, 163–4. Emphasis in original.)

Independence and equality are thus abstractions in the head and abstractions in reality. Most importantly, what Marx is insistent upon is that this process is understood as a set of relations, not as a thing. Therefore, capitalism is not a thing, but a set of relations. The great error that is made by economists, philosophers and individuals alike (according to Marx) is to mistake what is relational for that which is actual. Indeed, what is meant by fetishism is the mistaking of relations for concrete entities; for example, when categories are taken as actual and primary and not as relational concrete abstractions which are themselves productions. This is an example of what Whitehead terms "the fallacy of misplaced concreteness" which treats as a fact that which is an abstraction: 'the accidental error of mistaking the abstract for the concrete' (SMW, 64). 'This fallacy consists in neglecting the degree of abstraction involved when an actual entity is considered merely so far as it exemplifies certain categories of thought' (PR, 7–8). In terms of Marx (and capitalism), this entails that the relations between persons and other persons, or between persons and things, or between things and things, are not treated primarily as relations, or as in process, but as things in themselves. In capitalism, things have become persons and relations have become things (commodities have their own lives) and relations have become entities as well. Sayer (1987, 93) cites Marx's description of this as the '"enchanted, perverted, topsy-turvy world" of capitalism with its "personification of things and conversion of production relations into entities"'.[16]

So, civil-society and the free interchange of individuals in the market is not "unreal", but it is peculiar. It was wrung into freedom in its apparent abstraction from the state as posited within capitalism; but such an abstraction is not simply ideological. 'The relation of exchange between capitalist and worker becomes a mere semblance belonging only to the process of circulation, it becomes a mere form, which is alien to the content of the transaction itself, and merely mystifies it' (Marx 1990, 729–30). The creation of a "free" market both heightens and obscures that which is central to capitalism, that control over people is effected through control over things (rather than through forced loyalty, for example, as was the case in feudalism). And *labour as such* is a thing. But such thingness is guaranteed and substantiated by abstractions. This is a very strange state of affairs, but it is one that we take for granted. It is not so much a question of the bourgeoisie imposing their dominant values so that they appear normal and natural, as Marxists often argue. It is more than that. Reality is peculiar; reality is warped: semblances, forms and abstractions have taken hold of the world and of us and it is within and through them that we think and exist.

Hence, the link between religion and capitalism is not, as it is with Weber, a question of creating a certain frugal, ascetic attitude, but rather Protestantism's contribution to the effectiveness of the concept of abstraction. 'Christianity with its religious cult of man in the abstract... is the most fitting form of religion' (Marx 1990, 172). And the very individuality which supposedly underpins economic freedom also underpins political freedom. As Sayer states: 'Individuals are *citoyens* only as "abstract" individuals – individuals, in other words, divorced from the material circumstances and social relations which concretely make them what they are' (Sayer 1987, 104; emphasis in original). This proliferation of abstraction, of effective abstractions, is what possesses capitalist society and what possesses its members. It makes bankers into metaphysicians. Karatani (2005) has described the nineteenth-century British, supposedly down-to-earth, antirationalist approach to finance as follows:

> The investors thought it a matter of course that they got interest from their savings as well as dividends from their stock investments. That is to say that speculative philosophy turned into a daily event, as it were. The drive for expansion without production and circulation is like the drive for 'metaphysics' in Kantian philosophy, namely, the expansion of cognition *without* synthetic judgement. (Karatani 2005, 156. Emphasis in original.)

Such speculation is not limited to the nineteenth-century banker; it suffuses us, our society, our relations and relationships. We are all metaphysicians in our thoughts and our everyday lives, especially bankers. This makes Whitehead's recourse to a novel metaphysics even more compelling and relevant; it clarifies the extent of relationality and the importance of the quality of such relations which constitute the existence of capitalism rather than relying on any notion of either a base or a superstructure.

Value-*Form*

On the reading of Marx being presented here, abstractions, reality, the "economic", are all of a jumble. It is impossible to start with one idea, fact or social relation and build an edifice of political economy on it. Population, land, labour, commodities all presuppose one another and rely upon each other. This is why Marx approaches and reapproaches concepts and entities such as commodities and labour throughout *Capital*, and it explains why they take on different aspects and metamorphose as the argument proceeds. Marx is trying to account for the *process* of society. There is not one starting point, but there are definite moments within the process. Importantly, the landscape will look remarkably different depending on which moment you start from. This emphasis on process suggests that there is no such *thing* as capitalism. It is not an object; it is a set of relations (which are not immediately or solely human; such relations are constituted by the relations of humans and things, commodities). To assume or to posit any thing as the foundation of capitalism is to misunderstand the whole point of it, and of Marx's analysis of it, namely, that it is relational (for example, surplus-value presupposes the separation of the ownership of labour from the means of production, yet it is the relation between them which constitutes capitalism). Abstractions are real but they are not objects, as usually conceived. But then again, nor are objects simply objects, anymore. Objects within capitalism are now commodities which are simultaneously the embodiment of relations, the conveyors of relations, and the producers of relations (it depends on where you are in the cycle). In this respect they can no longer be construed as innocent, passive objects or receptacles of matter.

For Marx, it is the commodity *form*, it is value-*form* which are the keys to capitalism (not commodities and value, as economists think). In his account, commodities and value are in themselves relational. And they are located, historically and socially, in a specific context.

> The value-form of the product of labour is the most abstract, but also the most universal form of the bourgeois mode of production; by the fact that it stamps the bourgeois mode of production as a particular kind of social production of

a historical and transitory character. If we then make the mistake of treating it as the eternal natural form of social production, we necessarily overlook the specificity of the value-form, and consequently of the commodity-form. (Marx 1990, 174)

So the abstract value-form is universal but not eternal. This is a crucial distinction. For, to be universal, according to Marx, means that within the current, capitalist system of production, any thing which is produced has to conform to the commodity form. It is not possible to set up a factory or workshop or gallery which is not located within the nexus of exchange of commodities (no matter how hard one wishes). This universality is a real universal (a real abstraction) as it is that which touches all commodities. But it did not and will not define or create all those things which have ever been or ever will be produced. It is not eternal. It is a universal aspect of a specific group of relations which make up the contemporary production process. This is perhaps best explained by Whitehead's notion of "societies" (see Chapter Five) which he describes as the capacity of previously distinct elements to cohere insofar as they have a common manner of experience, of coming-to-be, of enduring; they thus have a common form. Viewed in these terms, the commodity form designates one such manner of coherence and endurance which affects and effects all such commodities, and is thus universal. But this form is not abstract, eternal, or external to such commodities; they are not Platonic or idealist forms. Rather, the commodity form is a description of the way in which things inhere and endure. It is another example of the adverbial character of existence. So, this emphasis on a recast notion of form entails that to believe that there really *are* productive forces, relations of production, etc. which subtend different ways (modes) of producing things, is to mistake the outcome of a specific historical era and mode of thought for a transhistorical concept which can be applied backwards and forwards (eternally), when they are in fact products of (or tied to) the society that generated them (see Sayer 1987, 141ff.).

This emphasis on "form" returns us to the inherence of quality which suffuses existence, as espoused by Whitehead (see Chapter Four). For the relations that make up capitalism are not inert or passive. They always occur in a certain way. Indeed, it is the specific manner of their occurrence which marks them out as specifically capitalist as opposed to feudal, for example. As such, there is always a "subjective form" (see Chapter Five) to the becomings which, in becoming, instantiate, reproduce and further capitalism. Such forms are identifiable, they are able to be analysed but they are not, in and of themselves, substantial. They inhere in neither a base nor a superstructure and they do not subtend society. Instead, the subjective forms, the different qualities of relations, are there as part of each event of production and consumption;

in "Just-In-Time" stock systems, flexible labour patterns, state-controlled capitalism, team-working, and so on. But none of these are things. They are ways of doing things, they are adverbial in that they are kinds of production and consumption. In this way they are hard to get hold of in reality and in terms of analysis. The adverbial and nonsubstantial character of capitalism helps account for its slipperiness. It is nigh on impossible to grasp, to invert, to revolt against, precisely because it is not a thing but a way of doing things. The task is to change our analytic and practical approach, to pay heed to the manner of existence and to change our modes of thought and action.

There is a need to move beyond the fallacy of taking certain categories or concepts as immediately and objectively real when they are really abstractions. There is a need to understand those abstractions which help the world operate. That which appears to be concrete may turn out to be an abstraction, and what appears to be a simple and straightforward category may be only one aspect of the complex of relations of which it is a part. Uncritical acceptance of such a category might lead us to, for example, believe the market to be a real place where free and equal individuals meet, as opposed to seeing it as a moment within the more general set of relations whereby the process of production continues (the "existence" of markets is therefore, in a Whiteheadian sense, doubtful). 'It is not that people mistake what they see, what they see misleads them, for thoroughly objective reasons to do with how it presents itself to their consciousness.' We are 'bewitched' by capitalism (Sayer 1987, 42–3). It is in this sense that capitalism operates as a form of sorcery rather than simply through ideology (see Pignarre and Stengers 2005). The point is not that there is an objective base out there (the economic) which we have to know (as both traditional and Marxist economists would seem to think), rather, it is that there are relations which are always presented in a certain way (there are *market-like* relations rather than markets in which such relations occur). There is no objective base, there is just the manner of the presentation which is itself a necessary element of the presentation. There is no such thing as the economic which could or could not determine the superstructure (Sayer 1987, 91–2, 135–8). To think in that way is to accept the partial abstractions of capitalism at face value when they are, precisely, what we are trying to understand.

Conclusion

Interestingly, Marx uses the term "organically" related when describing the reality of the process or production which economists have misunderstood. 'In bringing things which are organically related into an accidental relation, into a mere reflective connection, they display their crudity and lack of conceptual understanding' (Marx 1973, 88). Once again, the relations have been mistakenly conceived of as separate entities. Once this is done it appears impossible not to render one as causal of the other; hence the real foundation (the economic structure) is seen as necessarily prior to and as causing, producing, determining, the legal and political, the social life of humans and their thoughts (even if they are granted some level of relative autonomy). This is the worldview of determinist Marxism. But if there is a genuine organic relationship between the two, then the question of temporality and of cause and effect is misplaced. Rather, what is required is a fuller account of such a form of relation. Notably, Whitehead describes his own philosophical approach with the phrase 'philosophy of organism' (PR, 7 and passim). In adopting this term Whitehead aims to account for the utter integration of the material, conceptual, potential, qualitative, historical and actual into items which are not externally determined but which comprise the utter unities of existence. They are organic wholes. This is not to make them material or biological, for these very terms have been refigured. By "organic" is meant the creation of a unit constructed through the infusion of the actual, the potential, the living and the nonliving without any hierarchical distinctions between any of these elements and without recourse to ossified notions of the natural and the social (see Chapter Seven).[17] In the same way, Marx sees the relations between forms of production, the legal sphere, and the (human) social relations associated with these to be an organic whole with no element having priority or causal power over the other. The task is to analyse the manner of the relations which constitute the specificity and process of that whole. And, as Whitehead states, what is central to the reality of these unities is the process of their becoming, which always occurs in a certain way. This emphasis on organic unity is not, however, to assert that society as usually conceived, is a unity. Marx, like Whitehead, is wary of viewing human society as either originary or explanatory. It needs, itself, to be explained as constituted by and through the specific relations, and the quality of these, which make up the contemporary world, its objects and subjects.

> To regard society as one single subject is, in addition, to look at it wrongly; speculatively. With a single subject, production and consumption appear as moments of a single act. The important thing to emphasize here is only that, whether production and consumption are viewed as the activity of one or of many individuals, they appear in any case as moments of one process, in which production is the real point of departure. (Marx 1973, 94)

To posit society, the social or the economy as the real foundation or starting point of analysis is erroneous. To suggest that there is any unique thing which can be analysed solely on its own terms is mistaken. Furthermore, production and consumption are not two balanced elements which go to make up a unity (of society or the economy). Rather, they are elements within a process. However, there is clearly a relation between such production and consumption. They are not identical, but nor are they alien to each other.

> Without production, no consumption; but also, without consumption, no production; since production would then be purposeless...the product...proves itself to be, *becomes*, a product only through consumption. Only by decomposing the product does consumption give the product the finishing touch. (Marx 1973, 91. Emphasis in original.)

Hence, Karatani (2005, 205–11) is correct in identifying the spatial and temporal time-lag which is assumed by the commodity form. That is to say, a commodity is not created (in the sense of finished) once it leaves the factory. This is only one part of its adventure. It needs to enter in the realm of exchange and be sold. But it also needs to be consumed. Such consumption does not affect the value of a commodity. And it is not consumption (or demand) which drives the process. Consumption is integral to the process. At the prosaic level; the very production of a commodity involves consuming some materials (electricity, heat, wood, brain-power, etc.) 'Production is also immediately consumption' (Marx 1973, 90) but, more interestingly:

> Consumption is also immediately production... It is clear that in taking food, for example, which is a form of consumption, the human being produces his [sic] own body. But this is also true of every kind of consumption which in one way or another produces human beings in some particular aspect. Consumptive production. (Marx 1973, 90–1)

Or, as Whitehead puts it: 'life is robbery' (PR, 105). Our bodies are produced within and through the process and, equally, our bodies contribute to the process of production. Here, Marx is drawing the notion of production beyond the narrow limits imposed on it by political economy and extending it to suffuse the more general process of production within which the 'process always returns to production to begin anew' (Marx 1973, 99).

Production is not a flat, empirical, objective affair; it is not a simple, mechanical production system. It also produces the manner of production; its qualities.

> Hunger is hunger, but the hunger gratified by cooked meat eaten with a knife and fork is a different hunger from that which bolts down raw meat with the aid of hand, nail and tooth. Production thus produces not only the object but also the manner of consumption. (Marx 1973, 92)

Often, such statements by Marx are taken as evidence that he is both totalizing and in some way technologically determinist. That is to say, a certain system of production produces certain tools and technologies which therefore force all those who inhabit this system to adopt and behave in identical ways. 'You must use your knife and fork to eat your dinner'. This is to mistake as concrete that which is in fact a relation or a nexus of relations. Furthermore it is to misrecognize the quality of existence, the manner of existence, through which every moment and actuality gains its specificity, and hence its objectivity. There is an adverbial element to all production and consumption ('the manner of consumption'). It is not as if there are needs, wants or desires which exist inertly and are sated (or not) through certain modes of production. Desires, wants, needs always occur in certain ways and are met in certain ways, through "modes of production" (in a nontraditional Marxist sense) and modes of consumption, which always occur in certain ways. These "certain ways" are not added on to the bare fact of need or production but are its integral elements. The process of existence has an essentially qualitative aspect.

To render production or consumption as objective elements, shorn of the manner of their operation, is to replicate the very mistake that Marx accuses traditional political economists of making. That is, of taking as fixed, eternal, and transhistorical, a category or concept which is an element within a specific context or milieu. There is no such thing as Population, Land, Exchange, Value, Labour, in the sense that these can be understood in isolation or in separation from the contexts, the realities in which they are produced or within which they operate, or have effects. The point is not to try to fix those true objective categories, concepts or abstractions which explain all of the present, illuminate the past, and predict the future. The task is the rather more complex one of understanding the manner of the interrelation of abstractions, concepts and reality. For Marx, reality is the lived lives of real people, and this is not a bad starting place. However, it is not necessarily the ending place. As mentioned previously, *Capital. Volume 1* is a critique of political economy; it is "simply" an attempt to understand capitalism and to shift the ontological basis of political economy from a focus on supposedly concrete entities (Land, Labour, Property) so as to make clear the real and ongoing relations which suffuse the current system and manner of production. As Sayer puts it, intriguingly using Whitehead's own terminology but without citing him:

> Instead of operating with analytic categories which replicate the *misplaced concreteness* of reified forms like value and capital as conventionally conceived, we can begin empirically to recover the material ways in which, through time, these forms were constructed in the intercourse of 'real, living, individuals'. (Sayer 1987, 135. Emphasis added.)

Capitalism is, therefore, abstract on at least two levels. It is abstract in that it relies upon abstractions in order to operate, and it is not a substantial thing. This is not to say that it has no existence. Rather, it is to reapproach the question of what constitutes existence; this is where the work of Whitehead is so important. Just as societies, in the Whiteheadian sense, are defined by the like manner in which its members prehend the world, entailing that it is a common form of experience which links them together (PR, 89), so Marx sees capitalist relations as expressing the common characteristic of existence in many contemporary aspects and elements of society:

> In all forms of society there is one specific from of production which predominates over the rest, whose relations thus assign rank and influence to the others. It is a general illumination which bathes all the other colours and modifies their particularity. It is a particular ether which determines the specific gravity of every being which has materialized within it. (Marx 1973, 107)

Such statements have been used to criticize Marx for a totalizing approach in which everything is reduced to or explained by the economic system of production. There does seem to be such a danger here, in claiming that production is the be all and end all of reality and of explanation. However, perhaps this should not be seen as a danger but as an opportunity. The point is not to retain the traditional notion of economic production but to envisage production in the broadest sense. That is to say, it is indicative of the processes through which every being and thing is materialized. That which links all entities is not some mechanized system of production (although a mechanized system might be materialized within that form of production); nor is a certain level of technology or division of labour that which characterizes a form of production. Rather, it is a way of doing things; it is a quality, a manner of thinking, being and doing. This links disparate elements together and provides the unmistakeable yet diffuse character of an epoch. It is what remains unsaid, unthought, but which makes us what we are. This returns us to the very notion of a culture of thought which has been the main theme of this book. At the outset it was suggested that Whitehead takes on the difficult task of attempting to identify the 'general form of the forms of thought [which]...like the air we breathe...is so translucent, and so pervading, and so seemingly necessary, that only by extreme effort can we become aware of it' (AI, 14). 'As we think, we live' (MT, 87). And, for Marx, it is the manner of production which is indicative of the limits of life and thought. Again, this may give the impression of reducing him to some kind of economic determinist but this is only the case if a narrow, humanized notion of production is adopted. If, as with Whitehead's notion of experience, society and subjectivity, the notion of production is posited as an aspect of existence, of which human examples are a subset and not the ground, then it might be possible to develop a more fruitful link between the interrelation of production and thought. "Economic" production is only one aspect of the wider notion of the process of production. This is not to insert an ineluctable dialectic into nature, and it is not to insist that there is a natural march through history toward certain events and modes of being. For such approaches take for granted that which is meant by nature, history and progress. The real challenge is to reconceptualize, to shift the very theoretical stanchions which enable such concepts to arise. Perhaps the best way to do this is by rendering production in terms of Whitehead's notion of creativity.

To recap, the point is not to equate production with either political economy or an economic structure. It is not the economic which produces everything else, as this would be to fetishize the economy and to deny its inherently relational character. Rather, it is necessary to extend the concept of production, to expand it to its maximal definition.[18] But this is not to create an irrelevant abstraction. Once again:

> *Production in general* is an abstraction, but a rational abstraction in so far as it really brings out and fixes the common element and thus saves us repetition. Still this *general* category…is itself segmented many times over and splits into different determinations. Some determinations belong to all epochs, others only to a few… No production will be thinkable without them. (Marx 1973, 85. Emphasis in original.)

So, the first move is to isolate that which constitutes the simplest notion of production, that which enables something to be produced, consumed, and thereby become an element for a future production. This is a "rational abstraction". In this sense, production is creativity, in that it elicits the repetitions, novelty and process of the world. But the development of such a novel metaphysical abstraction is only worthwhile if it is adequate in relating to contemporary forms of production. Having gone through this stripping down, it will also be possible to enlarge this concept's capacity so as to include everything which is involved in contemporary production. Social theory should use this abstraction to develop descriptions of contemporary production which encompass what really happens in the real world and this will incorporate things, people, nature, society, economy, life and death, which all populate the ongoing process. This is not to suggest that creativity is inherently good or should be celebrated. Creativity, in this sense, simply demands that we pay attention to the process and dynamism of relations and to the manner of their deployment. Creativity can be "bad". Slavery was *created* (was an outcome of creativity), as were a whole host of techniques, implements, discourses, material items, practices, punishments, laws, thoughts and sanctions in order to enable the system of slavery to *create* goods and profit. It should also be noted that the processes which were instantiated by US and European slavery in the United States, Africa, Europe and the Caribbean are not simply in the past; they have not worn themselves out. They are still ongoing in the legacies of housing, education and the very existence of certain art galleries, such as the Tate in the UK which is still part of the unfolding of events of the nineteenth-century sugar trade and which clearly demonstrates the naivety of modelling any notion of creativity as simply an exemplum of that which is best about humankind.

In this way, the work of Marx and Whitehead can dovetail to make a set of demands upon us. To refuse a world of subject and objects, but to insist upon the reality and quality of those relations which constitute and sediment into the subjects and objects which punctuate our contemporary experience and existence. The emphasis thus shifts beyond the positing of a primary substance or economic base as constitutive of production, to a requirement to account for the mode and manner of production of the world and of that which occurs within it, without granting priority or authority to any element of analysis or reality. The wonder of the world is not that it is there at all but that it is such a peculiar place, with peculiar reasons and histories, riddled with inequalities. Social theory must try to account for the processes through which these events come to be. In doing so, it can, assume nothing and rule nothing out. It must widen its stance and develop a new culture of thought.

NOTES

Chapter One: A Culture of Thought – The Bifurcation of Nature

1 Stengers' *Penser Avec Whitehead* is currently being translated into English for publication by Harvard University Press. All the quotations from this work in this and later chapters are my own; they are not always elegant but are offered as the most literal and faithful renderings that I could achieve.

2 See also, Haraway 1976, 45; 1997, 141–8.

3 A conference on the inter-relations of the work of Whitehead and Judith Butler was held at Claremont Graduate University, California, 3–5 December 2009. Butler attended this conference and gave a paper on Whitehead which is to be published in a forthcoming edited collection titled *On the Occasion*.

4 The concept of nature as dead has been discussed by various theorists. Adorno and Horkheimer comment on how Enlightenment thought reduced matter to an object which could be mastered: 'From now on, matter would at last be mastered without any illusion of ruling or inherent powers, of hidden qualities' (Horkheimer and Adorno 1973, 6). Carolyn Merchant has traced the effect of conceiving nature as dead with especial reference to the lack of any sense of the "organic" which further points to the importance of Whitehead's attempt to delineate a "philosophy of organism": 'The removal of animistic, organic assumptions about the cosmos constituted the death of nature - the most far-reaching effect of the Scientific Revolution. Because nature was now viewed as a system of dead, inert particles moved by external, rather than inherent forces, the mechanical framework itself could itself legitimate the manipulation of nature' (Merchant 1983, 193). These correlations help indicate the direct relevance of Whitehead's work to specific questions in social theory; questions which will be discussed further in later chapters.

Chapter Two: Introducing Whitehead's Philosophy – The Lure of Whitehead

1 The notion of an "introduction" to the work of Whitehead is a problematic one. He offers such a radical philosophical construction that it is more of a question of immersing oneself wholesale within his thought. Indeed, Deleuze once wrote: 'I only remember being hypnotized by the great surge of bizarre categories at the beginning of *Process and Reality*....What a book!' (Deleuze, from a letter cited by Villani 1996, 245; my translation). However, Leclerc (1958) offers a clear account although this

text is not readily available, and Rose (2002) provides a lucid explanation of key Whiteheadian concepts. Debaise (2006) has produced an exemplary and succinct reading of *Process and Reality* though it is yet to be translated from French. Stengers' (2002) monumental *Penser Avec Whitehead* is not just an incisive rendering of Whitehead's concepts but a major contribution to contemporary philosophy and thought. In the Anglophone world, Shaviro's (2009) recent book *Without Criteria: Kant, Whitehead, Deleuze, and Aesthetics*, with its scholarly yet vivid analysis is probably the most rewarding place to start.

2 Hence the term "phenomenology" will not be used in this book, in order to emphasize the very particularity of Whitehead's approach and so as not to compare it or subsume it to an already existing set of debates. Interestingly, however, the closest contemporary commentator, in terms of his approach to the dislocation of experience from intentional consciousness in order to produce what he terms an "objective phenomenology" is perhaps Badiou (2009, 199–220).

3 The term "actual occasion" is one which Whitehead deploys to refer to an actual entity which has temporal and spatial extension: 'the term "actual occasion" is used synonymously with "actual entity"; but chiefly when its character of extensiveness has some direct relevance to the discussion, either extensiveness in the form of temporal extensiveness, that is to say "duration," or extensiveness in the form of spatial extension, or in the more complete signification of spatio-temporal extensiveness' (PR, 77). For simplicity's sake, the term actual entity has been used throughout the analysis offered here.

4 As will be seen in Chapter Five, these specific renderings of the public and private and their link to moments of individuality and sociality will lead to dramatic implications and opportunities for contemporary conceptions of the individual and society and their interrelation and, consequently, for debates around structure and agency.

5 The quote is from Book II, Chapter XXI, Section 1 of Locke's *An Essay Concerning Human Understanding* (1690).

Chapter Three: 'A Thorough-Going Realism' – Whitehead On Cause and Conformation

1 As Staten (1984) argues, this ultimately derives from the rather strange emphasis in Greek philosophy that that which subtends and explains existence is exactly that which subtends and explains rational thought and accurate perception of the world. This is the role of the concept of "eidos" (Staten 1984, 6–11).

2 See Haraway (1997, 145–7) for a fuller account of the relevance of Whitehead for contemporary understandings and misunderstandings of genes and Halewood (2005) for a discussion of this.

3 See, for example, the competing approaches of Archer (1995, 2003), Benton (1977, 1981), Bhaskar (1978, 1979, 1989), Elder-Vass (2010).

4 There is a link here to another crucial concept within Critical Realism, namely that of "emergence", whereby wholes develop distinct and greater properties than those possessed by their parts. The problem is similar to that of Critical Realism's stratification of reality in that there is a danger of producing a hierarchy of being through the concept of emergence, even if such emergence is conceived of as entirely relational as is the case with Elder-Vass (2010, 13–39).

5 See Shaviro (2009, 34–5, 48–51, 64, 77, 81).

NOTES   173

6 Technically this example could be seen as a mixed mode of perception involving Causal Efficacy (which will be discussed later on) in that the body is providing long-term data. However, for the moment, what is to be noted is Whitehead's critique of usual accounts of sense-data and his emphasis on the centrality of the body.

7 Whitehead's notion of symbolism and the reorientation it offers thought about the relation between language and reality and, more specifically, language and the body, will be taken up in Chapter Six. This will also involve a discussion of Butler on the materiality of the body.

8 Her work signals both an important contribution to the philosophy of science and to Whitehead's impact in developing fuller modes of thought. The analysis presented here is deeply indebted to and relies upon her work and ideas to an extent which may not be evident from the number of citations and references proffered in this book.

Chapter Four: The Value of Existence

1 The term "eudaimon" is one used by Aristotle to describe the "fulfilled" life – "the good life". It is not easily translated into English and the use of the word "happy" is not entirely accurate or satisfactory (Ross 1954, vi–vii). The difficulty of both translating and easily understanding this term may, indeed, point to the major difference between Greek conceptions of virtue and value and contemporary renditions of these concepts.

2 Interestingly, Parsons was a student at Harvard when Whitehead was teaching there and was clearly influenced by his ideas as is evidenced in the many but sporadic references to certain Whiteheadian concepts in Parsons' early work. See Halewood (2008) for a fuller discussion of this and of other early receptions of Whitehead in sociology by Mead and Schutz.

3 On two occasions it is actually the word "values" that occurs and is presented by Whitehead in inverted commas to signal that he is not directly affirming the sense of the word at that point (PR, 84, 104). At least 4 times, the reference to value comes in descriptions of his notion of "Propositions". Here he is explaining how judgements are not a question of deciding if something is true or false; he is describing their value (worth) as 'elements of feeling' (PR, 185 – he uses "value" three times on this page, and in the same manner on 191). Twice he uses the phrase "pragmatic value" to describe how the specific satisfactions of superjectivity qualify transcendent creativity (PR, 87, 88). That is, "pragmatic value" describes how completed actual entities contribute to and qualify the world.

4 There is a crucial distinction between eternal objects considered as sensa and complex eternal objects which are linked with some notion of sense-data through their relations with conceptual feelings. More complex eternal objects are referred to, by Whitehead, as "relational": 'qualities, such as colours, sounds, bodily feelings, tastes, smells, together with the perspectives introduced by extensive relationships, are the relational eternal objects' (PR, 61). The distance of such definitions from any kind of "thing" is furthered in that the terms "sensum" and "sensa" are intended by Whitehead precisely to differentiate them from the notion of sense-perception. Even more complex eternal objects, and more complex relations between them, are to be found in Whitehead's account of "propositions" (especially in PR, 184–208, 256–65).

5 Whitehead's specific notion of sociology, the social and societies will be addressed in the next chapter.

Chapter Five: Societies, the Social and Subjectivity

1 The importance of "form" within the work of Marx will be taken up in Chapter Eight.
2 German original given in the English translation.
3 Marx's approach to the status of society and capitalism will be taken up in Chapter Eight where a more Whiteheadian slant will be read into his work.
4 "Sociology" is a term that he only uses once in *Process and Reality* (PR, 5) and on this occasion the term only refers to its broad and generally agreed meaning as an academic discipline, and seems to have slipped in as part of a list, along with physics, physiology and psychology. This usage of "sociology" as a marker of an academic discipline is the rarest of Whitehead's deployment of the term.
5 This notion of the "maximization of a concept" is one that I took directly from a conversation with Didier Debaise and indirectly from Isabelle Stengers.
6 See Halewood and Michael (2008) for a discussion of some of the implications of Whitehead's work for methodological practices and procedures within sociology.
7 It could be argued that there is a further, gendered, aspect to this with sweeping studies of social structures appearing masculine and heroic thereby implying (mistakenly) that studies of the personal are intimate and hence feminized.
8 Having said that it is always necessary to take care with Whitehead's terminology, and recognising that when Whitehead says "subject" here, he is using it in his own specific sense, it is still important to indicate how Whitehead's work offers a way beyond the problem of knowing other people's minds. This is a problem which (indirectly perhaps) led to the rise and influence of the neo-Kantian school in the nineteenth century and ultimately to the reflected bifurcation of nature in the distinction between the methodologies of the natural and social sciences (see Lash 1999).
9 See Haraway (1976) for a discussion of Needham and Whitehead; Bono (2007) for a discussion of Whitehead and Waddington.

Chapter Six: Language and the Body – From Signification to Symbolism

1 It is customary within social theory to use the term "sex", that is, to put the word in scare quotes, when attempting to refer to that which is supposed to constitute the anatomical, biological bodily which is envisaged as distinct from the realm of gender. There are many good reasons for this. However, given that this text and discussion is attempting to reconsider and reconstruct some of the assumptions which apparently subtend such distinctions, it has been decided not to prioritize any element as either more or less immediately obvious or dubious.
2 Butler has recently stated that she accepts that her conception of nature in her earlier writing was problematic. Importantly and interestingly, she made this statement in a lecture on Whitehead, a philosopher to whom she is now returning. The lecture was titled 'On This Occasion' and was presented at a conference '*Becomings, Misplacements, Departures: Butler and Whitehead as Catalysts for Contemporary Thought*' held at Claremont Graduate University, California, December 3–5, 2010, organized by the Whitehead Research Project. A collection comprising Butler's lecture, other selected papers, and responses, is due to be published in 2011.
3 Having said this, Whitehead does tend to use examples from the "human level" in his discussions of all forms of symbolism.

4 There can be symbolic reference between two items in the same mode, this is not ruled out by Whitehead, but it is not the primary example of symbolic reference which involves the evocation and intersection of presentational immediacy and causal efficacy (PR, 181).

5 It is, perhaps, worth noting that the child playing at detective is involved in a more complex operation than the mere detective.

6 I have taken this notion of how Whitehead makes us slow down, consider, and dramatize our experiences and thought from the work of Stengers (2002, 2008a). I am deeply indebted to her work and thoughts on Whitehead.

Chapter Seven: This Nature Which Is Not One

1 This is especially pertinent to Freudian and Lacanian approaches. Also see Laqueur (1990) for an account of some of the historical shifts and complexities with regard to the conceptualization of distinctions within "one sex" or between sexes.

2 Examples of both positions within Irigaray are to be found in the following quotations: 'Sexual difference probably represents the most universal question we can address. Our era is faced with the task of dealing with this issue, because, across the whole world, there are only, men and women' (Irigaray 1996, 47); 'the couple that man forms with the other sex – woman. This couple forms the elementary social community. It is where sensible desire must become potentially universal culture, where the gender of the man and of the woman may become the model of male human kind or of female human kind while keeping to the singular task of being *this* man or *this* woman. In realising the transition from nature to culture...the couple formed by the man and the woman ensures the salvation of the community' (Irigaray 1996, 28; emphasis in original).

3 Whitehead's retention of the term 'Man' and 'Mankind' are especially unfortunate here, given the argument that is being made. But it does not vitiate his concepts although the assumptions of his writing should be noted.

4 It is at this point that elements of Butler's notion of performativity could be of use not as a founding explanation of the sex-gender dyad but as a mode of tracing its instantiations.

5 This relates back to the work of Butler as discussed in the previous chapter.

Chapter Eight: Capitalism, Process and Abstraction

1 Similarly, and with regard to the vector character of prehensions, Whitehead also stresses the link between movement and existence (see Chapter Two). He also points to the etymological root of this notion when he states that the word vector comes 'from the Latin *veho*, I draw or carry' (IM, 85; emphasis in original).

2 Pignarre and Stengers (2005) use the term "sorcery" to explicate the peculiar manner in which capitalism operates as a bewitching of contemporary relations and thought.

3 I have not indicated the remaining unnecessarily gendered pronouns in this citation but they should be noted.

4 The version mostly used in the analysis presented here is that published as the 'Introduction' to the *Grundrisse* (Marx 1973, 83–111). This is a translation (by M. Nicolaus) of the original German text as published in Volume 13 of the collected edition of his work (Marx 1964, 615–43). The original German text has been consulted to check to see if Marx consistently used the same term for that which has been translated using one term in English. Despite my lack of knowledge of German, I also was able

to quasi-translate the occasional word, using dictionaries, to confirm the general sense of a word. This 'Introduction' has also been published in a different English translation (by S. W. Ryanzanskaya) as an 'Appendix' to *Contribution to the Critique of Political Economy* (Marx 1971, 188–217). Extracts from it have also been published in another English translation (Marx 1977, 345–60) – edited and translated by D. McLellan). As the 'Introduction' is an unfinished manuscript and was written in a hurry, it can be somewhat unclear or even clumsy. The other two translations have therefore been consulted at points to clarify my understanding of Marx's ideas but have not been referenced throughout.

5 In the footnote to this passage, Marx discusses how Aristotle described this limitless accumulation in his distinction between economics and "chrematistics". For further discussions of the notion of "chrematistics" as well as the instantiation of the intertwining of the circularity yet infinite development of commodities, money and time (see Alliez 1996, 1–25).

6 To put it very briefly, "surplus-value" is a key process within capitalism, according to Marx, whereby the labour-power purchased by the capitalist is used to generate more value than that which is embodied in the exchange-value for which the capitalist acquires that labour-power. In this sense it is the answer to the question "How does money make more money?" Yet, within *Capital Volume 1*, the discussion and explanation of surplus-value both relies upon and presupposes other elements of analysis such as the separation of labour from property (Marx 1990, 729–30) which itself has to be explained, historically, by the actual events which constituted "primitive accumulation". In this way, surplus-value might be seen as the motor of capitalism but it is, in and of itself, relational and processual.

7 Another answer to the question of how capitalism initially produced that capital which became the lifeblood of its ongoing process is the notion of "primitive accumulation". This is that first moment whereby the nascent capitalists appropriated land or property which had previously been held in common. Interestingly, Marx's account of this aspect of the process makes up the very last part of *Capital. Volume 1* in the chapter titled "So-Called Primitive Accumulation". The positioning of this aspect of his account at the end not the beginning suggests that whilst this does provide the correct historical account of the development of capitalism, "Primitive Accumulation" does not explain its ongoing process and continuation. To have started with a historical account rather than a general account of the commodity form would have been to run the danger of historicism. Marx's aversion to historicism will be discussed further below.

8 The phrase "in the head" is one translation of Marx's original German text, as will be seen. Althusser, in providing an extended commentary on this 'Introduction' (see Althusser 1969, 182–218), talks not of "abstractions in the head" but of the '*concrete-in-thought* which is a knowledge' (Althusser 1969, 186; emphasis in original). This gives another indication of the flavour of Marx's argument here. However, whilst Althusser's discussion is fascinating, his concern is with accounting for knowledge and science.

9 German original given in the English translation.

10 I have noted Marx's appropriation of a Hegelian term but have not commented on it directly, as I want to develop a version of Marx's approach to abstraction which is not seen as simply an inversion of Hegel's approach. The importance of establishing a move beyond the apparent Hegelian foundations of Marx's terminology is very well put by Althusser (1969, 193–200).

11 German original given in the English translation.

12 See Murray (2000a, 2000b) for a detailed discussion of what he has termed "practically abstract labour" and which is designated here by the phrase *labour as such*.

13 'If we make abstraction from its (the commodity's) use-value, we abstract also from the material constituents and forms which make it a use-value. It is no longer a table, a house, a piece of yarn or any other useful thing. All its sensuous characteristics are extinguished. Nor is it any longer the product of the labour of the joiner, the mason or the spinner, or of any other particular kind of productive labour. With the disappearance of the useful character of the products of labour, the useful character of the kinds of labour embodied in them also disappears; this in turn entails the disappearance of the different concrete forms of labour. They can no longer be distinguished, but are all together reduced to the same kind of labour, human labour in the abstract. Let us now look at the residue of the products of labour. There is nothing left of them in each case but the same phantom-like objectivity; they are merely congealed quantities of homogenous human labour… As crystals of this social substance, which is common to them all, they are values – commodity values' (Marx 1990, 128).

14 Toscano (2008b) discusses this in terms of the contemporary development of "cognitive capitalism" 'which makes abstraction into an essential moment in the process of production' (Toscano 2008b, 284).

15 Sayer (1987) produces an excellent summary of these: 'First, the society must be a commodity producing one. This supposes a definite historical form of social division of labour. Second, labour must be "free" in Marx's double sense: free from constraints of serfdom or slavery, and free of means of production of its own… Third, the means of production must be constituted as the private property of capitalist employers… All of these…presume a requisite level of development of the productiveness of labour' (Sayer 1987, 132).

16 The citations are from *Capital. Volume 3.*

17 This notion of an "organic unity" which is neither natural nor social but is, in a sense, both has clear resonance with the terms "hybrid" and "cyborg" as used by Latour (e.g. 1993b) and Haraway (1991) respectively.

18 This is a phrase and approach that I have taken directly from a conversation with Didier Debaise and indirectly from Isabelle Stengers.

BIBLIOGRAPHY

Adorno, T. and M. Horkheimer. 1997. *Dialectic of Enlightenment*. London: Verso.

Alliez, E. 1996. *Capital Times. Tales from the Conquest of Time*. London: University of Minnesota Press.

Althusser, L. 1969. *For Marx*. Harmondsworth: Penguin.

————. 1984. *Essays on Ideology*. London: Verso.

Archer, M. 1995. *Realist Social Theory: The Morphogenetic Approach*. Cambridge: Cambridge University Press.

————. 2003. *Structure, Agency, and the Internal Conversation*. Cambridge: Cambridge University Press.

Aristotle. 1954. *Nichomachean Ethics* (translated and edited by D. Ross). London: Oxford University Press.

Badiou, A. 2009. *Logics of Worlds. Being and Event 2* (translated by Alberto Toscano). London: Continuum.

Barad, K. 1998. 'Getting Real: Technoscientific Practices and the Materialization of Reality.' *Differences: A Journal of Feminist Cultural Studies*, 10.2: 87–128.

Baudrillard, J. 1983. *In the Shadow of the Silent Majorities or 'The Death of the Social'*. New York: Semiotext(e).

Beauvoir de, Simone. 1972 [1949]. *The Second Sex*. London: Penguin.

Belaief, L. 1975. 'A Whiteheadian Account of Value and Identity.' *Process Studies*, 5.1: 31–46.

Benton, T. 1977. *Philosophical Foundations of the Three Sociologies*. London: Routledge & Kegan Paul.

————. 1981. 'Realism and Social Science. Some Comments on Roy Bhaskar's "The Possibility of Naturalism."' *Radical Philosophy*, 27: 13–21.

Bernard Cohen, I. 1994. *Interactions. Some Contacts between the Natural Sciences and the Social Sciences*. Cambridge, MA: MIT Press.

Bhaskar, R. 1978. *A Realist Theory of Science*. Hassocks: Harvester Press.

————. 1979. *The Possibility of Naturalism. A Philosophical Critique of the Contemporary Human Science*. Brighton: Harvester Press.

————. 1989. *Reclaiming Reality. A Critical Introduction to Contemporary Philosophy*. London and New York: Verso.

Bono, J. 2007. 'Perception, Living Matter, Cognitive Systems, Immune Networks: A Whiteheadian Future for Science Studies.' *Configurations*, 13.1: 135–81.

Bordo S. 1995. *Unbearable Weight: Feminism, Western Culture and the Body*. Berkeley: University of California Press.

Butler, J. 1990. *Gender Trouble: Feminism and the Subversion of Identity*. London: Routledge.

————. 1993. *Bodies That Matter: on the Discursive Limits of 'Sex'*. New York and London: Routledge.

————. 2004a. *Precarious Life. The Powers of Mourning and Violence*. London and New York: Verso.

————. 2004b. *Undoing Gender*. London and New York: Routledge.

Castells, M. 2000. *The Rise of the Network Society*. Oxford: Blackwell.

Cheah, P. 1996. 'Mattering.' *Diacritics*, 26.1: 108–39.

Collins English Dictionary. 1986. (Edited by P. Hanks). London: Collins.

Debaise, D. 2006. *Un Empirisme Spéculative. Lecture de Procès et Réalité de Whitehead*. Paris: Vrin.

Derrida, J. 1976 *Of Grammatology*. Baltimore and London: Johns Hopkins University Press.

Dewey, J. 1937. 'Whitehead's Philosophy.' *The Philosophical Review*, 46.2: 170–7.

————. 1958 [1925, revised 2nd edition 1929]. *Experience and Nature*. New York: Dover Publications.

Dilthey, W. 1976. *Selected Writings*. Cambridge: Cambridge University Press.

Du Bois, W. E. B. 1994 [1903]. *The Souls of Black Folk*. New York: Dover Publications.

Durkheim, E. 1964 [1895, 2nd edition 1901]. *The Rules of Sociological Method*. Glencoe, IL: The Free Press.

————. 2008 [1915]. *The Elementary Forms of the Religious Life*. New York: Dover Publications.

Eder, K. 1996. *The Social Construction of Nature*. London: Sage.

Elder-Vass, D. 2010. *The Causal Powers of Social Structures. Emergence, Structure and Agency*. Cambridge: Cambridge University Press.

Elias, N. 1982. *The Civilizing Process*. Oxford: Basil Blackwell.

Faber, R. 2009. '"O bitches of impossibility!" – Programmatic Dysfunction in the Chaosmos of Deleuze and Whitehead.' In K. Robinson (ed.), *Deleuze, Whitehead, Bergson: Rhizomatic Connections*, 200–17. Basingstoke: Palgrave Macmillan.

Faber, R., and A. Stephenson (eds). 2010. *Secrets of Becoming. Negotiating Whitehead, Deleuze, and Butler*. New York: Fordham University Press.

Fararo, T. 1992. *The Meaning of General Theoretical Sociology*. Cambridge: Cambridge University Press.

————. 2001. *Social Action Systems: Foundations and Synthesis in Sociological Theory*. Westport, CT: Praeger.

————. 2006. 'On the Foundations of Action Theory: Four Imperatives.' In H. Staubmann (ed.), *Action Theory: Methodological Studies*, 83–106. London: LIT Academic Books.

Foucault, M. 1972. *The Archaeology of Knowledge*. London: Tavistock.

————. 1974. *The Order of Things*. London: Tavistock.

Fraser, M. 2002. 'What is the matter of feminist criticism?' *Economy and Society*, 31.4: 606–25.

————. 2006. 'The ethics of reality and virtual reality: Latour, facts and values.' *History of the Human Sciences*, 19.2: 45–72.

Fuss, D. 1990. *Essentially Speaking. Feminism, Nature and Difference*. London: Routledge.

George, A. 2004. 'Ultimate Value.' *Process Studies*, 33.2: 284–302.

Giddens, A. 1984. *The Constitution of Society: Outline of the Theory of Structuration*. Cambridge: Polity Press.

Grosz, E. 1994. *Volatile Bodies. Toward a Corporeal Feminism*. Indianapolis: Indiana University Press.

Grosz, E., and E. Probyn. 1995. *Sexy Bodies: The Strange Carnalities of Feminism*. London: Routledge.

Halewood, M. 2005. 'A. N. Whitehead, Information and Social Theory.' *Theory, Culture and Society*, 22.6: 73–94.

————. 2007. 'On Whitehead and Deleuze – The Process of Materiality.' *Configurations*, 13.1: 57–76.

————. 2008. 'Introduction to a Special Section on Whitehead.' *Theory, Culture and Society*, 25.4: 1–14.

————. 2009. 'Language, Subjectivity and Individuality.' In K. Robinson (ed.), *Deleuze, Whitehead, Bergson: Rhizomatic Connections*, 45–60. London: Palgrave Macmillan.

————. 2010. 'Butler and Whitehead on the (Social) Body.' In R. Faber and A. Stephenson (eds), *Secrets of Becoming. Negotiating Whitehead, Deleuze, and Butler*, 107–26. New York: Fordham University Press.

Halewood, M. and M. Michael. 2008. 'Being a Sociologist and Becoming a Whiteheadian: Concrescing Methodological Tactics.' *Theory, Culture and Society*, 25.4: 31–56.

Haraway, D. 1976. *Crystals, Fabrics, and Fields. Metaphors of Organicism in Twentieth-Century Developmental Biology*. New Haven and London: Yale University Press.

————. 1991. *Simians, Cyborgs, and Women. The Reinvention of Nature*. London: Routledge.

————. 1997. *Modest_Witness@Second_Millenium.FemaleMan©_Meets_OncoMouse™ Feminism and Technoscience*. London: Routledge.

————. 2000. *How Like A Leaf*. London: Routledge.

Harman, G. 2009. *Prince of Networks. Bruno Latour and Metaphysics*. Melbourne: re.press.

Horkheimer, M. and T. Adorno. 1973. *Dialectic of Enlightenment*. London: Allen Lane.

Irigaray, L. 1985a. *Speculum of the Other Woman*. Ithaca, NY: Cornell University Press.

————. 1985b. *This Sex Which Is Not One*. Ithaca, NY: Cornell University Press.

————. 1993. *Je, Tu, Nous. Toward a Culture of Difference*. New York and London: Routledge.

————. 1994. *Thinking the Difference. For a Peaceful Revolution*. London: Athlone.

————. 1996. *I Love To You. Sketch for a Felicity Within History*. New York and London: Routledge.

————. 2000a. *Democracy Begins Between Two*. London: Athlone.

————. 2000b. *To be Two*. London: Athlone.

————. 2002. *Between East and West. From Singularity to Community*. New York: Columbia University Press.

Karatani, K. 2005. *Transcritique. On Kant and Marx*. Cambridge, MA: MIT Press.

Kirby, V. 1997. *Telling Flesh. The Substance of the Corporeal*. London: Routledge.

————. 1999. 'Human Nature.' *Australian Feminist Studies*, 14.2: 19–29.

Kline, G. (ed.) 1963. *Alfred North Whitehead: Essays on His Philosophy*. Englewood Cliffs, NJ: Prentice-Hall.

Kupiec, J-J. and P. Sonigo. 2000. *Ni Dieu ni Gène. Pour une Autre Théorie de l'Hérédité*. Paris: Éditions de Seuil.

Lacan, J. 1977. *Écrits. A Selection*. London: Tavistock.

Laqueur, T. 1990. *Making Sex: Body and Gender from the Greeks to Freud*. Cambridge, MA: Harvard University Press.

Lash, S. 1999. *Another Modernity. A Different Rationality*. Oxford: Blackwell.

Latour, B. 1993a [1984]. *The Pasteurization of France*. Cambridge, MA: Harvard University Press.

————. 1993b. *We Have Never Been Modern*. Harlow: Prentice Hall.

————. 1999a. *Pandora's Hope. Essays on the Reality of Science Studies*. Cambridge, MA: Harvard University Press.

————. 1999b. *Politiques de la nature. Comment Faire Entrer les Sciences en Démocratie*. Paris: Éditions La Découverte.

————. 2005. *Reassembling the Social. An Introduction to Actor-Network-Theory*. Oxford: Oxford University Press.

Leclerc, I. 1958. *Whitehead's Metaphysics. An Introductory Exposition*. London: George Allen & Unwin.

Locke, J. 1988. *An Essay Concerning Human Understanding*. London: J. M. Dent.

Lowe, V. 1990. *Alfred North Whitehead. The Man and His Work Volume II*. Baltimore: Johns Hopkins University Press.

Lukes, S. 1992. *Émile Durkheim. His Life and Works: A Historical and Critical Study*. London: Penguin.

Marx, K. 1964. *Einleitung [zur Kritik der Politischen Ökonomie]*. In K. Marx and F. Engels. *Werke, Band 13*. Berlin: Dietz Verlag.

———. 1971. *A Contribution to the Critique of Political Economy*. London: Lawrence & Wishart.

———. 1973. *Grundrisse*. Harmondsworth: Penguin.

———. 1977. *Selected Writings* (edited by D. McLellan). Oxford: Oxford University Press.

———. 1990. *Capital Volume 1*. London: Penguin.

Meillassoux, Q. 2008. *After Finitude. An Essay on the Necessity of Contingency*. London: Continuum.

Merchant, C. 1983. *The Death of Nature. Women, Ecology and The Scientific Revolution*. London: Wildwood House.

Meyer, S. 2007. 'Introduction. Whitehead Today.' *Configurations*, 13.1: 1–33.

Mitchell, J. and J. Rose (eds). 1982. *Feminine Sexuality. Jacques Lacan and the École Freudienne*. Basingstoke: Macmillan Press.

Murray, P. 2000a. 'Marx's "Truly Social" Labour Theory of Value: Part I, Abstract Labour in Marxian Value Theory.' *Historical Materialism*, 6: 27–65.

———. 2000b. 'Marx's "Truly Social" Labour Theory of Value: Part II, How is Labour that Is Under the Sway of Capital *Actually* Abstract?' *Historical Materialism*, 7: 99–136.

Noble, D. 2006. *The Music of Life*. Oxford: Oxford University Press.

Oakes, G. 1986. 'Rickert's Theory of Historical Knowledge.' In H. Rickert, *The Limits of Concept Formation in Natural Science*. Cambridge: Cambridge University Press.

Parsons, T. 1949 [1937]. *The Structure of Social Action. A Study in Social Theory with Special Reference to a Group of Recent European Writers*. Glencoe, IL: The Free Press.

———. 1991 [1951]. *The Social System*. London: Routledge.

Parsons, T. and E. Shils (eds). 1962 [1951]. *Toward a General Theory of Action*. New York: Harper & Row.

Peirce, C. S. 1958. *Selected Writings*. Mineola, NY: Dover Publications.

Pignarre, P. and I. Stengers. 2005. *La Sorcellerie Capitaliste. Pratiques de Désenvoûtement*. Paris: Découverte.

Plato. 2008. *Cratylus* (translated by Norman Jowett). Charleston, SC: BiblioBazaar.

Rickert, H. 1986 [1902]. *The Limits of Concept Formation in Natural Science*. Cambridge: Cambridge University Press.

Rickman, H. 1976. 'Introduction.' In H. Dilthey, *Selected Writings*. Cambridge: Cambridge University Press.

Riley, D. 1988. *Am I That Name? Feminism and the Category of 'Women' in History*. London: Macmillan.

Robinson, K. (ed.) 2009. *Deleuze, Whitehead, Bergson: Rhizomatic Connections*. Basingstoke: Palgrave Macmillan.

Rose, N. 1996. 'The Death of the Social? Re-figuring the Territory of Government.' *Economy and Society*, 25.3: 327–56.

Rose, P. 2002. *On Whitehead*. Belmont, CA: Wadsworth.

Ross, D. 1954. 'Introduction.' In Aristotle, *Nichomachean Ethics* (edited by D. Ross), v–xxiv. London: Oxford: University Press.

Sandford, S. 1999. 'Contingent Ontologies. Sex, gender and 'woman' in Simone de Beauvoir and Judith Butler.' *Radical Philosophy*, 97: 18–29.

Saussure, F. de. 1983. *Course in General Linguistics*. London: Duckworth Press.

Sayer, D. 1987. *The Violence of Abstraction. The Analytic Foundations of Historical Materialism*. Oxford: Basil Blackwell.

Sennett, R. 1977. *The Fall of Public Man*. Cambridge: Cambridge University Press.

Shaviro, S. 2009. *Without Criteria: Kant, Whitehead, Deleuze, and Aesthetics*. Cambridge, MA: MIT Press.

Shindler, D. 1983. 'Whitehead's Inability to Affirm a Universe of Value.' *Process Studies*, 13.2: 112–31.

Sohn-Rethel, A. 1978. *Intellectual and Manual Labour. A Critique of Epistemology*. London: Macmillan Press.

Soper, K. 1995. *What is Nature? Culture, Politics and the non-Human*. Oxford: Blackwell.

Spinoza, B. 1992. *The Ethics. Treatise On The Emendation Of The Intellect. Letters* (translated by S. Shirley). Indianapolis: Hackett Publishing Company.

Staten, H. 1984. *Wittgenstein and Derrida*. Oxford: Basil Blackwell.

Stengers, I. 1997. *Power and Invention. Situating Science*. Minneapolis: University of Minnesota Press.

———. 2000. *The Invention of Modern Science*. Minneapolis: University of Minnesota Press.

———. 2002. *Penser Avec Whitehead. Une libre et sauvage creation de concepts*. Paris: Éditions de Seuil.

———. 2007. 'Whitehead's Account of the Sixth Day.' *Configurations*, 13.1: 35–55.

———. 2008a. 'A Constructivist Reading of *Process and Reality*.' *Theory, Culture and Society*, 25.4: 91–110.

———. 2008b. 'Experimenting with Refrains. Subjectivity and the Challenge of Escaping Modern Dualism.' *Subjectivity*, 22: 38–59.

———. 2009a. 'Thinking with Deleuze and Whitehead: A Double Test.' In K. Robinson (ed.), *Deleuze, Whitehead, Bergson: Rhizomatic Connections*, 28–44. Basingstoke: Palgrave Macmillan.

———. 2009b. 'William James. An Ethics of Thought.' *Radical Philosophy*, 157: 9–19.

Stone, A. 2006. *Luce Irigaray and the Philosophy of Sexual Difference*. Cambridge: Cambridge University Press.

Stones, R. 2005. *Structuration Theory*. Basingstoke: Palgrave Macmillan.

Thomson, G. 1972. *The First Philosophers*. London: Lawrence & Wishart.

Toscano, A. 2008a. 'The Culture of Abstraction.' *Theory, Culture and Society*, 25.4: 57–75.

———. 2008b. 'The Open Secret of Real Abstraction.' *Rethinking Marxism*, 20.1: 273–87.

Urry, J. 2000. *Sociology Beyond Societies. Mobilities for the Twenty-First Century*. London: Routledge.

Villani, A. 1996. 'Deleuze et Whitehead.' *Revue de Metaphysique et de Morale*. 101.2: 245–65.

Weber, M. 1949. *The Methodology of the Social Science*. New York: Free Press.

———. 1978. *Max Weber. Selections in translation* (edited by W. G. Runciman). Cambridge: Cambridge University Press.

Whitehead, A. N. 1922. *The Principle of Relativity with applications to Physical Science*. Cambridge: Cambridge University Press. (PRPS)

———. 1927 [1926]. *Religion in the Making*. Cambridge: Cambridge University Press. (RM)

———. 1927. *Symbolism. Its Meaning and Effect*. New York: The Macmillan Company. (SYM)

————. 1929. *The Aims of Education and Other Essays*. London: Williams and Northgate. (AE)

————. 1932 [1925]. *Science and the Modern World*. Cambridge: Cambridge University Press. (SMW)

————. 1933. *Adventures of Ideas*. Cambridge: Cambridge University Press. (AI)

————. 1938. *Modes of Thought*. Cambridge: Cambridge University Press. (MT)

————. 1948. *Science and Philosophy*. New York: Philosophical Library. (SP)

————. 1964 [1920]. *The Concept Of Nature*. Cambridge: Cambridge University Press. (CN)

————. 1978. [1929] *Process and Reality. An Essay In Cosmology* (Gifford Lectures of 1927–8), corrected edition (edited by D. Griffin and D. Sherburne). New York: The Free Press. (PR)

————. 2007 [1911]. *An Introduction to Mathematics*. Seaside, OR: Rough Draft Books. (IM)

Whitehead, A. N. and B. Russell. 1973, *Principia Mathematica to *56*. Cambridge: Cambridge University Press.

Wilson, E. A. 1999. 'Introduction: Somatic Compliance – Feminism Biology and Science.' *Australian Feminist Studies*, 14.29: 7–18.

Wright Mills, C. 1967. *The Sociological Imagination*. Oxford: Oxford University Press.

INDEX

Lightning Source UK Ltd.
Milton Keynes UK
UKHW041946100219
336957UK00001B/59/P